HIRE

with your

HEAD

FOURTH EDITION

HIRE

with your

HEAD

USING **PERFORMANCE-BASED HIRING**

TO BUILD OUTSTANDING DIVERSE TEAMS

LOU ADLER

WILEY

Published by John Wiley & Sons, Inc., Hoboken, New Jersey.
Published simultaneously in Canada.

Library of Congress Cataloging-in-Publication Data

Names: Adler, Lou, author.
Title: Hire with your head : using performance-based hiring to build outstanding diverse teams / Lou Adler.
Description: Fourth edition. | Hoboken, NJ : Wiley, [2022] | Includes index.
Identifiers: LCCN 2021033440 (print) | LCCN 2021033441 (ebook) | ISBN 9781119808886 (hardback) | ISBN 9781119808930 (ePDF) | ISBN 9781119808916 (ePub)
Subjects: LCSH: Employee selection. | Employees—Recruiting. | Employment interviewing.
Classification: LCC HF5549.5.S38 A35 2022 (print) | LCC HF5549.5.S38 (ebook) | DDC 658.3/112—dc23
LC record available at https://lccn.loc.gov/2021033440
LC ebook record available at https://lccn.loc.gov/2021033441

Cover Design: Wiley
Cover Image: © DesignAB/Shutterstock

SKY10028799_080521

Contents

Foreword

As part of my research on individual performance as described in *The End of Average*,[1] I argued that modern science has conclusively shown that there simply isn't an average person. Instead of relying on this outdated myth, the principles of individuality offer a better way to understand how people perform at school, at work, and in life. The three principles of individuality are as follows:

1. *The jaggedness principle*: All characteristics we care about are multidimensional and those dimensions do not correlate with each other like we think they do, which means that we cannot reduce human performance to a single score.

2. *The context principle*: Human behavior cannot be understood independently from the immediate context in which that behavior occurs.

3. *The pathways principle*: For any outcome that matters, there are always multiple paths to achieving that outcome.

In trying to better understand how companies hire people given this definition of human performance, it became clear in most situations that there was too much of a one-dimensional approach to the entire process. As a result it was unlikely companies would be able to hire stronger and more diverse talent using traditional processes. In fact, I was concerned that little has changed over the years, with companies still depending on outdated competency models and relying too much on skills and experiences to screen and assess candidates. This approach eliminated highly qualified

[1] Rose, Todd. *The End of Average: How We Succeed in a World That Values Sameness.* Harper One, 2016.

people who had a different mix of skills and experiences and totally ignored the context of the job.

My research in this area led me to Lou Adler and his Performance-based Hiring system. At the time I was trying to discover if there was any work being done that emphasized differences rather than similarities or emphasized the uniqueness in people based on the three principles of individual performance.

Performance-based Hiring does this by recognizing that individual performance is as much about ability to do the work as it is about the context underlying the work. Context in this case is considered the environment in which the work occurs, the culture of the organization, its level of sophistication, the pace and intensity of the situation, and above all, the people involved, especially the hiring manager. All of these factors will impact individual performance. For example, we've all seen situations where highly capable people underperform due to these contextual factors. And just as often, but less visibly, we've seen people who have what appear to be unremarkable backgrounds excel given these same factors.

Adler has somehow put all of this together and succinctly captured it in his hiring formula for success. Simply stated: the ability to do the work in relationship to fit is what drives motivation to excel. And without the right fit, motivation, engagement, satisfaction, and performance will suffer.

According to Adler, ability consists of both the hard skills (i.e., technical, creative, and problem-solving) and the soft skills (i.e., organizational, interpersonal, leadership, and managerial) required to properly handle the job. This is where Adler's Performance-based Hiring process begins to expand the talent pool and ends the notion completely that people are average. By defining work as a series of performance objectives rather than as a list of skills and competencies, everyone who can do this work is considered a potential candidate. People are then assessed on their past performance doing comparable work in similar situations. Given this approach, Adler embeds the three principles of individuality directly into the hiring process. This is why I find Performance-based Hiring so fascinating.

While fit is essential, just as important is to recognize that there is no such thing as an average person – and that if you want to really understand a person you have to understand them as an individual (and from our scientific perspective that means understanding those three principles of individuality). This insight has transformed every field it has touched, from medicine and nutrition to sports and education, but the one place where we continue to rely on average-based thinking is in the place that arguably matters the most: how we hire people. Given how profoundly important work is to most people – it can be the source of fulfillment or of frustration – we simply cannot afford to continue with the Frederick Taylor–inspired approach to one-size-fits-all hiring. It doesn't work, and it hurts both companies and individuals. That's what got me so excited about Performance-based Hiring – it accurately captures the principles of individuality and uses them to create a hiring formula that actually works.

This new edition of *Hire with Your Head* offers new insight into the hiring process, especially the increased focus on Win-Win Hiring – hiring for the anniversary date rather than the start date. This requires a long-term decision-making approach for both the hiring manager and the candidate, especially on the fit factors. While challenging, it's the best way companies can ensure an *End of Average* mindset and create a culture where every person can excel based on their innate ability and individuality.

TODD ROSE

Todd Rose is the cofounder and president of Populace, a think tank committed to a positive-sum world where all people have the opportunity to live fulfilling lives in a thriving society. Prior to Populace, Dr. Rose was a professor at Harvard University where he served as the faculty director of the Mind, Brain, and Education program, as well as led the Laboratory for the Science of Individuality. Todd is the author of two best-selling books, *The End of Average* and *Dark Horse*, as well as the forthcoming *Collective Illusions* (February 2022). He lives in Burlington, Massachusetts.

Introduction: Performance-based Hiring, Four Editions Later

As I was finishing this book, I asked Don Spear, CEO of OpenSesame – a hugely popular curated online course marketplace – why he decided to implement Performance-based Hiring in his company. His answer surprised me. He said, "It gives us a framework for ensuring that we're attracting high-quality candidates who meet our performance hiring standards while also reducing bias from our hiring teams. We believe diversifying our workforces makes our company better by bringing a variety of perspectives and voices to serve our customers."

He went on to say that their company wanted to aggressively increase the diversity of the workforce and that the Performance-based Hiring interview guides and talent scorecard rubric were some of the tools used to achieve the goal. Using these tools, managers are now confidently able to assess ability, fit, and potential, ensuring that those hired meet the company's standards of excellence. Just as important was to send a clear message to those hired under this program that they met the company's rigorous selection standards and threshold of excellence. He said hiring outstanding people is essential in order for the company to meet its aggressive growth goals.

While the Performance-based Hiring tools described in this book will allow managers and companies to build outstanding diverse teams, it's up to the leaders of these companies to fully commit to doing it. This, it turns out, is often the more difficult step to take.

■ A SHORT HISTORY ON THE IMPORTANCE OF HIRING TOP TALENT

In the introduction to the first edition of Hire with Your Head in 1997, I described a situation where I first learned about the importance of investing extra time into hiring outstanding talent. In this case it was in 1972 in my first management job as the manager of capital budgeting for a large industrial products manufacturing company. I was only 26 and had just received my MBA a year earlier. My boss, who just convinced me to relocate from Southern California to the Detroit area, called me late one morning demanding I drop everything and meet him at the University of Michigan to interview MBA students. Many more than were expected signed up to be interviewed. While I protested, given weeks of 12- to 14-hour days ahead and a critical report to the executive team the next morning, he was unrelenting. I can still hear his words from 50 years ago: "Nothing is more important than hiring outstanding people. Nothing." Then he hung up. After sitting in with Chuck for the first 30-minute interview I then interviewed another six students on my own, with Chuck interviewing about 15 over the whole day. We then took seven who we thought had the most potential out to dinner that night in Ann Arbor. From this group we made five offers and hired four outstanding people.

We got back to the office that night around 10 p.m. and by 4 a.m. we completed the detailed review of the group's financial performance. At the 9 a.m. meeting the next day the president of the group asked why the report was handwritten. Chuck told him what we were doing and why. He understood and said to us and to every other senior manager in attendance that there is nothing more important than hiring great people. Nothing.

While the big takeaway from that 24 hours was the importance of hiring great talent, there were some equally important tactics learned as well. The biggest one was once you've figure out if the person was clearly top notch, you need to provide a vision of where the job could lead if the person is successful. Our division was going through a huge turnaround moving from an old-time manufacturing company to one using advanced financial planning and management tools to drive growth, profitability, and performance. As part of this we needed a number of MBAs with manufacturing backgrounds to handle some major projects, and those taking the challenge would be rewarded for their successes. Creating the career ladder and proving that climbing it was a real possibility turned out to be more important than the size of the starting date compensation package. We were competing with some hot companies at the time – Ford, IBM, and P&G – and even though our jobs didn't have a lot of consumer appeal, we hired all but one person who also had other offers from these companies.

■ BEING MORE EFFICIENT DOING THE WRONG THINGS IS NOT PROGRESS

Around 1998 there was talk that the war for talent would be won with the advent of job boards, the creation of in-house corporate recruiting departments, new screening and assessment technology, and the use of applicant tracking systems (ATS). Based on these trends, companies were promised that hiring the best talent would be less costly, more efficient, and seamless. At that time I publicly contended this was pure fiction and that little would change in terms of improving quality of hire, increasing job satisfaction, and reducing turnover.

The cartoon in Figure I.1 was drawn to demonstrate this belief. My overriding contention was that doing the wrong things more efficiently was not progress. In fact, the same problems highlighted in the cartoon still exist today despite the billions of dollars spent on job postings, new technology, more sophisticated testing, and the use of artificial intelligence. LinkedIn was one of the few exceptions to this, and while it has had diminishing returns since everyone is now using it, it still is a powerful recruiting tool when used creatively and in the proper hands. These techniques will be revealed throughout this book.

Gallup's recent employee engagement survey summarizes the dismal results of this overriding focus on process efficiency rather

Figure I.1   Hiring circa 1998.

than improving quality of hire.[1] While their quarterly results show a very modest increase in employee engagement over the past 20 years, these same surveys still indicate that approximately 55% of the workforce is partially or totally disengaged with their work. This situation has changed little since the birth of the Internet and job boards. Job postings are just as boring, and these jobs are just as hard to find now as they were decades ago. And with them it's just as unlikely today that companies are going to be able to attract the strongest and most in-demand talent by offering them what on the surface appears to be an ill-defined lateral transfer and then forcing them to suffer the demeaning and burdensome application and assessment process.

[1]Harter, Jim. "Historic Drop in Employee Engagement Follows Record Rise." *Gallup.com*, Gallup, 19 Nov. 2020, www.gallup.com/workplace/313313/historic-drop-employee-engagement-follows-record-rise.aspx.

While there are many variables involved when it comes to hiring, lack of clarity around job expectations and the attempt to speed up the decision-making process reward the wrong behaviors. The impersonal nature of the process makes it too transactional with the size of the start date compensation package valued more highly than the career opportunity the role represents. Given this, job hopping becomes the acceptable norm with the need to avoid mistakes being more important than hiring the best person available. Band-Aid solutions are then used to solve a strategic problem: a broken hiring process designed to weed out the weak rather than one designed to attract the best.

Without a fully integrated and end-to-end system, improving overall hiring results is not possible. These types of loose business processes leave too much to chance, letting bias, hiring manager desperation, and the competency of those involved in the sourcing and selection decision dictate the quality of the people hired and their ultimate performance. That's why little progress has been made in the past 25 years. This is both a strategic and a process design problem. The overriding objective of this book is to demonstrate that it can be solved by using Performance-based Hiring.

■ CREATING A WIN-WIN HIRING CULTURE

More important than the process itself is the need for a company to embrace the idea that hiring success shouldn't be measured on the start date; instead it should be measured on the first-year anniversary date. This is called Win-Win Hiring. Demonstrating how this can be achieved on a consistent basis is the overriding purpose of this book.

A positive Win-Win Hiring outcome after one year means the new employee is still fully satisfied with the role and his or her career progression, and the hiring manager still fully supports and endorses the person. In these situations both are glad an offer was made and accepted one year after working together. Achieving this important hiring outcome changes how the hiring process is designed, managed, and implemented, including how both the hiring manager and the candidate make their decisions to move forward in the process and make and accept offers. Getting all of these critical steps properly aligned starts with the right talent acquisition strategy.

This boils down to the overarching idea that you can't use a surplus of talent strategy designed to weed out the weak when there isn't a surplus of talent. In those situations where there is a scarcity of talent, you need to use a high touch and highly personalized process designed to attract the best. This is possible by spending more time with fewer people, as long as they're the right people.

With this strategic supply versus demand starting point, it's important to recognize that there are three major hiring challenges most companies face. These are described below and shown in Figure I.2. Given this segmentation it's important to note that the same hiring strategy and associated processes can't be used to solve all three challenges, especially when the overriding goal is to achieve more consistent Win-Win Hiring outcomes. While high tech can be part of the solution, it can't be the primary solution,

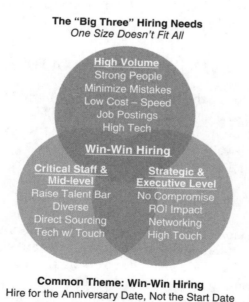

The "Big Three" Hiring Needs
One Size Doesn't Fit All

High Volume
Strong People
Minimize Mistakes
Low Cost – Speed
Job Postings
High Tech

Win-Win Hiring

Critical Staff & Mid-level
Raise Talent Bar
Diverse
Direct Sourcing
Tech w/ Touch

Strategic & Executive Level
No Compromise
ROI Impact
Networking
High Touch

Common Theme: Win-Win Hiring
Hire for the Anniversary Date, Not the Start Date

Figure I.2   The "Big Three" Hiring Needs.

especially in those situations when the demand for talent far exceeds the supply. In these cases more customization and high-touch involvement will be required from the recruiters and the hiring managers involved.

■ THE BIG THREE HIRING CHALLENGES

➤ **Hiring at Scale.** The focus here is filling high-volume roles with strong people while minimizing mistakes. This is largely a high-tech process, but it can be improved by making jobs easier to find and more compelling. As you'll discover in Chapter 12 on sourcing, eliminating the "Apply Now" button is a good first step.

➤ **Hiring to Raise the Talent Bar.** Improving quality of hire needs to be the goal when filling critical professional staff and mid-management positions. This requires a process targeting outstanding and diverse people who all have significant upside potential and who would likely see the role as a career move worthy of consideration. Most of these people will be passive and/or hard to find. While technology and advanced sourcing tactics are needed to identify them, just as important are excellent recruiters who can reach out and engage with them in a consultative manner and hiring managers who are willing to engage with these potential prospects very early in the process.

➤ **Strategic Leadership Hires.** Absolutely the best people must be hired to fill critical technical and executive level roles that have a direct bearing on the company's future success. This requires a high-touch process emphasizing networking and the need to invest the time necessary to convert any strangers into acquaintances long before an offer is made.

Regardless of the mix of high touch and high tech used, better results can always be achieved when a Win-Win Hiring outcome is the overriding objective used to decide whom to hire and why. This entire process will unfold and become apparent as you read this book and apply the concepts described.

■ CLARIFYING JOB EXPECTATIONS UP FRONT IS THE KEY TO HIRING OUTSTANDING PEOPLE

A more recent story will help set the stage for implementing this current version of Performance-based Hiring. It ties the idea of what's required to ensure a positive Win-Win Hiring outcome with some old and new ideas on how to find, interview, and recruit the strongest people.

One of our clients called just before the manuscript for this book was being finalized and asked for some advice on preparing a performance profile for their new VP of Data Analytics. The company was already an adherent of the Performance-based Hiring process, but since this was a new position, they wanted our help to define the performance objectives for the role. To get started I asked the COO to describe what the person would need to accomplish during the first year that everyone would consider an outstanding achievement. It went something like this:

> *Architect and implement a mobile-ready data information system that provides everyone in the company the real-time information needed to effectively manage their jobs, projects, and departments to meet their budget and performance objectives.*

We then developed the calendarized subtasks required to achieve this major objective, starting with evaluating the current situation, developing each user's needs, understanding the technology platforms and the technical challenges, putting the detailed plans together, obtaining the resources, and then building and deploying a functioning system.

Since the person leading this hiring effort was familiar with the Performance-based Interview, he only needed a short reminder that when interviewing candidates he had to be sure to ask the person to describe his or her accomplishments most comparable to these performance objectives. Then as part of the subsequent fact-finding have the candidate describe step by step how the project was started, planned, and completed. Making the assessment involves comparing the candidate's major accomplishments and the process used to achieve them to the performance objectives of the open role.

Defining work as a series of key performance objectives is the foundation of the Performance-based Hiring process. This list of performance objectives is called a performance-based job description or performance profile. The idea underlying this is that as long as the person has done comparable work in similar situations, the person will have all of the skills, experiences, and competencies necessary to successfully handle the job. With this starting point, it's possible to broaden the talent pool to include more diverse, high-potential, and nontraditional candidates who have a different mix of skills and experiences. Just as important, in order to achieve a Win-Win Hiring outcome and get these people hired, they need to see the role as the best career move among competing alternatives rather than an ill-defined lateral transfer with the biggest compensation package.

By moving the definition of hiring success to the first-year anniversary date from the start date, everything changes about how candidates are found and interviewed, how they're recruited, how offers are negotiated, and how the person is managed and developed post-hire. This includes delivering on the promise after they're hired. In many ways this entire concept is comparable to embedding a modern post-hire performance management and personal development program into the pre-hire process. It all starts by defining the job as six to eight performance objectives rather than the common list of skills, required experiences, generic competencies, and "must have" personality traits.

■ WHY PERFORMANCE-BASED HIRING IS THE RIGHT BUSINESS PROCESS FOR HIRING

Before I became a recruiter, I had 10 years of industry experience as a control systems engineer, a corporate financial analyst, a capital budgeting and planning manager, a director of logistics, and a VP/GM of a manufacturing company with 300 employees. These positions were in a variety of industries including aerospace, consumer electronics, and automotive with three different Fortune 500 companies.

This was a great background for being a recruiter since I fully understood the jobs I was filling, but the primary reason I quit a good position with lots of upside opportunity and became a recruiter was to find a different job. The problem was that my boss – the group president – and I didn't get along very well. I wanted as little direction as possible, and he wanted everything done his way. This was a very demotivating experience for me the three to four times a month he showed up. As a result of this I realized that the additional need for ensuring a good managerial fit – meaning that the hiring manager's and new hire's working styles meshed reasonably well – was just as important as technical competency, project and team management skills, and motivation to excel in order to achieve a positive Win-Win Hiring outcome.

While how to properly assess candidates on all of the factors affecting post-hire performance was imperative, on a big-picture level just as essential was the idea that hiring needed to be a true business process, not an unstructured hodgepodge of tactics and techniques. This is where my background in manufacturing and process control became valuable. It made no sense to me that a hiring manager would ever need to see more than three or four strong people to confidently hire someone. No one in manufacturing would ever continue making bad parts if the first few were out of spec hoping a few good ones would eventually be produced. In this case the production line would be stopped and fixed before starting up again. But this is not the case in hiring. Hiring managers frequently ask their recruiters if they have any more candidates rather than trying to figure out why the first few weren't good enough. Most often, it's the lack of understanding of the performance objectives of the job.

Without this insight about the real job, hiring managers aren't able to conduct an accurate assessment and recruiters aren't able to convince the strongest people that the jobs they're trying to fill represent potential career moves worthy of consideration. Bridging this gap and giving both sides the information needed to achieve Win-Win Hiring outcomes is how Performance-based Hiring came into being. Done properly a hiring manager never needs to see more than three or four strong candidates and will never need to ask, "Do you have any more candidates?" When and if they do, it's time to stop and figure out what's wrong.

When viewed in this light, Performance-based Hiring is comparable to most business processes using measurable objectives, metrics, and process control feedback applied to the unstructured world of hiring, recruiting, interviewing, onboarding, and performance management.

While the basic principles of hiring are still relevant, this fourth edition of *Hire with Your Head* has been updated to take into account the important things that have changed and improved in the past 20 years. As before, it's written for hiring managers and recruiters with a focus on what's required to find great candidates, interview and assess them accurately and objectively, and negotiate offers on fair and equitable terms. Implementing it starts before the job requisition is approved and doesn't end until at least a year after the person is hired.

Performance-based Hiring is different than traditional hiring practices. However, all of the ideas and the associated tactics described in this book have been validated by one of the top labor attorneys in the U.S. (see Appendix 1), by a number of top researchers and public research. Achieving the results, though, does require some significant reengineering of the more traditional hiring processes used by most companies today. As mentioned earlier, these changes are both strategic and tactical, emphasizing more high touch and less high tech. The idea is that by spending more time with fewer prequalified candidates it is possible to improve quality of hire, increase assessment accuracy, reduce turnover, and increase job satisfaction, all while reducing cost-per-hire and time-to-fill. In the process it will allow hiring managers to spend more time making their strongest people better rather than wasting time trying to get those who shouldn't have been hired in the first place to become average performers.

As you read this book, I urge you to consider these words I heard so long ago: "There is nothing more important than hiring outstanding people. Nothing." They're still true today.

Chapter

1

Define Your Talent Strategy Before You Design Your Hiring Process

■ STOP MAKING TACTICAL EXCUSES FOR A STRATEGIC PROBLEM

A Catch-22, based on Joseph Heller's book[1] of the same title, refers to a situation where someone is trapped and wants to get out of the situation but can't because of some policy, law, or regulation.

Hiring is like that.

For example, too many HR leaders believe that job descriptions must include laundry lists of skills, experiences, and generic competencies in order to be considered objective in the eyes of the law. Yet I asked one of the top labor attorneys in the U.S. if describing a performance objective like "determine the root cause of the manufacturing yield problem and put a plan together to solve the problem" was as objective as "must have 5+ years of experience and a degree in manufacturing engineering." He said it was not only more objective from a compliance standpoint but it was far better than the arbitrary list since it opened the talent pool to more diverse and nontraditional candidates who had a different mix of skills and experiences but who could do the work. (His whitepaper is included in Appendix 1.)

Another part of this Catch-22 is the continued use of generic competency models in combination with structured behavioral interviewing to screen and assess candidates. A structured interview is a great technique to remove bias, but just asking candidates to describe their major accomplishments related to the actual requirements of the role would achieve a bigger benefit by not only reducing bias but also understanding if the person can successfully handle the actual job.

I talked to a number of senior scientists at the firms that use these types of statistically validated tools, including psychometric prescreening tests, and they agree that their tools are far less than perfect. Making them even more imperfect is the lack of a job analysis for every job that's using a generic competency model in combination with behavioral interviewing to assess candidates.

Few companies actually do this, yet it's an essential requirement made abundantly clear in Schmidt and Hunter's exhaustive

---

[1]Heller, Joseph. *Catch-22*. Vintage, 1997.

research on which selection methods are most effective.[2] Harvard Professor Todd Rose and I discussed this same missing link idea when Todd was writing his book *The End of Average*. The collective scientific conclusion is that without understanding the job (this is the *performance profile* in Performance-based Hiring terminology) and the underlying context (these are all of the fit factors in the Hiring Formula for Success), a behavioral interviewing process using generic competencies is fundamentally flawed.

Yet despite the logic, the statistics, and the scientific evidence, HR executives continue to make some Catch-22 excuses for not changing or even using some type of A versus B test to see what approach is most effective.

But there's an even bigger and far more important Catch-22 at play when it comes to hiring. This one has to do with the importance of strategy over tactics. Let me explain this with a story from long ago.

The Importance of Having the Right Talent Strategy

I learned very early in my pre-recruiting career that strategy drives tactics – it's not the other way around. At the time I was a new financial analyst at the headquarters of a Fortune 50 company listening in on a business unit presenting its annual plan to the corporation's executive team. After about 30 minutes the CFO stood up and lambasted the president of a $5 billion group (today's dollars) with seven operating divisions.

It's been almost 50 years now, but I can still hear those words as if they were said yesterday:

Strategy drives tactics – it's not the other way around. And I don't care how good your tactics are, your strategy doesn't make any sense. Your operating plan will not be approved until you have a strategy to grow your business, not just run it more efficiently.

---

[2]Schmidt, Frank L., and John E. Hunter. "(PDF) The Validity and Utility of Selection Methods in Personnel Psychology." ResearchGate, www.researchgate.net/publication/232564809_The_Validity_and_Utility_of_Selection_Methods_in_Personnel_Psychology.

When it comes to hiring stronger talent, the root cause of most problems is typically the wrong strategy or the lack of the right one by default. This experiment will help you appreciate the importance of getting the talent strategy right before you start looking for candidates.

Supply versus Demand Needs to Drive Talent Strategy

The primary business of my company now is to train hiring managers and recruiters how to implement the Performance-based Hiring process described in this book. At the beginning of each of these programs I always ask the attendees to think about their most important hiring requirements to demonstrate the importance of getting the talent strategy figured out first. I then ask if, given these hiring needs, is there a surplus of great candidates to fill these positions or is there a scarcity? Before reading further, how would you answer this question for the critical positions that need to be filled at your company?

Do you have a scarcity of great talent for your critical roles or a surplus?

In normal economic times it's not surprising that 90% of the time the answer is scarcity. This was the same answer when I first asked the question to a group of 15 TEC/Vistage CEOs at my first resource presentation in 1990 and the same answer for the thousand or so workshops since then.

Given a scarcity of talent, this simple strategy change must be the first taken:

You can't use a surplus of talent strategy and process when there isn't a surplus of talent. In this case you need to implement a scarcity of talent program designed to attract the best, not weed out the weak.

The primary intent in a surplus of talent strategy is to cast a broad net, weed out the unqualified, and hope a few good people remain. This is the classic hiring process most companies still use today and why little has changed from a results standpoint over the past 30 years. It's why doing the wrong things more efficiently, even with the addition of AI and the best ATS on the planet, won't improve overall hiring results.

A scarcity of talent strategy is a high-touch process focused on prequalifying outstanding people, engaging in exploratory career conversations, and recruiting the strongest. This is what Performance-based Hiring is designed to achieve. In our training programs we use the graphic in Figure 1.1 to demonstrate the importance of having the talent strategy define the process rather than the process defining the strategy.

To understand how to achieve the strategy of raising the talent bar in a talent-scarce market, it helps to categorize the major steps in the hiring process into one of these four groups:

➤ **The Having**: The job description itself, including the skills, experiences, and "must have" competencies

➤ **The Getting**: The offer package and what the person receives on the start date, including the title and location

➤ **The Doing**: The actual work the person will be doing, not the list of responsibilities

➤ **The Becoming**: The learning opportunity and the upside potential of the job

While this categorization is a good simplification of a complex hiring process, the direction of the process is what matters

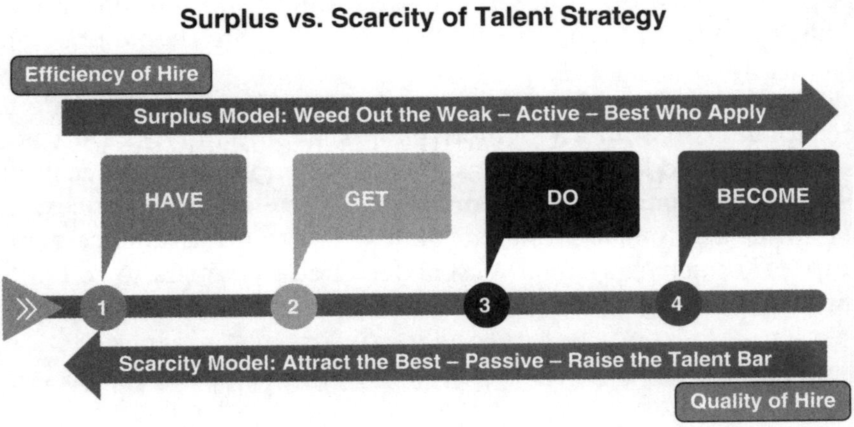

Surplus vs. Scarcity of Talent Strategy

Figure 1.1 Surplus versus Scarcity of Talent Strategy.

the most in terms of achieving the desired results of attracting and hiring strong people on a consistent basis. This is where the "strategy drives tactics" concept becomes important. Here are the differences when looking at the hiring process from a directional point of view.

> A *Left-to-Right Surplus of Talent Process*: This is a transactional hiring process designed to fill jobs with the best person who applies or responds to an email as efficiently as possible. It's appropriate for high-volume hiring when the supply of talent is greater than the demand. Properly weeding out the unqualified is the key to the effectiveness of this strategy and process.

> A *Right-to-Left Scarcity of Talent Process*: This is a more complex hiring process designed to identify and attract the strongest talent possible by offering the best career opportunity among competing alternatives. Spending more time with fewer but prequalified people and understanding their ability and career needs is the key to the effectiveness of this strategy and process.

With these definitions as a guidepost, it's obvious that using a left-to-right process designed to weed out the weak as efficiently as possible will be ineffective when the demand for talent exceeds the supply. The reason is that the best people just won't apply or won't be interested in spending time learning about what appears to be on the surface nothing more than a possible lateral transfer.

To get the best people to consider changing jobs or decide to accept yours requires a lot more effort similar to the discovery and solution-based selling process involved in more complex customized sales situations.[3] This requires a right-to-left hiring process.

While this might seem logical, it's hard to achieve since every applicant tracking system (ATS) is designed by default to go left to right, somehow assuming there's a surplus of talent.

---

[3]Rackham, Neil. *Spin Selling*. McGraw Hill Book Company, 1988.

Paraphrasing the words of the CEO, "This is backwards since the strategy is wrong, so the tactics don't matter no matter how good they are."

The Catch-22 in this is that HR leaders know the left-to-right process design is conceptually flawed, especially when they realize referrals are found and hired using some version of the right-to-left process. They're just not sure how to rework it, thinking they're trapped by their ATS design, corporate bureaucracy, legal compliance, hiring manager reluctance to change, and the need to focus on efficiency and cost rather than quality of hire.

Rather than getting overwrought by the challenges involved in making the shift, let's first figure out what it would take to reengineer the hiring process given a talent scarcity situation. Then we'll demonstrate that Performance-based Hiring is an effective means to accomplish this including modifying the ATS to make it all work at scale.

Comparing the Scarcity of Talent versus a Surplus of Talent Strategies

No matter how efficient, a surplus of talent strategy won't work when a surplus of talent doesn't exist.

Filtering people on their skills (the HAVE in Figure 1.1) and what a person gets on the start date (title, location, compensation) before even considering them makes no sense since the best and most diverse people have a different mix of skills and experiences. That's why excluding this group from consideration based on factors that don't predict performance is counterproductive. As important, what people GET on Day One are all factors that are negotiable if the job represents a significant career move. This point is explained in more depth in Chapter 3 comparing the skill set of the strongest performers to those who meet the requirements listed in the job description.

Doing this left-to-right process faster and even using AI to boost it to warp speed is akin to a dog chasing its tail faster and faster and wondering why it can never catch it.

By slowing down, thinking more "high touch" versus more "HR Tech," and spending more time with the right people, these problems go away. Here are the big mind-altering ideas that need to take place to make it happen one hire at a time.

■ WIN-WIN HIRING: HIRING FOR THE ANNIVERSARY DATE, NOT THE START DATE

Hiring for the anniversary date, rather than the start date, and addressing how candidates are onboarded and managed post-hire, has a direct influence on how they're sourced, assessed, and recruited pre-hire. A positive Win-Win Hiring outcome means the hiring manager and the new hire both agree it was the right decision after working together for one year. Recognizing the longer term and dual decision-making involved in this type of process forces both parties to spend more time ensuring they're making the right decision. Achieving this is not possible unless the DOING and BECOMING are clearly defined early in the process.

Part of this is a more in-depth assessment process focusing not only on the ability to do the work but also on ensuring all of the fit factors are properly aligned. Just as important is the need to provide the candidate all of the information needed to compare opportunities being considered from a longer-term perspective.

Develop an Ideal Candidate Persona to Achieve More Win-Win Hiring Outcomes

When the goal is to hire stronger people for the long term, rather than to fill jobs as cheaply and as quickly as possible, it seems logical to first figure out how these stronger people actually change jobs, why they stay, and why they continue to perform at peak levels. This analysis is comparable to a traditional marketing problem associated with the development of any new product. It starts by developing an ideal customer profile that defines what the customer wants, how to reach the customer, and what messages work best. When it comes to hiring, the equivalent is called the "ideal candidate persona." There is a template in Appendix 2 summarizing how to prepare this important marketing document. In Chapter 12 this form will be used as the basis for developing a whole series of sourcing plans and compelling messages with the goal of dramatically increasing top candidate response rates.

As you'll discover, posting boring jobs and hoping a top person applies is not the most effective means to find these top people. In a scarcity of talent situation, the focus needs to be narrowed to semifinalists rather than just people who apply. A semifinalist is someone who is clearly a top performer in the required field and who would also see the role as one worth at least considering. The value of this is that when done properly a hiring manager only needs to interview three or four semifinalists to make one outstanding hire. The challenge in achieving this is first getting both parties open-minded enough to talk to each other. This is why defining the DOING is so important.

In Chapter 7, describing the details of developing a complete performance profile, there are a number of techniques to overcome hiring manager reluctance. This story describes the simplest and most important.

I remember working with a CEO for a Silicon Valley firm who wanted to hire a VP of Marketing who had at least 10 years' experience in a related field and an MBA and BSEE from a top school. When I asked the CEO what the person needed to do with this, he said, "Lead the development of a detailed product roadmap that incorporated all of the new tech trends." When I asked him if he'd at least talk to someone who had done this work, even if the person didn't have the exact experience and academic background, he said, "Of course." Without defining the DOING as a performance objective, getting this agreement would not have been possible.

Describing the BECOMING is no less important. Developing it starts by asking the hiring manager what the long-term opportunity is for someone who successfully achieved the results required. In this same VP of Marketing example, it related to architecting the future direction of a company that would soon be going public. This became a key part of the messaging that convinced some remarkable people to at least begin the conversation who wouldn't have been interested otherwise.

The key to successfully implementing a scarcity of talent program rests on the idea that fewer people need to be seen to make one outstanding hire. But finding these remarkable people and convincing them to at least consider what's being offered requires exceptional recruiters and fully engaged hiring managers. Yet even with this as a foundation piece, how the job is defined is the tipping point for success. Unfortunately, there are a lot of institutional Catch-22 barriers required to make the DOING and BECOMING shift a companywide initiative.

Remove the HAVING Mindset and Shift to a Performance-Qualified Screening Standard

The biggest bottleneck in making the shift to a scarcity of talent process from the traditional hiring process is the skills-laden job description.

Consider the premise that in a scarcity of talent situation there are few top people desperate enough to apply to a job that appears on the surface to be an ill-defined lateral transfer. From a more practical standpoint, it's pretty obvious that few of the people who do apply read these job postings anyway. In fact, published research from the ATS vendors handling over 60 million applications from 2015 to 2020 reveals that only 1% were hired who applied and roughly 4% actually interviewed.[4] This means that 96% of the effort involved in managing, reviewing, and contacting those who do apply is a wasted and unnecessary overhead expense. Making it worse, their continued use requires companies to spend extra time and resources to deal with these unqualified people, including the creation of a "Positive Candidate Experience" function to ensure the people you say no to don't feel bad.

I have a related HAVING concern with competency models when it comes to using them for screening and assessment purposes. One big one is that they're pretty much all the same. Just about everyone wants to hire people who are hungry, humble, and smart.[5] Others want to hire the same kinds of people but use different terms like results-oriented, have great team skills, think creatively, or are detail-oriented. Just recently I was working with a group of IT hiring managers at a well-known national restaurant chain who were required to screen for cultural fit. While they all said it was important, there was little agreement when I asked them to define their company culture and how they screened for it. In fact, they actually started arguing amongst themselves when trying to define what it actually was.

The problem, as Professor Rose pointed out, without context the use of required skills and generic competencies are ineffective for screening and assessment. Interviewers can define them

---

[4]ATS research from SmartRecruiters.
[5]Rose, Todd. *End of Average: The Science of What Makes Us Different*. Harper One, 2015.

any way they want, resulting in just as many false positives as false negatives.

As shown in the example earlier, converting generic competencies, "must have" personality traits, or any essential skill is easy. Just ask the hiring manager how it's used on the job and if she/he would talk with someone who achieved something comparable. The bigger point here is that you never need to compromise performance, ability, or potential when the work is defined as a series of performance objectives. This is what "performance qualified" means.

To prove the person is competent, all you have to do is dig deep into the candidate's comparable accomplishments to see if there's a fit. If so, you'll discover the person will have all of the skills, experiences, competencies, and personality traits needed to successfully handle your job.

However, it will likely be a different mix than what's listed on the job description. As important, emphasizing these performance objectives in your job postings and outbound messages will attract a broader and more diverse pool of people who will quickly see the role as a potential career move.

Regardless of the common sense in all of this, the Catch-22 excuse relates to being more comfortable using some tried-and-true method that other companies use. This is a much safer approach than trailblazing.

■ NEGOTIATE WITH THE END IN MIND

As long as the DOING and BECOMING are better than the other opportunities the person is considering, what the person gets on the start date (compensation, title, benefits, etc.) becomes less important. It takes extra time for a person to fully understand this, which is why a "high-touch" go-slow process is essential for attracting, hiring, and retaining top performers. Presenting offers and negotiating this way is a skill all recruiters need to possess, including those hiring managers who want to make offers directly to their candidates. Of course, it's not possible without using a performance profile to make the comparison.

While these techniques are covered in the sourcing and recruiting chapters (Chapters 12 and 13), the basic premise is to advise candidates not to make long-term strategic career decisions using short-term tactical thinking.

■ MORE HIGH TOUCH AND LESS HIGH TECH: CONVERT STRANGERS INTO ACQUAINTANCES

Although many HR leaders balk at this entire scarcity of talent mindset and process design, this approach is not as radical as it might seem. For evidence, just compare this entire sequence of steps to those used to find and promote people we know, including former co-workers, or to attract and hire referrals from trusted sources. In some way these are all acquaintances or "weak connections" in the words of Reid Hoffman, the founder of LinkedIn.[6]

What is surprising is that we hire strangers using a totally different process that's designed based on a surplus of talent mindset. That's why this whole concept boils down to this commonsense idea: In a talent-scarce situation it's important to hire strangers like we hire acquaintances – based on their past performance doing comparable work. And by spending more time with these people, it's possible to convert these former strangers into acquaintances before they're hired.

[6]Hoffman, Reid. "Allies and Acquaintances: Two Key Types of Professional Relationships." LinkedIn, November 26, 2012, www.linkedin.com/pulse/20121126205355-1213-allies-and-acquaintances-two-key-types-of-professional-relationships/.

Chapter 2

Step-by-Step Through the Performance-based Hiring Process

■ WIN-WIN HIRING: HIRE FOR THE ANNIVERSARY DATE, NOT THE START DATE

Everyone wants to hire great people. But achieving a Win-Win Hiring outcome, where the new hire is still satisfied with the role one year into the job and the hiring manager is still pleased the person was hired, involves a lot of variables. All of these are embedded in the Performance-based Hiring system covered in this book and summarized in Figure 2.1.

The ultimate goal of the process is to raise the talent bar for every position being filled. Achieving this requires a different hiring approach. It must be recognized – but rarely is – that if a company decides to do the same things more efficiently or decides to implement processes with the objective of avoiding mistakes, the result will be hiring people just like it always has. Performance-based Hiring is designed to raise the level of talent, not just to maintain it.

Performance-based Hiring Is Designed to Raise the Bar

This chapter will provide a broad overview of each of the components of the Performance-based Hiring process. Although this appears as

Performance-based Hiring → Win-Win Hiring™

Hire for the Anniversary Date, Not the Start Date

Figure 2.1   The Performance-based Hiring Business Process.

a sequence of steps, the time-based phases below the sequence of steps tell a slightly different story. For one thing, the process is nonlinear. The first five steps take place over a month or two and the last step takes another 12 months before it's known if the hiring process was successful. To make it even more nonlinear is the idea that sourcing, interviewing, and recruiting all take place concurrently when reaching out and engaging with prospects. This could be as soon as just a few days after the job is defined.

This is comparable to the concurrent engineering product development process[1] that started in the 1980s and the agile software development process that started a decade later. As some wise HR executive told me as she began implementing Performance-based Hiring at her company, "Better late than never."

Suboptimization Prevents Win-Win Hiring Outcomes

However, it turns out that integrating a number of independent steps is easier to design than to implement. The creators, vendors, and suppliers of these independent steps aren't much interested in the greater good since it might have a negative impact on their businesses. They'd rather propose efficiency improvements, not better Win-Win Hiring outcomes. As a result this leads to an even bigger problem: suboptimization.

This definition will help you understand this critical and often misunderstood issue:

Suboptimization refers to the practice of improving one step in a total system or process while ignoring the effects on the entire system.

For example, while psychometric tests have great value later in the hiring process, when used for screening purposes they can eliminate many strong candidates who won't take the assessment until they learn about the job first. Just as bad is that the combination of

[1]"What is Concurrent Engineering," Concurrent Engineering. https://www.concurrent-engineering.co.uk/what-is-concurrent-engineering.

false positives and false negatives is about 50% for those who do take them before they're even considered.

Benchmarking How the Best People Find Jobs and Get Hired

These and related suboptimization problems are avoided by designing and implementing an end-to-end hiring process that is designed based on how the strongest and most talented people look for new jobs, compare and accept opportunities, and perform at peak levels once on the job. A big part of this is the need to treat these candidates as equal decision-makers at every step in the process from first contact to the final close and beyond. This requires full disclosure and full transparency.

In order to implement Performance-based Hiring as described here, recruiters and hiring managers must work the process in tandem as equal partners, not in the more traditional customer-vendor relationship. Since the quality of the people seen by the hiring manager will be equivalent to the quality of the recruiters handling their jobs, recruiters need to be treated as the hiring managers' trusted sales representatives, not as subordinates.

The importance of this collaborative and parallel versus sequential process will become clear as you see the Performance-based Hiring process unfold. It starts with how the job is defined. But this is just a starting point. How this is used as the foundation for everything that follows is what really matters.

■ HIRING A GREAT PERSON STARTS WITH A GREAT JOB

Hiring a great person starts with a great job, not a laundry list of skills, experiences, a list of responsibilities and "must have" competencies. This "great job" concept then needs to be carried out throughout the entire sourcing, recruiting, and assessment process in order for the candidate to fully understand that the job being discussed represents the best career move among competing alternatives. This way the size of the opportunity, not the size of the compensation package, becomes the reason the person accepts or rejects an offer.

But the process doesn't end on the new hire's start date. During the onboarding process job expectations need to be clarified and prioritized without any surprises of the "I didn't know that was part of the job" sort, or "I didn't know the hiring manager was a jerk to work for." Given this type of full disclosure and transparency, the company must then deliver on the promise.

Here are few more details on each of these critical steps.

Define Success as Performance Objectives, Not Skills and Experiences

To get started with Performance-based Hiring, job expectations need to be clarified up front, including some overriding statement as to why the job is worth consideration. This is called the employee value proposition, or EVP. Not only is clarifying objectives up front the foundation of good management, but when tied to an important company initiative or mission, it helps increase the number of people who will engage in exploratory career conversations. For example, describing a software development role with a standard list of skills and some generic employer branding statement won't have nearly the impact of describing how the projects the person will be working on and the role played will help drive market share, improve customer satisfaction, or push the envelope on some particular technology.

From what I've seen, every job, from the mail room to the CEO, can be defined by six to eight key performance objectives (KPOs) defining the task, the action required, and some measurable result. These are also called OKRs – objectives and key results. For example, for a business analyst it's better to write, "Build an auditable dashboard tracking multi-unit sales and gross margins by territory and sales rep within six months," than to post that the person must have an MBA (CPA preferred), three-plus years of experience with SQL and Tableau, excellent communication skills, a strong attention to detail, and a can-do attitude. To capture the EVP in the job posting or email message, saying something about how the role will help the company control its accelerating sales growth with real-time information adds another dimension to the importance of the role.

Advertising jobs emphasizing skills, experiences, and generic competencies combined with hyperbole and superficialities is not only bad marketing, it's also demeaning to those applying. These types of job descriptions won't attract the strongest people who see them as ill-defined lateral transfers, but even worse they're too generic to filter candidates properly or to conduct an accurate assessment.

Source Semifinalists

In a "scarcity of talent" situation, you can't hope a good person will apply. Instead, you need to proactively find outstanding and diverse talent who would see the role as a career move. Then you need to spend time and effort with these people just to convince them to talk to you and seriously consider your opening. This is the collective role of the hiring manager and the recruiter working together as partners. When there is little contact between the hiring manager and the recruiter – who is actually talking with the prospects first – other than a resume sent via email, finding a top person is comparable to playing pin the tail on the donkey. Figure 2.2 depicts this game and why it's a waste of valuable time and effort.

"This is more precise than objectively reviewing resumes."

Figure 2.2   Pin the Tail on the Donkey.

By targeting semifinalists and prequalifying them before making contact, the job of finding great hires is somewhat easier. It's important to emphasize the point that a semifinalist is someone who has been recognized for doing outstanding work in the field required AND someone who would also see the job as a possible career move. (If you didn't know it, the "AND" is a Boolean search term that recruiters and sourcers need to use to find qualified candidates.)

Many of the people identified this way should be called prospects rather than candidates since they have only agreed to have a preliminary conversation to determine if the job is something worth serious consideration. In fact, until they agree to have the first conversation, they're just potential prospects. That's why an exploratory phone screen is a critical extra step in the Performance-based Hiring process. (Conducting this phone screen is covered in Chapter 8. There is an interview guide and scorecard available in Appendix 2.)

While assessing general fit and competency is part of the conversation, hiring managers also have the responsibility of convincing a candidate who's on the fence that the role is worth serious consideration. Hiring managers are more open to conducting these types of exploratory conversations with people who look strong, and the strongest candidates are also more open to continuing the exploratory evaluation if the job seems like it might offer a better career trajectory.

Getting hiring managers and strong prospects to agree to the conversation is an important step in reducing the number of candidates who are seen onsite. Typically the first phone call is with the recruiter, and if the person meets the basic conditions he or she will be forwarded to the hiring manager for the next call. If the prospect is not perfect for the role for any reason, it's up to the recruiter to network with the person and proactively ask for referrals. This is part of the high-touch parallel processing that takes place during the phone screen. It combines interviewing, recruiting, and sourcing in order to ensure only a few people need to be invited onsite in order to make a great hire. Chapter 12 on sourcing and metrics describes why this is important, what to track to make sure the process is functioning properly, and when to stop the process entirely if too many candidates need to be phone screened.

Conduct the Two-Way Performance-based Interview

Most people think the primary purpose of the interview is to assess competency and fit. And while this is important, it's not the only part. As important is demonstrating to the strongest people that your job is the best among other opportunities the person is considering. It's also important to make this case without overselling the job. It's best if this is done in parallel with the interview rather than after the interviewer has determined that the person is competent to handle the job. When recruiting is done after the interview, it often comes across as overselling, demeaning the job in the process.

It's a two-way street when it comes to hiring the most talented people. These people are just as discriminating about accepting an offer as the company should be in deciding to make one. The quality of the interview itself is a critical part of the candidate's decision-making process. Given this broader perspective, here are the factors that are most important:

1. The recruiter, hiring manager, and everyone on the interviewing team need to fully explain real job needs.

2. Everyone on the interviewing team must be prepared and on time. This will naturally occur if those conducting the interview consider the candidate an equal partner in the decision-making process.

3. The professionalism and depth of the interviewing process demonstrates the standards of the company, the leadership qualities of the hiring manager, and the importance of the job.

4. Demonstrate sincere interest by asking in-depth questions about the person's accomplishments rather than overselling.

5. Have the candidate fully appreciate the career opportunity represented by the job by understanding the key challenges involved and the importance of the role.

All of this is possible by describing the performance objectives of the job and having candidates describe their most comparable major accomplishments. When candidates see the job explained this way as part of a give-and-take process, they're apt to become excited if the work itself meets their career needs and motivating job interests. While there's more to the complete interview than this, it is the most important part for ensuring the person is both qualified and intrinsically motivated to handle the role.

Measure and Predict Quality of Hire

Measuring Quality of Hire has been an elusive metric, one that most companies, if they do it at all, do after a person has been on the job for at least a few months or longer. Even then, there's a lot of debate on what factors should be used to measure it and how the information should be used to improve it.

Regardless, waiting months after the person is hired is too late. It's comparable to figuring out if you've arrived at the correct destination after you've arrived. If there is anything that HR should have learned about the quality control and Six Sigma movement of the 1980s, it is that real-time process control metrics are essential in order to provide instant feedback when a manufacturing process is producing bad parts or a business process is broken in some way. Under these conditions you don't continue business as usual; you intervene and stop the process or fix it on the fly, not three to six months later. By waiting this long before taking corrective action, you won't know if it's worked for another three to six months.

The Hiring Formula for Success described in detail in Chapter 6 and summarized in Figure 2.3 defines all of the factors required

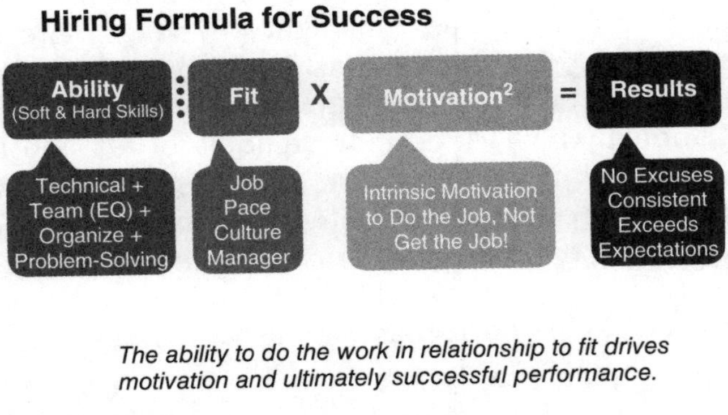

Hiring Formula for Success

| Ability (Soft & Hard Skills) | : | Fit | X | Motivation^2 | = | Results |

| Technical + Team (EQ) + Organize + Problem-Solving | Job Pace Culture Manager | Intrinsic Motivation to Do the Job, Not Get the Job! | No Excuses Consistent Exceeds Expectations |

The ability to do the work in relationship to fit drives motivation and ultimately successful performance.

Figure 2.3   The Hiring Formula for Success.

to accurately predict on-the-job success and control it in real time when things go amiss. Getting to this point starts by predicting Quality of Hire by collecting evidence of past performance doing comparable work in similar situations and completing the talent scorecard described later in this book. Since the assessment is made in comparison to real job needs, this same scorecard can be used to measure Quality of Hire post-hire to figure out what needs to be changed if the prediction is not correct.

What we've discovered based on years of tracking predicted and actual performance is that raw technical ability and intellect are the easiest of the factors to accurately assess, and the person's soft skills are more challenging because in many ways they're dependent on the fit factors. For example, a brilliant person might find it difficult to deal with a demanding boss or the pressures of making quicker decisions without enough time to gather the needed information. On the flip side a person with solid but not spectacular technical credentials might be an exceptional hire under the exact same conditions.

How to control the entire recruiting process using these hiring success factors in combination with related recruiting funnel metrics is described in Chapter 12 on high-touch sourcing. Used this way, a company will have a means to adjust its hiring process to meet the competing objectives of Quality of Hire, productivity, cost, and time-to-fill.

Unexpectedly, it turns out the most important of all of these yield metrics is the number of candidates needed to be phone screened before one is considered a serious semifinalist. While a bit counterintuitive, it turns out that whenever more than two candidates are needed before considering one seriously, it indicates the recruiter and the hiring manager are not in sync on what's needed. Normally it's lack of understanding of real job needs or the recruiter's inability to attract the strongest talent. Of course it could also be that either the recruiter or the hiring manager isn't a great interviewer. Regardless of the root cause, the process should be stopped to figure out the problem rather than continuing to present candidates in the hope that one passes muster.

Close on Career Growth, Not Compensation Maximization

You'll rarely have enough money in your compensation budget to attract the best people. And even if you do, you shouldn't spend it all. Instead, it's best for the candidate to fully understand the career opportunity of the role in balance with the compensation package before accepting an offer.

Here's a quick overview of how this is done. Early in the hiring process tell your candidates that a good career move must offer a 30% nonmonetary increase consisting of some combination of job stretch (a bigger job), a mix of more satisfying work, better work/life balance, a job with more impact, and one with a faster multi-year growth rate. Go on to say that the purpose of your interviewing and assessment process will be designed to allow the candidate to gather this information, while in parallel the company will determine the person's ability and interest in handling the job.

You might even want to share the infographic in Figure 2.4 after the first phone screen and ask the person to rank the factors shown in order of importance. Highlight the fact that your company's interviewing process will offer the chance for the candidate to learn about all of these factors as well as for the company to determine if the person is both competent to do the work and intrinsically motivated to do it.

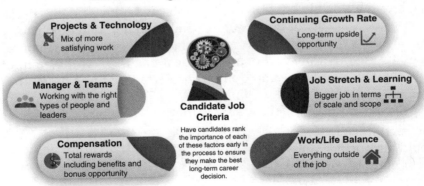

Win-Win Hiring: Career vs. Job Comparison

Projects & Technology — Mix of more satisfying work

Continuing Growth Rate — Long-term upside opportunity

Manager & Teams — Working with the right types of people and leaders

Candidate Job Criteria — Have candidates rank the importance of each of these factors early in the process to ensure they make the best long-term career decision.

Job Stretch & Learning — Bigger job in terms of scale and scope

Compensation — Total rewards including benefits and bonus opportunity

Work/Life Balance — Everything outside of the job

Figure 2.4 Have Candidates Rank These Factors in Order of Importance.

At the end of the process, but before making the formal offer, ask the candidate to ignore the compensation package for a moment and describe why the person wants the job. If the person can't describe the nonmonetary factors comprising the 30% in detail, an offer shouldn't be extended. In this case a Win-Win Hiring outcome is unlikely. It also means that the interview process was short-circuited in some way. On the other hand, if the candidate can describe the 30% and is excited about it, a fair compensation package can likely be negotiated.

Use Onboarding to Clarify and Prioritize the Performance Objectives

While there are a lot of administrative aspects to the onboarding process, as far as I'm concerned, the most important is to review the performance objectives of the job with the new hire soon after the person starts. If the interview and closing process was conducted properly, there will be no surprises. On the other hand, if there are surprises, HR must intervene at once.

This happened to me twice early in my pre-recruiting career, so I'm personally aware of the potential pain it can cause and why I go out of my way now to ensure it never happens to candidates I'm representing. The first time it happened to me was when I started on my first full-time engineering job and the second was just after getting my MBA. In the first job the fault was mine. I took an offer because it got me to sunny southern California from snowy upstate New York. My boss took the fact that I was a mechanical systems engineer instead of an electrical engineer with a grain of salt, though. He just assigned me to projects that I was more able to do and interested in handling.

The MBA was a different story entirely. I accepted an offer to handle investment analysis work for new R&D projects, but when I started, I was assigned to handle overhead budgeting and was working for a different manager than promised. The matter was corrected in a few days after I had a frank discussion with my new manager and his boss that this was not the job I had agreed to take. Both agreed and personally got me reassigned to the right group, but it was an uncomfortable situation for a few days until it was resolved. This was a great learning experience and one every candidate, recruiter, and hiring manager should go out of their way to prevent from happening to them.

But there's more to this than just preventing potential negative problems when a person starts on a new job. According to Gallup in their landmark book *First Break All the Rules: What the World's Greatest Managers Do Differently* and Google's *Project Oxygen*, clarifying job expectations is the number one trait of every successful manager.[2,3] That's why it's important to capture this information as part of preparing the job requisition. During the interview process this will be clarified and likely modified based on the person being hired. During the onboarding process the hiring manager and new hire need to review these objectives in detail, put them in priority order and agree to a plan of action.

After a hiring manager does this a few times, he or she will recognize the importance of preparing performance-based job descriptions during the requisition phase and the time savings involved both pre- and post-hire. Some hiring managers balk at doing this at first until they realize that it needs to be done anyway, especially when the best people start asking about the performance objectives of the job during the interview to determine if the job is worth serious consideration.

Deliver on the Promise

Part of the value of the Performance-based Hiring process is the ability to accurately predict Quality of Hire pre-hire using the same talent scorecard to measure Quality of Hire post-hire. This is possible as long as the performance objectives initially defined before the hire are reasonably the same as the ones assigned post-hire, especially the intensity of the environment and hiring manager's leadership style. A mismatch on any of these factors reduces the likelihood of the person being successful. Just as important is the need for the hiring manager to proactively help the new person achieve these objectives. However, the degree of coaching, training, and support needed to make this happen should have been

---

[2]Harter, J., 2016. *First, Break All the Rules*. New York: Gallup Press.
[3]"Project Oxygen," re:Work, Google. https://rework.withgoogle.com/subjects/managers/.

determined during the assessment process and understood before making the candidate an offer.

Regardless, it needs to be recognized that interviewing is not an exact science, even though the Performance-based Interviewing approach described in this book is as close as you're likely to get. Nonetheless, by comparing differences in predicted and expected performance using the Quality of Hire Talent Scorecard as the framework and using this as feedback, the entire process can be constantly improved.

While it won't be obvious at first, managers who use this process will quickly realize that Performance-based Hiring helps them become better managers by clarifying expectations up front. In many ways this is comparable to pulling the company's performance management process into the pre-hire process. As important is the need for managers to hire strangers the same way they evaluate and hire people they have worked with in the past: based on the person's past performance and potential combined with a job that represents a career move.

Consider this same process from the perspective of a former coworker being hired. This person knows the hiring manager's style and wouldn't consider working for the person again unless the fit was right and there was mutual respect. The person also wouldn't take the job without a clear understanding of the role, the expectations, an understanding of the new company culture and the environment, and why the job represented a good career move.

Now imagine if the hiring manager misled the person or reneged on any of this. It wouldn't happen, at least not more than once. And that's what delivering on the promise means when it comes to hiring strangers.

By spending more time with fewer people and getting to know them better during the assessment process, those hired will be more like acquaintances and less like strangers once the offer is made.

■ SUMMARY

Behind this end-to-end Performance-based Hiring process is the idea that hiring managers need to own the hiring decision and be responsible for achieving Win-Win Hiring outcomes. Without this mindset, shortcuts will be taken and blame will be placed on the talent department and HR. However, with this mindset and by clarifying expectations up front, spending more time with only semifinalists and offering candidates career opportunities, achieving Win-Win Hiring outcomes is not only possible, but likely.

Chapter 3

The Best Candidates Are Often Not the Best Hires

Throughout this book I make the contention that in order to achieve a positive Win-Win Hiring outcome you need to spend more time with fewer people in order for the company, the hiring manager, the recruiter, and the candidate to fully understand the job and to determine if the person being considered is competent and motivated to do the job. But these people need to be the right people or else this extra time is wasted.

In Chapter 12 on sourcing I define a great hire as someone who has been recognized for doing outstanding work in the field of interest and who would also see the job as a career move. When these two conditions are met it increases the likelihood the hiring manager would be open to meet this person and the person would more likely engage in a conversation and accept an offer if one were extended. I refer to these people as semifinalists.

While this idea is great in theory, it falls short in practice when those involved in the hiring decision have a different idea of what the "right people" actually means, how to define it, and how to find candidates who meet the criteria.

The graphic in Figure 3.1 highlights the differences between a great candidate and a great hire. It provides a means for getting people to agree that the people you want to spend more time with are those on the right (the great hires), not those on the left (the great candidates).

In our training programs we start with this graphic to convince hiring managers and recruiters that an overemphasis on skills, experience, and first impressions is a surefire way to wind up hiring the wrong people.

■ THE WORST CANDIDATES ARE OFTEN THE BEST HIRES

Understanding the "great candidate versus great hire" comparison starts by understanding what it means to be a "Great Candidate"

Figure 3.1   The Best Candidates Rarely Become the Best Hires.

and why these people are not necessarily the people you want to attract, interview, recruit, and hire.

Let's first debunk the premise that in order to be a great hire the person must first meet the three conditions on the left side to be seriously considered a worthy candidate. As you review these requirements, compare them to your company's current hiring process to determine what needs to be changed to achieve better hiring results.

Category 1: Great Candidates Must Have All the Basic Skills Listed on the Job Description

Aside from being arbitrary, the problem with this list is that having the skills, required experiences, and "must have" competencies doesn't mean the person will be an outstanding performer. By filtering people on these skills and ultimately hiring them, you wind up with a big bunch of "false positives." These are the people who are competent to do the work but who underperform if they find the actual work unsatisfying or below their current level of expertise.

Putting these lists in job postings is also a bad idea since they're so boring they turn off the most talented people with the skills but who won't apply to what appears to be a boring and ill-defined lateral transfer.

But there's an even bigger and more fundamental problem using these lists to filter and attract candidates – they generate too many false negatives. These are the people who can actually do the work but who have a different mix of skills and experience. The most talented won't apply either, because they assume they'll be considered unqualified.

Some hiring managers might want to minimize the impact of this false negative problem, but they tend to overlook the fact that the best people – including most diverse candidates – have achieved success because they're quick learners, have handled comparable but not identical assignments, and have either volunteered or been assigned to handle stretch projects. In this group of people include everyone who has ever been promoted, since by definition a promotion means the person is being assigned to a new role to learn new skills.

Why anyone would want to exclude this talented group of people from consideration makes no sense, but that's what happens when skills and experiences are used to attract and screen candidates. So if your company is filtering people on this type of listing, recognize you're not seeing the strongest talent available and by default putting a lid on the quality of the people you'll be seeing and hiring.

Category 2: Great Candidates Must Agree to the Terms of an Offer Before Knowing the Job

There are very few outstanding people willing to agree to a compensation range, a job title, and location before first knowing what the job is all about. Yet that's what we expect a person to do before he or she has a chance to get an interview with a hiring manager.

This highlights the need to eliminate the transactional short-term thinking that's embedded into the hiring process of most companies by default. By spending more time with fewer people – as long as they're semifinalists – compensation can be used as a negotiating item, not a filter to have a conversation.

This is also true for the job titles and to a lesser degree location. As long as the job is bigger, or at least equivalent in terms of scope and scale, the title should not be a stumbling block to having an initial conversation. Unfortunately it is, and most recruiters find it difficult to overcome the concern when a strong prospect refuses to even have an exploratory conversation. Location is a bigger problem, but it can often be overcome by having a number of very preliminary "let's get to know each other" conversations with the senior team and the candidate over an extended period of time. With remote work becoming more common, location is not that big an issue anyway.

Again, the requirement for considering a person for a role that filters them on factors that are less relevant, negotiable, or explainable prevents companies from seeing the strongest people and building a deep referral network. But this is common when short-term thinking and efficiency become the measures of hiring success.

Category 3: Great Candidates Need to Be Prepared, Make a Great First Impression, and Be Good at Presenting Themselves

Consider the illogic of this hiring process that is used by most companies: to be granted an interview with the hiring manager, a potentially great candidate must possess the laundry list of skills and experiences listed on the job description *and* must first agree to the terms of an offer. Recruiters who make this determination, despite the obvious flaws, contend they do this to save time.

But the problems continue for those who make it through the initial screening maze. Sadly, the traditional interview itself is an ineffective means to determine if someone is competent and motivated to do the work required. Instead the person is judged through a cloudy and biased lens based on their technical or intellectual brilliance and their personality and presentation skills. Now while many companies use behavioral or some type of structured interview to minimize the damage, most often the rules are short-circuited. Also ignored from the validation studies is that the subset of candidates being assessed is not representative of the best people available since many of these people were filtered out earlier.

There are a number of chapters later in the book on how to conduct more objective and bias-free interviews, but they will be far less effective if the strongest people are never even seen or considered. It's also important to note that the strongest people, many of them passive candidates who could ultimately be great hires, are often less prepared and less formal than those who are more anxious to get hired right away. Since the strongest people are more selective, they want to learn more before getting too excited about a new job. This reluctance or lack of initial enthusiasm is considered a negative by most hiring managers, yet it might actually be a positive indicator of a more discriminating top performer.

It's also important for all interviewers, and hiring managers in particular, to recognize that the strongest people might not be the strongest interviewees even if they are prepared, on time, and excited about the role. Too often this is not the case, and the person hired is the person who makes the best presentation, not the one who is the best performer.

■ SOME GREAT CANDIDATES BECOME GREAT HIRES, BUT MANY MORE DON'T

It's hard for me to comprehend the idea that a great candidate is defined as someone who has applied for the job AND possesses some arbitrary skill set AND agrees to the offer package before knowing the job AND is a good interviewee despite its biased and imperfect nature. Yet this is the process most companies are trying to automate with the promise that artificial intelligence will cure all of the ills.

The solution to the problem is to stop trying to find and hire great candidates and start over. And starting over starts by understanding what it takes to be considered a great hire and then working backwards to figure out what it takes to find, interview, and hire these people. The first step in this backwards thinking process is shifting your emphasis to what is shown on the right side of the graphic in Figure 3.1.

Great Hires Are Easy to Define but Hard to Hire

One way to vividly see the difference between a great candidate and a great hire is to write down the attributes of people you know who are top performers. We've been conducting this same exercise for the past 30-plus years at each of our workshops. Not surprising, the answers are pretty much the same regardless of the job, company, or location. On a big-picture level the common theme among these outstanding people is their ability to consistently achieve or exceed their performance objectives. On a deeper level the specific attributes can be subdivided into the three groups described below and shown in Figure 3.1.

Category 4: Great Hires Deliver the Results without Making Excuses

Once a person gets up to speed, it's easy to spot exceptional performance. Exceeding expectations is often part of this, including taking responsibility for additional work and consistently delivering on the promise. Overcoming bottlenecks and setbacks and not making excuses is a common denominator of great hires. Clues also abound about whether the person will be successful soon after starting. Some include taking the initiative to learn more, going the extra mile, working harder to get up to speed, volunteering for special projects, being resilient and flexible, and doing whatever is necessary to meet deadlines and commitments.

Little of this is predictable using the definition of a great candidate as a starting or filtering point. Some interviewers equate being prepared, on time, and enthusiastic about the job as predictive of work ethic. Unfortunately, initiative to get the job is not the same as intrinsic motivation to do the job.

Category 5: Great Hires Collaborate with Others and Build Strong Teams

There's no dispute that strong team skills are an essential component of being considered a great hire. What's disputed is how to assess them properly during the interview. One problem with assessing team skills is first determining what good team skills actually means. At our workshops we address this by asking attendees to define what great team skills look like once a person is on the job. Here's what we typically hear:

- Strong cross-functional collaboration skills
- Sincere interest and ability to fully understand someone else's point of view

- If person is a manager, able to build and develop a strong team and keep the team motivated despite the typical challenges and frustrations faced
- Proactively coaches and helps peers
- Fits with the culture and the company's way of doing business

Knowing what good team skills look like on the job is a good starting point for assessing them properly. We cover these "how to" techniques in the chapters on interviewing and developing performance-based job descriptions.

Category 6: Great Hires Effectively Organize and Manage Themselves and Their Teams

In some course long ago, I heard that the pillars of good management involved planning, controlling, managing, budgeting, and team development. It turns out these are just as important whether a person is an individual contributor, a member of a team, a project manager, or someone directly managing a team. Everyone has to get their work done on time and on budget.

Even non-managers have to organize teams and manage projects, overcome challenges, obtain resources, make important decisions, and figure out what to do when things go awry. Yet these critical drivers of success are rarely evaluated directly during the interview. The assumption is that the person must possess them if they have the right title and experience working at the right companies. It's a bad assumption.

The competencies related to this are responsibility, commitment, and taking the initiative, but without job-related context these important characteristics are mere buzzwords.

■ WOULD YOU RATHER HIRE A GREAT CANDIDATE, OR SOMEONE WHO DELIVERS GREAT RESULTS?

In Chapter 9 on describing how to conduct a Performance-based Interview, you'll learn how to accurately predict if someone will become a great hire and achieve a Win-Win Hiring outcome.

You'll also discover there's little correlation between these great hires and those who are also great candidates.

In our training we build the great candidates versus great hires comparison one step at a time. Once completed as shown in Figure 3.1, we ask the attendees who they'd rather hire: someone who has all of the skills or someone who can deliver the results. Just about everyone selects the great hires, not the great candidates. This is somewhat obvious, but the next question is the one that really matters.

How well do the criteria defining a great candidate on the left predict the likelihood of a great hire as defined by the factors on the right?

While some initially answer "somewhat," they all respond "probably not" when asked if they've ever met someone who turned out to be a great hire but who had a different mix of skills and experiences than listed on the job description.

They also all agree that what a person gets on the start date in terms of an offer package are all negotiable terms once a candidate learns about the job. In fact, just about all agree that compensation is still an important factor but less important if the job represents a significant career move.

In addition, they all say they know people who are remarkable performers who don't make a great first impression or were a little nervous at the start of the interview.

What they say, though, when asked if they've ever hired someone who met all of the criteria of a great candidate but who underperformed after they were hired, is "Of course."

■ SUMMARY: AVOID THE 90-DAY WONDERS

When it comes to hiring, a 90-day wonder is someone who has been hired but 90 days later you wonder why. More times than not the cause of the problem can be found somewhere in the "great candidates versus great hires" difference described in this chapter.

It's important to highlight the idea that a process designed to produce great candidates more efficiently is a bad process. Doing the wrong things faster, even though they've been validated by flawed statistics and wrapped around state-of-the-art technology and AI, doesn't mean you'll be hiring stronger talent.

Consider that when we hire or promote people we know, it's based on their past performance doing comparable work. In most cases, to attract the person the job itself needs to represent a clear career move superior to other opportunities the person is considering. Given this, and even though there are some unknown factors involved, the likelihood the person will be successful is quite high.

Yet when we hire people who are strangers, we throw out these valuable "best practices" and start over with a bunch of rather dumb ideas. The worst is that these strangers must pass through the "Great Candidate" filtering system, endure a demeaning hiring process, and be willing to accept what amounts to an ill-defined lateral transfer based on some pre-agreed compensation range. This is not how you hire great people.

> *Converting strangers into acquaintances before hiring them is one step. Assessing their past performance doing comparable work is the second step. Offering them a significant career move is the third step.*

This is how you hire great people. This is how you achieve more Win-Win Hiring outcomes.

This is Performance-based Hiring. This is what you'll learn how to do in this book.

Chapter 4

Developing a Bias-Free Hiring Process

This chapter is about controlling interviewer bias. It is the most important chapter in the book since more hiring mistakes are made due to bias than any other cause. In fact, if you read only this chapter

10 Ways to Eliminate Interviewer Bias

Conduct a Pre-hire Performance Review Based on Real Job Needs

Use Panel Interviews
Replace the 30 minute 1:1 Interview with a 2-3 person organized panel.

Script the Interview
Conduct work history review & ask about major accomplishment.

Be a Juror, Not a Judge
Hear all of the evidence before deciding yes or no.

Conduct a Phone Screen First
The phone minimizes the visual part of first impression bias.

No Gladiator Voting
Share evidence in a formal debriefing session using the Talent Scorecard.

Use Reverse Logic
Become cynical with those you like and open-minded with those you don't.

Treat the Person as a Consultant
Assume the person is extremely competent and treat with respect.

Measure First Impression Last
Determine if the person's first impression will help or hurt OTJ performance.

Wait 30 Minutes

Figure 4.1   Conduct a Pre-hire Performance Review.

before conducting another interview and use these techniques for overcoming bias, you'll reduce you're hiring mistakes by at least 50%. (See Figure 4.1.) Part of this reduction will come by not hiring someone who makes the best presentation but won't or can't do the work. The other part of the reduction is more important: hiring a great person you normally wouldn't have by being more objective.

Here's why controlling bias is so important in making an accurate assessment. In my 45-plus years as a recruiter, one thing I learned was that strangers get a bad deal when it comes to being accurately assessed during interviews. While people who are known to the hiring manager are assessed on their past performance, strangers are judged on their motivation to get the job, a bunch of generic competencies, the depth of their technical knowledge, and the quality of their presentation skills. Not only are these terrible predictors of on-the-job performance, worse is they're viewed through a biased lens filled with misconceptions, flawed logic, and a bunch of myths.

For example, if a candidate who's a stranger makes a positive first impression, the interviewer looks for facts to justify the candidate as strong. This is called the halo effect or affinity bias: hiring people who seem most like us. Conversely, if another candidate who's also a stranger makes a negative first impression for whatever reason, the interviewer looks for facts to justify excluding the candidate. Not surprisingly, it's simple to find facts to justify either situation.

Because of this, it's imperative to prevent biases from creeping into the interview as much as possible in order to make accurate and objective hiring decisions. Here are some of the techniques I've found work best. Some of these ideas can be institutionalized, while others require brute force.

■ CONDUCT A PRE-HIRE PERFORMANCE REVIEW

The most important tactical step in the entire Performance-based Hiring process is defining the job as a series of performance objectives rather than a laundry list of skills, experiences, and competencies. This point is mentioned, highlighted, clarified, explained, described, and summarized in just about every chapter in this book, but the repetition is justified. Without doing this as part of preparing the job requisition, you will not be able to achieve a Win-Win Hiring outcome.

It's important to recognize that a list of skills and the like is not a job description, it's a person description. A job description is a list of things the person needs to DO to be successful, NOT a list of things the person needs to HAVE. If it can be proven during the interview that a candidate has successfully handled similar work, it's clear the person has all of the skills and experiences necessary. Typically, this will be different from what's listed on the job description. Outstanding diverse and all high-potential candidates will have a different mix of skills and competencies, but the one thing they'll have in common is their ability and motivation to do the work required.

The Performance-based Interview described in this book is comparable to a pre-hire performance review. It starts by digging into the candidate's past accomplishments and then comparing them to the performance objectives of the new job. This opens the talent pool to everyone who can do the work without compromising performance, fit, or potential.

Never Meet Anyone in Person Before Conducting a Phone Screen

Only Invite Semifinalists for the Full Interview

There's a semi-scripted exploratory phone screen interview guide in Appendix 2 with complete instructions on how to use it most effectively. Its value cannot be overstated. I contend that while all of the other steps that follow are important for controlling bias, conducting the phone screen is the most important for multiple reasons.

For one, the less personal nature of the phone screen naturally reduces bias by eliminating visual clues and focusing on general fit and the person's track record of growth and performance. This is even true for a video interview.

For another, you'll be able to attract stronger people who might be willing to have an exploratory phone call with the hiring manager before becoming seriously interested in the role. This is a great technique for a recruiter to move the process forward by convincing a person who's on the fence to learn more about the role without becoming a fully committed candidate.

For a third reason, you'll save time by only inviting candidates onsite for a full interview who are reasonably qualified and who see the role as something worth investing serious time into fully evaluating. In this case the hiring manager has the responsibility for determining if the person is qualified and if so, convincing the person to become a fully committed candidate.

And last, and maybe most important of all, you'll establish the primary reason for coming onsite: the career growth opportunity inherent in the job, not the size of the compensation package. Making this case is the responsibility of both the recruiter and the hiring manager. This was the recruiting step described in Chapter 2 introducing the Performance-based Hiring process. The idea is to gain a concession from the candidate as a condition for moving forward in the process. This is only possible if the job represents a career move, but that's the purpose of the phone screen: to make the case that it is, if possible.

By establishing an initial connection with the candidate via the phone screen, the candidate's onsite first impression – strong or weak – is far less impactful since you already know the person is capable of doing the work. By getting to know someone this way, you've also started making the shift into converting a total stranger into an acquaintance.

■ USE ORGANIZED PANEL INTERVIEWS

Eliminate the 30-Minute One-on-Ones

A panel interview where the interviewers are allowed to ask their own pet questions, interrupting the candidate and each other, is worse than useless. Maybe worse is the 30-minute series of one-on-one interviews where everyone is invited to make an instant, biased assessment.

However, a well-organized panel interview of about 75 minutes with two to three people is a powerful way to increase assessment accuracy while eliminating bias from the assessment process. The Performance-based Interview described in this book involves asking candidates to describe their major accomplishments most comparable to the performance objectives of the open job. One panelist needs to lead the process asking the major questions, with everyone else asking for clarifying details. The business-like nature of this type of panel interview ensures that the appropriate information is collected based on real job needs rather than each interviewer's perception of these requirements.

The complete Performance-based Interview guide found in the Appendix can be used for conducting an effective panel interview.

The next bias-preventing idea I suggest is giving candidates the answers to the questions. When asking about accomplishments during a panel interview, you might want to describe what constitutes a good answer. (See Figure 4.2.) It will help if you put this on

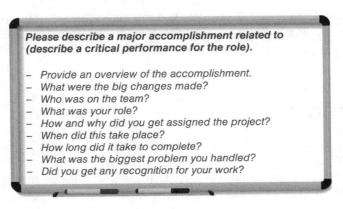

Please describe a major accomplishment related to (describe a critical performance for the role).

- *Provide an overview of the accomplishment.*
- *What were the big changes made?*
- *Who was on the team?*
- *What was your role?*
- *How and why did you get assigned the project?*
- *When did this take place?*
- *How long did it take to complete?*
- *What was the biggest problem you handled?*
- *Did you get any recognition for your work?*

Figure 4.2 Ways to Reduce Interviewer Bias.

a whiteboard or screen for the candidate to provide the information without prompting. Then all members of the panel can ask for clarifying details.

■ SCRIPT THE INTERVIEW AND GIVE CANDIDATES THE QUESTIONS

Football coaches script and practice the first 20 plays of every game. This ensures the game gets started properly. By using pre-scripted interviews, you reduce the chance of going off-script due to the interviewer's emotional reaction to the candidate. In Appendix 2 you'll find a series of interview guides for a variety of different jobs and situations. They all have the same basic Performance-based Interview format of conducting a work-history review, followed by detailed questions about the candidate's major accomplishments. Most important, though, is that using this type of pre-scripted semi-structured interviewing approach minimizes the chance bias will impact the assessment.

Interviewing Tip: Tell candidates you'll be asking about their major team and individual accomplishments and ask them to prepare short fact-filled summaries before the interview. This type of preparation reduces candidate nervousness and results in a smoother and more timely flow to the entire process. During the follow-up fact-finding, the interviewer will be able to validate the information since facts and dates can be verified. In some cases I've given these write-ups to the hiring manager and asked them to review them with the candidate during the interview. This forces the hiring manager to focus on the candidate's major accomplishments. This doesn't require any interview training either.

■ WAIT 30 MINUTES BEFORE MAKING ANY YES OR NO DECISION

My first retained search was with In-N-Out Burger – a highly regarded regional hamburger quick-service restaurant chain in the western U.S. It was around 1990 and the search assignment was for their CFO. I met the CEO at a Vistage/TEC event (a worldwide group supporting

CEOs of midsize companies), where I was a resource providing an overview of Performance-based Hiring. The CEO called me a few weeks later and said one thing stood out at my presentation that resonated the most with him: "Wait 30 Minutes" before making a yes or no hiring decision. He had just tried the technique and it worked as described. While he liked the person at first, by waiting 30 minutes he realized the person wouldn't fit the company's culture despite his superb qualifications. We not only placed the CFO with his firm, but also six other senior-level managers and executives over the next few years who all turned out to be outstanding performers.

Assessment accuracy will increase by collecting evidence before deciding if a candidate is worth considering seriously. This idea is represented by the gauge in Figure 4.3.

While "Wait 30 Minutes" is a simple idea in words, it can be hard to apply in practice since human nature often intervenes, pushing us to make an instant decision based on first impressions. This is the friend versus foe response.[1] Objectivity can be maintained by waiting at least 30 minutes at the beginning of the interview before making any yes or no decision. During this time ask every candidate the same questions, whether your initial reaction is positive or negative.

Figure 4.3   Collect Evidence Before Making Decisions.

---

[1]Trudeau, Michelle. "You Had Me at Hello: The Science Behind First Impressions." NPR, May 5, 2014, www.npr.org/sections/health-shots/2014/05/05/308349318/you-had-me-at-hello-the-science-behind-first-impressions.

Be a Juror, Not a Judge

If you have ever been on a jury trial or watched one on TV, you know the judge's instructions to the jurors are always the same: hear all the evidence before reaching a conclusion. Every interviewer should take the same advice. The idea here is to use the interview to collect the evidence to make a hiring decision, rather than making it during the interview. Despite the logic of this approach, it is very hard to do. Fighting the natural urge to quickly make an intuitive judgment about a person based on their first impression or technical depth requires brute force. Bringing your biases from the subconscious to the conscious level is the first step. Doing it over and over again for each interview will help you reprogram yourself. Even interviewing candidates who appear to be on the margin will help highlight how your biases affect your hiring decisions. Applying the other techniques described here will help you become a fair, impartial, and objective juror.

Use Reverse Logic to Reveal and Reprogram Your Subconscious Biases

This technique involves doing the opposite of what comes naturally. The natural response is for people to relax when they meet a candidate they instantly like and get uptight when this instant reaction is negative. I'm sure you've experienced this whenever meeting someone for the first time, regardless of the situation, business or social.

Make a note about this every time you meet a candidate to interview. A pattern will soon emerge. This will help you reveal your natural biases. Controlling them starts by recognizing you have them and how you act as a result. Most people seek out positive confirming facts for people they like and negative facts for people they don't like. You can neutralize your biases by doing the opposite. In the case of interviewing, this typically means becoming cynical with those you like and more open-minded with those you don't.

One of my clients put the candidate's resume on the right side of the desk when he liked the person and on the left when he didn't. At the end of the interview he wrote down what caused the reaction. Regardless of how you keep track, becoming aware of your biases will help you put them into the background and conduct a more objective interview.

■ TREAT CANDIDATES AS CONSULTANTS

Rather than trying to use the interview to prove the person isn't qualified, take the opposite point of view: assume the person is fully competent at the beginning of the interview regardless of your immediate reaction, positive or negative. This is the professional and courteous thing to do anyway, especially when a person has taken the time to be interviewed. By giving deference to someone who is a recognized subject matter expert or a highly regarded consultant, the interview is more like a discussion among equals. Ask about the person's major accomplishments, and if there's a fit, get into a professional dialogue about how the person would go about solving a realistic problem likely to be faced on the job. Within 30–45 minutes you'll know if the person is worth considering.

Another benefit of this approach is that hiring a person as a consultant doesn't have the same long-term performance risk as there is with hiring a full-time employee. Nor is there the same interpersonal requirement that exists when hiring someone you'll be working with on a regular basis. So separating the two decisions – technical competency and long-term fit – is one way to reduce bias.

Long ago I learned how to overcome interviewing bias by accident when asked to interview someone the company was considering for a short-term consulting assignment. The person came highly referred but I was instantly put off by his appearance, age, and accent. Regardless, since we weren't going to be best friends or even work together for very long, none of this mattered.

To get started I asked the person to give me a quick overview of his background and how he got to be an "expert" in the project area he was being considered to handle. It took 20 minutes to go through his work history and understand some of his major accomplishments and why he got assigned to them. It was readily apparent he was a quick learner, hard worker, and had the right background for handling projects comparable in scope, scale, and complexity to the process improvement project envisioned. After learning more about his accomplishments related to the project he would be working on, there was another big surprise. By the end of the hour-long interview I was dumbfounded that I barely noticed his accent, his appearance was far better than I first thought, and I realized his age had nothing to do with his ability. As important, I was looking forward to working with him on the project.

Kill the Gladiators

Use a Talent Scorecard to Share Evidence

It's essential to eliminate thumbs-up/thumbs-down "gladiator" voting where the person with the biggest thumb tilts the scale on who gets hired or not. In Appendix 2 you'll find a talent scorecard summarizing the factors we've seen that best predict on-the-job success. Biased versus objective evidence is instantly exposed when each member of the hiring team shares their reasons for justifying a score. This is a great learning experience too because everyone understands that objective evidence requires facts, dates, metrics, and specific details, not emotions and gut feelings.

This became instantly apparent when I first started using this type of Quality of Hire Talent Scorecard. As a recruiter I wanted to ensure the candidates I was representing were objectively evaluated since I didn't want to redo the entire search because someone misjudged the person. That's why I suggested having these formal debriefing sessions that I volunteered to lead. During one of these sessions for a VP of Operations for an automotive parts manufacturer, the VP of Sales didn't believe my candidate was strong enough to ensure the sales growth he forecasted could be sustained. His evidence was flimsy at best, filled with emotional jargon like "He just didn't have the right attitude," and "He doesn't seem like someone who would listen to the sales team." He changed his mind quickly, though, once a few others on the interviewing team provided specific recent and tangible evidence disproving his concerns.

While it's not possible to eliminate all forms of bias, you can implement techniques like these to first expose it and then root it out of your hiring process.

■ MEASURE FIRST IMPRESSIONS LAST

Last year during one of our hiring manager training sessions, a VP of Sales got upset that I said first impressions don't matter. She went on to say that for salespeople first impressions do matter, so she couldn't agree with this step in the Performance-based Interviewing methodology. I then asked her if everyone with a good first impression turns out to be great salesperson. She said, "Of course not." So I said why not wait until the interview is over to determine if the person's first impression will help or hinder the person's sales results. This way you won't be seduced one way or the other. She agreed this was a good idea.

Not surprisingly, when I checked in with her a few months after the initial training, she said that this idea worked even better than predicted. She rejected some sales candidates who made a great first impression but who had a spotty record of sales results. She also found a few people who didn't make a great impression but who had a strong track record of sales results whom she ultimately hired. To her surprise, she said that by deferring judgment until the end of the interview, it turned out these people's first impressions were not so bad.

This "surprise" happens all of the time for all types of jobs, including sales. Some people get nervous when talking about themselves. Some talk too much, others not enough. But by the end of the interview, when asked meaningful questions, people become their natural selves. It's an eye-opening experience for the interviewer as long as you can wait until the interview is over to have it. These people are often called the "hidden gems." They were always there; you just have to work hard to see their ability.

■ SUMMARY

While each of these tips will help minimize the impact of bias when interviewing, it's even better when all of the steps are embedded throughout your company's hiring processes. This will ensure you're not only seeing the strongest and most diverse talent possible, but also that each person is objectively assessed. And that's important, whether the person is a stranger or an acquaintance.

Chapter 5

Using the BEST Test to Reduce Unconscious Bias

This chapter will demonstrate how to use personality assessments, also called psychometric tests, in a few unique ways to help increase objectivity and improve interviewing accuracy. These are not the normal uses of these tests, but as you'll discover, that's what makes them much more useful. For example, to get the best results it's helpful for the interviewer to take the same tests to uncover their own biases and control them during the interview.

BEST personality test, introduced in this chapter, is a simple way to accomplish this in a few minutes. The idea behind this technique is that by becoming "least like" themselves personality style-wise, interviewers will learn a huge lesson in what it takes to fully understand someone else's point of view.

Another way to make these tests more useful is by asking candidates to describe their major accomplishments for each of the major personality types. This way you'll be able to determine the person's flexibility using different types and how effective they are when doing it.

■ TWO HUGE FLAWS IN PERSONALITY ASSESSMENTS THAT ARE OFTEN IGNORED

These two unusual ways to use psychometric tests will have a profound effect on improving assessment accuracy while overcoming these two big flaws:

1. When personality assessment tests are used as part of the early screening, they reward anti-diversity practices since companies are just hiring more of the people who have already been hired.

2. These tests only measure preferences, not competencies. Having the "right" personality style doesn't mean a person is good at it and having the "wrong" one doesn't mean the person is incompetent either.

While these assessments have value when used properly and at the appropriate time in the hiring process, these two problems are not insignificant. Let me first explain the "cloning" problem caused by using assessments too soon in the hiring process.

In Chapter 2 introducing the Performance-based Hiring process, the idea was presented on how suboptimization can exclude good candidates by seeming to make one step in a larger business process more efficient while ignoring the negative downstream impact. Psychometric and many preemployment assessments are perfect examples of this since they can inadvertently exclude the most talented and most diverse people. These are people who can excel at doing the work but achieve it with a different style. As part of the Performance-based Interviewing process, described in depth in Chapter 9, it's possible to determine this by delaying slightly when the assessment is used.

But first, some history is required describing how I learned about the problems associated with these tests and how they are improperly used for hiring purposes. Back in the '80s I took my first DiSC personality assessment and its cousin, the Predictive Index (PI). (In fact, during this time I visited the people who popularized these tests and learned how they originally were part of the same company.[1])

Like the Myers-Briggs Type Indicator (MBTI), these types of assessments involve a series of either/or questions, like "Would you rather attend a beer bust or do root cause analysis?" Given these types of "either/or" questions, the DiSC and PI tests concluded I liked to persuade people with a hammer and that I was a weak analyst. I took another updated version of the PI just recently with similar results. This assessment was incorrect 40-plus years ago and it's still incorrect today.

While I prefer to party and argue, these are not my core strengths. My core competency, which I'm really good at, is detailed multifunctional analysis of complex business processes. While this is somewhat anecdotal, it pretty much demonstrates the second biggest problem with these types of psychometric assessments: they measure preferences, not competencies. If you've ever hired someone who passed the test but flunked the on-the-job performance part of the exam, you have your own anecdotes for confirmation.

This is why these types of assessments generate so many false positives in the process. These are people who supposedly have

[1]"DISC: The History of DISC Personality Styles." *Disc Insights*, discinsights.com/disc-history.

the "right" personality profile but aren't very good at doing the work required. I remember one candidate who told me he was an ENTJ – "Life's Natural Leader" in Myers-Briggs terminology – with his buttons popping off. That was at least until I asked him to give me an example of his greatest leadership accomplishment. A few minutes later he timidly left my office when the example he used to prove his dominant strength was rather insignificant.

Statistical Validation Understates the Impact of False Negatives

Despite this huge flaw, the test vendors validate their results using statistical analysis that show reasonable but not remarkable correlation. In my opinion, being right and wrong 40% of the time just isn't good enough. This is only half the problem though.

Aside from the loose correlation and false positive problem, the false negatives are even worse. These tests totally ignore the fact that the strongest people are flexible and can modify their preferred style based on the needs of the situation even if their preferred style doesn't meet some contrived standard. These are the people who take the assessment but are screened out too early in the process and are never seen.

If all of the above is not enough to dissuade you from using these assessments to screen candidates, consider all of the best people, whether they have the "right" style or not and who are exceptionally competent but won't take the tests until they learn about the job.

This is why I contend these tests should never be used for initial screening purposes since they cause too many false positives, too many false negatives, and they prevent some of the best people who won't take the test before they learn about the job to be seen.

One way to eliminate some of these problems is using the two-step process described in Chapter 12 on sourcing. In this approach all candidates who reply to a job post are first invited to submit some type of work sample before officially being considered a candidate. By comparing this work sample to their personality profile, both the false positive and false negative problems will be eliminated.

The idea with the two-step application process (see Appendix I for the legal validation for this) is that if the major accomplishment isn't comparable to the requirements of the job, the person wouldn't be seen regardless of personality type. On the other hand, if the accomplishment is comparable, the person can then be invited to take the personality test to become an official candidate for the job. Used this way any differences between expected personality type and the actual accomplishment can then be discussed during the interview. For example, figuring out how a very analytical person handled a big project, making lots of decisions with limited data, or how a more influential and persuasive person got into the details before making an important decision.

■ PERSONALITY ASSESSMENTS ARE VALUABLE WHEN USED LATER IN THE HIRING PROCESS

Despite these concerns, these tests are quite useful for assessing the three to four finalists for a job to see how their natural style has impacted their individual and team performance either positively or negatively. In fact, I use and recommend these tests in combination with some cognitive skills testing to validate the results of the Performance-based Interviewing process described in this book. Used this way, these personality assessments are very helpful for generating additional questions to better understand the person.

Given my "use later in the process" suggestion, I talked to the CEO of one of the major test vendors when writing the first edition of Hire with Your Head to get his insight about my point of view. While he mostly agreed with the validity of my concerns, he said he was in the business of selling tests and if companies wanted to screen candidates using them with the proper cautionary statements, he was not going to change his business model despite the logic. And that's the problem with using these tests and why the vendors will never publicly agree with these conclusions.

It's important to note that my concerns about using these tests only refer to the prescreening process, nothing else. Using these tests post-hire to better understand how people make decisions and interact with others is appropriate and provides valuable insight.

■ TAKE THE BEST TEST BEFORE INTERVIEWING ANYONE

Given all of these pros and cons and in-betweens, let me make an offer you can't refuse:

➤ The BEST personality test is a better one-minute no-cost alternative. In fact, once you take it, you'll better understand the flaws involved in all of these types of psychometric tests and some of their hidden strengths.

➤ After studying the results of these tests for many years it was clear that two factors dominated the overall assessments. One involved the preference people had for how they made decisions – either fast or slow. This captured the intuitive versus analytical mindset found in all of these psychometric assessments. The other dimension related to how a person balanced the need for results versus their sensitivity to the needs of the people they work with. This factor captures the feeling and perceiving factors in the Myers-Briggs type indicator versus the less personal thinking and judging factors. This mapping might not be perfect, but this is less important than understanding how the two BEST factors can be used to improve your hiring results.

➤ The "Super Pareto" 90/10 version of these assessments is called the BEST test. The graphical version is shown in Figure 5.1. While you can and should use it for assessing candidates during the interview, it's even more useful for interviewers to take it just before they interview anyone to help expose and control their biases.

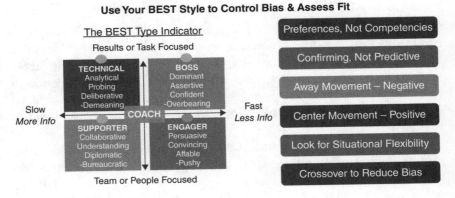

Figure 5.1 Use Your BEST Style to Increase Interviewing Accuracy.

Figuring out your BEST personality type starts with just these two questions:

➤ Put yourself on the right side of the 2X2 BEST matrix if you prefer to make quick decisions and on the left if you're more cautious. (Hint: If it takes you more than a few seconds to figure this out, you're on the left more cautious side.)

➤ Assign yourself to the top half if you tend to focus more on results than people and on the bottom half if the reverse is true. (Hint: If you're wondering what people will think of you as you figure out your answer, you're somewhere on the people-focused bottom half.)

Based on this analysis, you're either a **B**oss, **E**ngager, **S**upporter, or **T**echnical. Read the descriptions of each type to see if they're reasonably close for you and modify your position on the grid as appropriate. The center position is the coaching position. Flexible people adopt this style to better understand others' points of view. The descriptor with the minus sign at the bottom of each square indicates movement away from the center coaching position and describes how inflexible people react when under stress by becoming the worst-case versions of themselves.

Changes in BEST Style Reveal Growth and Flexibility

The descriptions below are generalizations of the four BEST styles, but I think you'll see that for a one-minute assessment they're quite accurate. As important, recognize the simplistic nature of the BEST test, and its predecessors, and why they're not accurate enough to be used for screening purposes. It provides a false and unjustified sense of being more efficient and more accurate when neither is the case.

The **B**oss: These people are primarily focused on achieving the results. As part of this they are comfortable making quick decisions with limited information as long as progress is made. They are more of the A-type "let's get it done as soon as possible" personality and have little regard for the impact this has on the people they manage or work with regularly. Under stress they can become belligerent and overbearing.

The **E**ngager: These people are more extroverted, with the people interactions and relationships driving their decision-making. They tend to be friendly and outgoing. They use persuasion and logic to move the team forward, even if the criteria they use is not fully developed or fully understood. Missing a few deadlines is less important to them than keeping the people they work with satisfied. Under stress they can become pushy and manipulative.

The **S**upporter: These people are more cautious. While focused on the team over the results, they don't want to make decisions until they've fully studied the situation and gathered as many facts as possible. They go out of their way to gain consensus with the team before moving forward on a plan of action. Their slowness can frustrate those who want to move forward more rapidly. Under stress they can become bureaucratic or political.

The **T**echnical: These are the classic analytical types. They get into the details and want to fully understand what the numbers, facts, and specifications mean and what their implications are. They certainly don't want to be rushed until their analysis is complete and are very uncomfortable making decisions without this information. They can be a bit impersonal and Spock-like when considering the impact of their approach on those they work with. Under stress they can become distant or demeaning.

While these descriptions are one-dimensional, what is more insightful is how a person's BEST style changes over time and under different circumstances.

Assess Team Skills by Observing Changes in BEST Type over Time

You'll be able to assess team and critical thinking skills by determining if a candidate naturally moves to the coaching position whenever the person is trying to fully understand all sides of an issue and whether this movement is situational or permanent.

One way to do this is to ask candidates to give a few different examples of team accomplishments over the past few years. As part of this, get examples of decision-making, problem-solving, and handling conflict where different BEST styles would logically be needed to fully understand the situation and find the best solution. After a few accomplishments at different periods in time, you'll see patterns emerge revealing whether the candidate modified his or her dominant BEST style to meet the needs of the situation or uses a "one-size-fits-all situations" approach. Raise the caution flag high when you see people who are this one-sided or who become more extreme in their natural style.

Assess Flexibility by Observing Changes in BEST under Stress

After working with hundreds of different managers over extended periods of time I've seen that the strongest people, regardless of their preferred style, adjust their dominant style and move towards the center or coaching position as they become more comfortable in their roles. This is how they're able to understand and collaborate with others more effectively. On the other hand, the least flexible people move away from the center when under stress, converting their core strengths into weaknesses. In these cases, the Boss becomes even more demanding, the Engager becomes in-your-face, the Supporter becomes rule-bound, and the Technical becomes hard-nosed.

While making this assessment is covered in the chapters on interviewing, you can get a sense of a person's flexibility using the different BEST personality styles by asking the candidate to provide an example of a major accomplishment for each one. For example, ask a person who's a strong-willed Boss to describe their biggest accomplishment related to achieving consensus among a very diverse team. This will also allow the interviewer to determine the person's competency level for each of the styles. In the Boss example, the person's competency would be pretty low if the example chosen was insignificant and pretty high if the person did something remarkable that was totally out of character.

However, you'll appreciate and understand this ability to adopt a different personality style depending on the situation even more once you step out of your own natural style while conducting the interview.

Increase Interview Accuracy by Becoming Your "Least BEST"

In addition to controlling your biases as described in Chapter 4, another way to become a more objective interviewer is by forcing yourself to move towards the coaching or center position shown in the graphic. You can accomplish this in real time by temporarily adopting the attributes of your diagonally opposite style during the interview. As part of this transformation, it's important to note that in general people get along best with those who are most like them or adjacent to them style-wise. Those who are least like themselves are their diagonal opposites. Their differences cause both conflict and misunderstanding.

By adopting this polar opposite style you'll be able to neutralize some of your own biases during the interview, which will allow you to better understand how a candidate's style impacted their accomplishments and if this approach would work within your organization. This is part of the cultural fit assessment described in Chapter 6, "The Hiring Formula for Success."

Here's how to become your "least BEST":

The Boss: By listening more before judging a candidate's answers and asking about team projects, the Boss can be more like a Supporter.

The Supporter: Getting lots of metrics and details about the results the candidate has achieved allows a Supporter to become Boss-like.

The Engager: Engagers can become like Techies by digging into the process the candidate used to achieve results rather than making instant decisions based on personality.

The Technical: Techies can become Engagers by shifting their emphasis from determining technical brilliance to finding out how the person collaborated and influenced people on their team projects to achieve results.

■ SUMMARY: USE THE BEST TEST TO CONFIRM RATHER THAN PREDICT

BEST and similar personality type indicators have their good and bad points. Since they only assess preferences, not competencies, these tests should not be used for screening candidates before they're interviewed. However, it is appropriate to use these types of tests for the short list of finalists to determine how they adapt their natural style based on the circumstances. More important is for interviewers to take this test ahead of time to override their natural decision-making approach to evaluate candidates more objectively. This is actually the BEST way to improve interviewing accuracy and hire the right person for the right reasons.

Chapter 6

The Hiring Formula
for Success

■ WIN-WIN HIRING BEGINS WITH THE END IN MIND

One of Stephen Covey's 7 *Habits of Highly Effective People*[1] is "Begin with the end in mind." This is great advice whenever doing any type of project work or planning, especially when it comes to implementing a new hiring process like Performance-based Hiring. In fact, I'd urge you to read the book since many of Covey's "7 Habits" are the core competencies the people you'll be hiring should possess, regardless of the role.

"Think win-win" is another one of Covey's seven habits. When it comes to hiring, this habit is doubly important. It means ensuring the new hire and the hiring manager both recognize the importance of making the right decision and both have all of the information needed to make the right one. This requires true transparency. Due to its importance this habit has been adopted as the overriding goal and theme of Performance-based Hiring and rightly called "Win-Win Hiring." It means hiring for the anniversary date rather than the start date. While a worthwhile and ambitious goal, ensuring successful performance throughout the first year requires a new way of thinking about the interviewing process and determining what information is required to more accurately predict a Win-Win Hiring outcome.

Getting to this new beginning starts by considering what hasn't worked in the past.

After years of tracking hundreds of people, it became obvious that most people get hired based on criteria that doesn't predict success: typically their individual contributor skills, their technical depth, an ability to interview well, how prepared they are, their forced enthusiasm for the job despite little insight about it, and their first impression. The problem with this is that when they underperform most of the time it's due to their lack of soft skills; poor decision-making; weak organizational ability; inability to fit with the team, manager, or company culture; or lack of motivation to do the actual work required. Some of the time, though, it's caused by situational circumstances that prevent the new hire from doing his or her best work.

---

[1] Covey, Stephen R. *The 7 Habits of Highly Effective People*. Franklin Covey, 1998.

Predicting Hiring Success Requires Much More Than Assessing Ability

The Hiring Formula for Success shown in Figure 6.1 was developed to address the wide difference between the factors assessed during the interview and what really occurs on the job. Simply put:

The ability to do the work in relation to fit drives motivation and ultimately successful performance. And because motivation to do the actual work is so important, it's squared in the formula.

In some way this is probably comparable to Einstein's Theory of Relativity[2] and Energy = mass times the speed of light squared ($E=mc^2$), but I'll leave this comparison to others to prove. Nonetheless, if you don't get the "motivation to excel" component of the formula properly assessed, on-the-job performance will suffer.

Underlying the formula is the idea that predicting on-the-job performance needs to consider all of the factors that not only define a person's ability to do the work but also those that impact a person's motivation to do this work. These are the environmental

Hiring Formula for Success

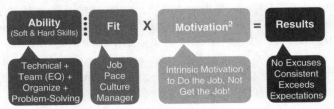

The ability to do the work in relationship to fit drives motivation and ultimately successful performance.

Figure 6.1   Hiring Formula for Success.

---

[2]"Theory of Relativity." Wikipedia, Wikimedia Foundation, March 7 2021, en.wikipedia.org/wiki/Theory_of_relativity.

or fit factors and include cultural fit, fit with the team, fit with the job itself, and fit with the hiring manager's style for managing, coaching, and leading.

From an interviewing standpoint, the formula highlights the need to put just as much effort into assessing the fit factors as done for assessing the person's ability to do the work. In addition to technical competency, this includes team skills, organizational and project management ability, soft skills, communication skills, upside potential, ability to learn, and problem-solving and thinking ability.

It's important to emphasize that without the right fit even the most capable person will underperform. We've all experienced this situation, whether in others we've worked with or through personal experience. It's easy to get demotivated when any of these external fit factors persist for any extended period of time. Under these conditions it's hard to consistently stay motivated and do our best work. According to Gallup,[3] the lack of the right fit has a huge impact on overall employee productivity. In fact, Gallup estimates[4] that the cost in lost productivity just due to unnecessary turnover is one trillion dollars per year just in the U.S. While their financial estimate seems overwhelming, it is a huge and correctable problem.

Gallup's studies show that employee engagement has plodded along at a dismal 30–35% for the past 20 years. This means that two-thirds of the workforce is somewhat or significantly dissatisfied with their jobs. Little has changed over the years to improve these outcomes despite the enormous investment made in new hiring tools and training. I contend the reason why this happens when hiring someone has to do with too much emphasis on the short-term issues and not enough on the long-term fit factors that drive motivation.

If fact, in his book *The End of Average*,[5] Harvard Professor Todd Rose considers fit the primary driver of personal performance and motivation. He refers to fit as the context of the job and without

[3]Gallup, Inc. "Employee Engagement." Gallup Topic, www.gallup.com/topic/employee_engagement.aspx.
[4]Wigert, Shane, and Ben McFeely. "This Fixable Problem Costs U.S. Businesses $1 Trillion." Gallup, January 29, 2021, hiring.tips/Gallup_trillion.
[5]Rose, Todd. *The End of Average: How We Succeed in a World That Values Sameness*. HarperOne, 2017.

fully considering it for hiring purposes individual success is problematic. According to Rose, context relates to how a person's skills and competencies are used on the job and in the environment in which this work takes places. All of these interrelationships have been captured in the Hiring Formula for Success.

The Hiring Formula for Success Captures the Dynamics of Actual Performance

The Hiring Formula for Success provides a good summary of the information needed to make an accurate hiring decision. The formula can also be used to organize the interview with each of the members of the hiring team given a few of the factors to own. During the interview they'll ask the candidates to provide examples of accomplishments that best demonstrate the factor being evaluated. This is comparable to behavioral interviewing, with one big difference: the example chosen to demonstrate the skill or competency needs to be directly related to one of the actual performance objectives of the job. Without this direct connection, the assessment will be flawed. During the debriefing session, each hiring team member will then share the evidence used to rank the person and how it compares to an actual job requirement. When it comes to making an accurate yes or no hiring decision, this is "the end in mind" we want to achieve.

Having personally been involved in more than 2,000 different hiring situations over the past 40 years and tracking the subsequent performance of many of those who were hired, it's clear most hiring mistakes are attributed to the following nontechnical factors:

➤ The hiring manager and the new hire don't work very well together.

➤ Lack of intrinsic motivation or full commitment to do the actual work required. Ability to do the work is far different than motivation to do it.

➤ Weak interpersonal skills. Much of this relates to the new hire's inability to collaborate cross-functionally, coupled with the lack of appreciation for the needs of others.

➤ Lack of flexibility dealing with change.

➤ Frustration with the pace of the organization including how decisions are made and the lack of available resources.

➤ An inability for the new hire to properly manage and organize his or her work properly. This is true whether the person is an individual contributor or a manager.

➤ For management roles, in addition to the above, it's an inability to build, manage, and develop the team assigned.

Some people group these factors collectively under the "soft skills" label. In my mind this minimizes their importance since without them people will underperform. Despite this, too many interviewers still focus too much on the person's technical ability – the so-called "hard skills" – and not enough on the factors that actually impact on-the-job performance.

Many HR leaders contend that generic competencies are a useful means to assess these nontechnical and personality factors. From what I've seen this is not sufficient, providing only incremental improvement, unless they're directly related to the actual job and the specific situation.

The Hiring Formula for Success addresses all of these issues by describing how a person's performance relates not just to the person's ability to do the work but also to the surrounding circumstances. It turns out that of all of the factors in the formula, technical ability to do the work is the easiest of the factors to assess and motivation to excel is the hardest.

Motivation to get the job is not the same as motivation to do the job. That's why getting the motivation assessment wrong happens so often.

While technical ability isn't simple to assess, it's pretty straightforward once you convert the major skills into performance objectives. The same is true for all of the nontechnical and soft skills like project management, resiliency, flexibility, and team skills. You'll assess these factors during the interview by asking about the person's most comparable accomplishments and spending extra time finding out how these technical and nontechnical skills were used to achieve the results obtained. The specific techniques on how to do this are covered in the chapters describing how to prepare performance profiles and conduct Performance-based Interviews. Interview guides and templates are provided in Appendix 2 to help you get started using this approach.

Motivation to excel turns out to be the hardest to measure since it fluctuates so much over time and depends on many different and variable circumstances. Too many interviewers assume motivation to get the job, assertiveness, and how prepared the person is for the interview are clues for measuring motivation to do the job. It's not that simple. Motivation to get the job is not the same as motivation to do the job. That's why getting the motivation assessment wrong happens so often. Since motivation is largely driven by the fit factors, measuring fit should be a dominant focus of most interviews. When it comes to achieving a Win-Win Hiring outcome, this represents the difference between a good hiring decision and a bad one.

■ THE BIG FOUR FIT FACTORS DRIVE MOTIVATION TO EXCEL

Without a complete assessment of the fit factors and how they affect motivation and performance, it's problematic if the person will achieve the performance objectives of the job defined when the job requisition was first prepared. All of these detailed "how-to" interviewing techniques will be covered in this book, but here's the "beginning with the end in mind" introduction focusing on the top four fit factors.

Define the Fit Factors as Part of the Job Description

It took me about 15 years to figure out and validate the Hiring Formula for Success. But developing it started around 1990 when one of my clients said he would give my staffing firm all of his company's search projects if I would give him a one-year guarantee on all of the placements we made. He even went further by saying he'd be an advocate for my firm to other members of his business group if I'd go along with this and if it was successful.

Word quickly spread, and we had more search work then we could handle given that no one else was offering a one-year guarantee. However, it took another three years to actually figure out that the fit factors were the critical ingredients to on-the-job performance and how to assess them during the interview.

When we first offered the one-year guarantee we had already started using performance-based job descriptions to define the job, but the circumstances underlying the job were less clear. Despite this shortcoming, in the 10 years before we offered a one-year guarantee we had very few candidates quit or get fired in the first year. In fact, for the roughly 500 mid-management placements we made in those earlier years, less than 15% ever left in the first year for any reason and over 50% either got promoted or their role was expanded. This success was all attributed to the use of a performance profile to define the job and developing the Performance-based Interviewing methodology. By defining the job this way as a prerequisite, making the leap to formally offer the one-year guarantee was more a matter of refining the interviewing process rather than a major overhaul.

Once we figured out the critical fit factors and how to assess them, our one-year success rate was even better: less than 5% left in the first year and over 60% got promoted or their jobs were expanded. This was based on an additional one thousand or so mid-level and senior management placements. But there were some important lessons learned in getting these results that highlight some of the problems other companies and hiring managers are likely to face when using these same techniques.

■ THE FIT FACTORS AND THEIR IMPACT ON JOB PERFORMANCE

As we started to interview candidates we placed after they started working, it became clear that motivation to do the work depended on all of the fit factors, with the most important being the hiring manager's style. If the hiring manager and the new hire didn't get along, performance would be rocky regardless of everything else. However, if the hiring manager was a strong leader, he or she would normally be able to compensate for any potential problems that might arise. Given a reasonable hiring manager to new hire relationship, intrinsic motivation to do the work then becomes the dominant factor driving long-term hiring success.

Since we started getting more search work from small and mid-size companies that were members of TEC/Vistage and YPO (Young Presidents Organizations) – these are business groups where CEOs meet on a regular basis – some things became readily apparent. The biggest ones were how the owner's style dominated the company culture, how decisions were made, how professional the company was, and how people were managed. Some of these CEOs were exceptional leaders and managers, others were more independent and free-wheeling, and some were just terrible. Giving a one-year guarantee under the more trying conditions required a lot more effort in understanding the factors that impacted the performance of every candidate we placed.

The Impact of Managerial Fit on New Hire Success

The biggest issue with these smaller companies – typically around $10 to $100 million in annual revenue – was how the hiring manager's typically dominant leadership style meshed with the new employee's need for coaching, direction, and management. I had to "fire" one of my biggest clients who turned out to be a very difficult person to work for. As a result he churned through many outstanding people, often in just a few months after they started. During this period of soul searching and investigation I heard about Ken Blanchard's program on Situational Leadership.[6] The idea behind this was for the hiring manager to adapt his or her style to better mesh with the needs of the team. For hiring purposes and to achieve more Win-Win Hiring outcomes, I reversed this idea and decided to find people who could mesh with the hiring manager's dominant style instead. This became the Managerial Fit piece in the Hiring Formula for Success.

In Performance-based Hiring terminology, *Managerial Fit* relates to how the person needs or wants to be managed and how this compares to how the hiring manager actually manages and develops

---

[6]Blanchard, Ken, and Spencer Johnson. *The One Minute Manager.* HarperCollinsBusiness, 1996.

people. In Chapter 9 on interviewing there's a chart describing how to determine the manager's style, ranging from hands-off to in-your-face micromanagement. During the interview you can find out the candidate's preferences by asking the person how their hiring managers helped or hindered their ability to achieve their goals. This will give you a sense of how the person's manager affected the person's success. Raise the caution flag very high if the soon-to-be hiring manager's style is at odds with how the person needs or wants to be managed.

(As an FYI, I quit my industry job running a business unit making automotive accessories to become a recruiter because my boss – the group president – and I clashed every time we met. He was a micromanager, and I wanted no direction whatsoever. This is a classic example of less than zero managerial fit!)

Job Fit: Intrinsic Motivation to Do the Work Actually Required

Job fit relates to work the person finds intrinsically motivating and how this compares to the needs of the job. If the person is not naturally motivated to do the actual work required, he or she will need too much direction and will likely underperform. When asking about accomplishments during the interview, get lots of examples of when the candidate took the initiative or went the extra mile. Patterns will soon emerge revealing the work the person finds intrinsically motivating. By comparing this to the performance objectives of the job, you'll be able to accurately predict job fit.

For example, if a candidate always seems to proactively work on difficult technical challenges without prompting but the job largely involves design improvement work, the person is not likely to get too excited if this is a major part of the new job. In these cases the hiring manager will need to intervene and constantly push or urge the person along. All hiring managers have been in this situation and it's terribly demotivating from their perspective. All of this wasted time can be avoided by preparing a performance profile when opening a new job requisition focusing on ensuring there is excellent job fit during the interview. On the other hand, if a candidate for a management role seems to make it a habit of making and implementing personal development plans for his or her team, you can be comfortable the person will continue to do this if it's an important part of the new role.

Team Fit and EQ

Team fit relates to how the person interacts with others. It's important to note that neither affability nor a great first impression are good predictors of team skills, yet too many interviewers get seduced by these factors.

A good indicator of team skills is if the person continues to be assigned to comparable teams and at different companies. To figure this out during the interview, ask candidates to describe the teams they've been assigned to, how they got assigned to the teams, the types of people who were on the teams, the role the person played, and if these teams were growing in size and importance over time. Then compare all of this to the types of teams the person will likely be assigned to in the new role. Even if there's a good fit on this measure, be concerned if the team's importance and/or the person's roles are not getting more important over time.

Cultural Fit Is More Than a Value Statement

Just about everyone is confused about how to define and measure company culture. Despite the challenge, it's necessary to figure it out since it's a critical fit factor and needs to be properly assessed.

In our training programs we ask hiring managers from the same company how important cultural fit is for people they hire. They all understand its importance but when asked to define it, few can. And despite their long-winded answers, there is little agreement. Try it out for yourself to see where your company stands on this measure. Typically the definitions relate to some value statement about how employees or customers are treated or some higher purpose. While these can sound nice, they have little value when interviewing someone. With no definitive consensus of company culture, this part of the assessment often boils down to first impressions, gut feelings, the person's age or ethnicity, or something even less insightful like the person's attire or how he/she treated the receptionist.

I've found that a good proxy for cultural fit relates to the pace of the organization, the organizational structure, the depth of resources available, and how decisions are made. If a person can't deal with whatever exists on these factors, he or she will underperform and often this will be attributed to lack of cultural fit. To assess this during the interview, ask about the person's major accomplishments and then find out how the cultural fit factors impacted the person's motivation, attitude, and performance. One way to get at this quickly is to have the person walk you through the process they used to make a few major decisions at different companies. Then ask if there was a preference for one approach over another and how this impacted the results. This will typically reveal many of these cultural differences and which ones are preferred.

From a cultural fit standpoint, it's great if the person has shown flexibility in different environments. At a minimum, though, there needs to at least be a fit with the pace and intensity components of cultural fit and how decisions are made. For example, someone from a large professionally run company with deep resources is unlikely to be at ease working more independently at a start-up with decisions being made on the fly with little information. This will be true despite candidates saying this is exactly what they are looking for and why they want to change jobs.

Be a cynic in this case unless you can prove the person has thrived in similar and recent situations. I was on an interviewing team recently where we raised this exact concern with a candidate for a senior marketing role. While she was a remarkable person with a great track record at a large well-run company, her best example of running a smaller team happened 15 years earlier, just after she received her MBA degree.

■ SUMMARY

Because motivation is at the core of exceptional performance, it's squared in the Hiring Formula for Success. Unfortunately, before even meeting the person, potential candidates are screened based on some arbitrary list of skills and academic requirements that have little to do with ability or motivation to do the work. Making matters worse, when deciding whom to hire, the person's motivation to get the job and their first impression dominate the yes/no hiring decision. The solution to this conundrum is recognizing that the fit factors drive success and unless they're assessed accurately, success is unlikely, no matter how capable the candidate is. The best managers can help their new staff members overcome many of these obstacles, but it's important to identify them before the person is hired.

By using the Hiring Formula for Success as a guidepost for collecting the best information to make an accurate Win-Win Hiring decision, it becomes a perfect example of how to begin with the end in mind.

Chapter 7

Understanding the Real Job Starts with a Performance Profile

■ DEFINE THE WORK BEFORE DEFINING THE PERSON DOING THE WORK

A performance-based job description, also called a performance profile, describes the work a person needs to do to be successful, not the skills and experiences required to do the work. The interview will be used to prove the person can do the work by finding examples of comparable accomplishments. It's obvious that if a person can do the work, he or she has all of the skills and experiences required, but normally these are in a different mix than what's written on the traditional job description. The interviewing and assessment process will be covered later in the book but for now it's important to learn how to develop these performance profiles for any type of job, from entry-level to chairman in any industry, with any company anywhere in the world.

Throughout this book reference is made to the terms KPI, KPO, and OKR. They're all similar, with some slight differences depending on how each is used. These definitions will help clarify these related terms:

1. KPI (Key Performance Indicator): This measurement is typically a single goal or metric. For example, a KPI for a sales rep could be "Make 10 cold calls per day."

2. **KPO (Key Performance Objective):** A KPO is typically more detailed than a KPI in that it describes the process used to achieve a KPI or is a more complicated measurable result. For example, "Within six months, build a software development team to develop new iOS apps that can be easily ported to the Apple MacBook Air with the new M1 chip."

3. **OKR (Objective and Key Results):** This is another term for KPOs, although it might have a few additional subtasks included as part of the major objective. In Performance-based Hiring terminology these subtasks would be separate KPOs. See John Doerr's *Measure What Matters*[1] for more on the importance of using performance objectives and OKRs to drive organizational success.

A graphical summary of a performance profile for a business intelligence analyst for a major corporation is shown in Figure 7.1. It highlights the differences between a traditional job description and a performance profile to give you a quick idea of what this chapter is all about and why it's so important to make the shift to performance-based job descriptions.

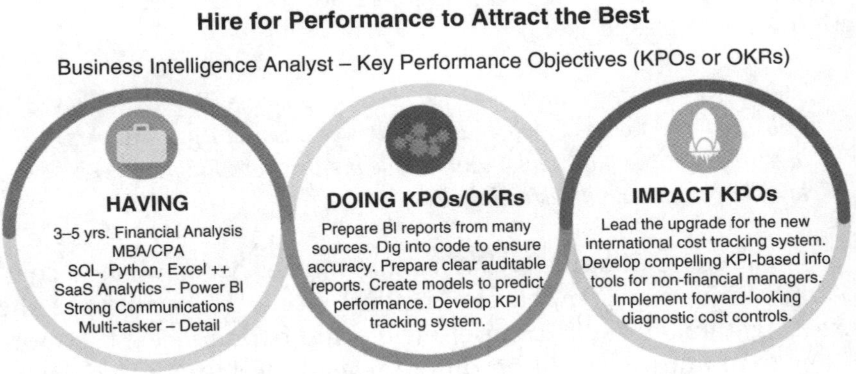

Hire for Performance to Attract the Best

Business Intelligence Analyst – Key Performance Objectives (KPOs or OKRs)

HAVING
3–5 yrs. Financial Analysis
MBA/CPA
SQL, Python, Excel ++
SaaS Analytics – Power BI
Strong Communications
Multi-tasker – Detail

DOING KPOs/OKRs
Prepare BI reports from many sources. Dig into code to ensure accuracy. Prepare clear auditable reports. Create models to predict performance. Develop KPI tracking system.

IMPACT KPOs
Lead the upgrade for the new international cost tracking system. Develop compelling KPI-based info tools for non-financial managers. Implement forward-looking diagnostic cost controls.

Figure 7.1   Hire for Performance to Attract the Best.

[1]Doerr, John. *Measure What Matters: How Google, Bono, and the Gates Foundation Rock the World with OKRs.* Portfolio/Penguin, 2018.

The performance objectives shown in the center image were created using the techniques described in this chapter. The circle on the right summarizes the reason why a top person would want this job. This is the employee value proposition, or EVP. In most cases some form of the EVP should be at the top of all of your posted job descriptions and email messages. These impactful statements help attract the strongest and most career-minded talent who are motivated not only by the content of the work but also the impact it could have. To get a sense of this, compare the two circles on the right to the original job description on the left and ask yourself, "Which job would a top performer be more interested in?" It's clear both versions of the same job are different, and each would attract a different type of candidate.

■ HIRE FOR PERFORMANCE TO ATTRACT OUTSTANDING TALENT

Since I started as a recruiter 40-plus years ago I must have reviewed more than 2,500 different job descriptions with hiring managers. Most start with the classic laundry list of "must-have" experiences and competencies, like those shown in the circle on the left of Figure 7.1 for the business intelligence analyst. As a result, they all got my classic response:

> *This is not a job description, it's a person description. A job does not have skills and experience. A job is about the work. So let's put the person description in the parking lot and first define the work the person needs to do to be considered successful.*

The idea behind this is that if someone has accomplished comparable things in comparable circumstances, they will have the exact right mix of skills, competencies, and experiences, but more times than not these will be different than the initial job description list. This concept is what led to this basic Performance-based Hiring truism:

> *It's what people do with what they have that makes them successful, not what they have.*

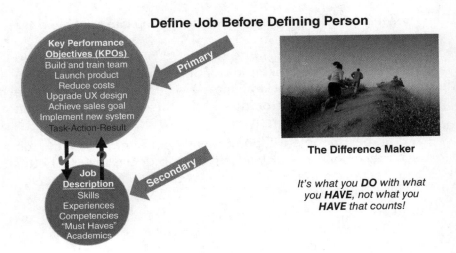

Figure 7.2 Define the Job Before Defining the Person.

The logical point here is that the work required is what determines what skills are required. It's not the other way around. This is shown in Figure 7.2. Having the laundry list of skills and competencies found on the traditional job description doesn't guarantee the person will be competent to handle the work successfully or be motivated to do it.

I contend that in addition to not using a scarcity of talent strategy designed to attract the best, the biggest reason companies struggle to hire outstanding diverse, nontraditional, and high-potential talent is that they continue to use job descriptions that require a skill set that doesn't predict on-the-job success. The continued use of these effectively puts a lid on Quality of Hire since many of the best people have a different mix of skills and experiences. Just as bad, the best people with the required skill set aren't interested in what appears to be an ill-defined lateral transfer. In essence the use of these types of job descriptions guarantees the company will hire people exactly like those they've already hired and not improve the quality or the diversity of the people hired.

Aside from these huge issues, here are a few other reasons these skills-laden job descriptions prevent companies from hiring the strongest talent or cause them to find out too late they hired the wrong person:

1. Assessing generic skills in combination with generic competencies using behavioral interviewing does little to improve interview accuracy or predict on-the-job satisfaction and performance.

2. The best people will opt out early in the process if the job expectations are unclear or if the job doesn't offer a better career opportunity compared to other situations the person is considering.

3. When expectations are unclear, you often need to pay an inflated compensation premium to convince the person your job is worth accepting.

4. You'll lose candidates to other companies if their other opportunities seem more attractive.

5. Job satisfaction and performance will decline, and turnover will increase when the actual job turns out to be different than what was promised or what the person thought was promised.

This chapter will describe how to minimize these problems by converting traditional job descriptions into performance-based job descriptions. The process starts by asking the hiring manager, "What does this person need to do over the next 6–12 months to be considered an outstanding performer?" Then, "Given this, what does the person need to do in the next 30, 60, and 90 days to ensure these major objectives are met?"

The importance of this approach can't be understated. In *The End of Average*[2] author Todd Rose (cofounder and president of Populace and professor at the Harvard Graduate School of Education) demonstrates that the context of the work is what drives individual performance. He proves that the circumstances of the job matter, the available resources matter, the culture matters, the hiring manager matters, the team matters, and the focus of the job matters.

---

[2]Rose, Todd. *The End of Average: How We Succeed in a World That Values Sameness.* HarperOne, 2017.

That's why you need to define all of these things ahead of time and find people who can deal with all of them. As important is the need to stop screening people on things that don't matter: their level of skills, their years of experience, their GPA, their behaviors, and their competencies.

■ THE LEGAL VALIDATION FOR USING PERFORMANCE-BASED HIRING

Achieving a positive Win-Win Hiring outcome starts by defining the positive outcome as a series of KPOs during the requisition process. While this seems commonsensical, many of those in HR use the excuse that it violates some government compliance issue or labor law. Hiring managers have a different series of excuses generally of the "no time" variety or they won't compromise on the skill set listed believing that without this prerequisite the person would require too much training and support to meet the basic needs of the job.

For the compliance-minded, you'll find the *General Legal Validation of Performance-based Hiring* written by David Goldstein eye-opening. There's a copy of his summary report in Appendix 1 with a link to the full version. David is a senior partner at Littler Mendelson, one of the top labor law firms in the U.S. As part of the research for this book I reached out to David to get his viewpoint on the use of performance profiles as a replacement for the more traditional job description. Here's his quick summary:

> *Because the Performance-based Hiring system does differ from traditional recruiting and hiring processes, questions arise as to whether employers can adopt Performance-based Hiring and still comply with the complex array of statutes, regulations, and common law principals that regulate the workplace. The answer is yes.*
>
> *In particular:*
>
> ➤ *A properly prepared performance profile can identify and document the essential functions of a job better than traditional position descriptions, facilitating the reasonable accommodation of disabilities and making it easier to comply with the Americans with Disabilities Act and similar laws.*

➤ Even employers that maintain more traditional job descriptions may still use performance profiles or summaries of performance profiles to advertise job openings. Employers are not legally required to post their internal job descriptions when advertising an open position. Nor is there any legal obligation to (or advantage in) posting boring ads.

➤ Under some circumstances, federal government contractors will want to include in their job postings objective, noncomparative qualifications for the position to be filled. Using SMARTe, employers can create performance-based job descriptions that include such objective, noncomparative elements. Requiring applicants to have previously accomplished specific tasks represents a selection criterion that is no less objective than requiring years of experience in some general area.

➤ Focusing on "Year 1 and Beyond" criteria may open the door to more minority, military, and disabled candidates who have a less "traditional" mix of experiences, thereby supporting affirmative action or diversity efforts.

Shifting to a Performance Qualified Definition of On-the-Job Success

Most jobs can be defined by six to eight key performance objectives (KPOs or OKRs, objectives and key results). At a minimum these performance objectives need to describe the task itself, some action the person needs to take to achieve the task (e.g., build, upgrade, design, maintain, prepare, etc.), and some measurable result or deliverable. For example, "Within 90 days complete the design of a new dashboard interface to be used by the sales management team to track sales rep performance to quota," is a well-written performance objective.

The Hiring Formula for Success shown in Figure 7.3 and described at length in Chapter 6 offers a good summary of the information needed to make an accurate prediction of on-the-job performance and what needs to be captured in the performance profile to accomplish this.

A person who can do the work required is considered "performance qualified." Proving a candidate can do this work involves getting examples of major accomplishments during the interview

Hiring Formula for Success

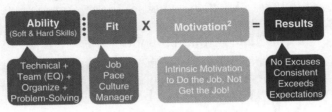

*The ability to do the work in relationship to fit drives
motion and ultimately successful performance.*

Figure 7.3 Hiring Formula for Success.

that are most comparable to the required performance objectives. Used this way the Hiring Formula for Success offers a good bridge between the performance profile and the Performance-based Interviewing process since it covers all of the factors needed in both steps. Chapter 12 on sourcing will cover how to use Google and LinkedIn to find and attract the best of these performance-qualified candidates using some of the action terms and KPOs developed for the performance profile.

Once you've interviewed a few actual candidates after shifting to this type of performance-qualified sourcing approach, you'll discover that the talent pool is expanded by targeting more diverse, high-potential, and passive candidates who can successfully do the work but who have a different mix of skills and experiences. The strongest of these candidates will have accomplished a great deal more than their peers from a quality and quantity standpoint because of this different mix. As important, these candidates will be more responsive to any outreach messages since the job will be seen as a potential career move rather than a lateral transfer.

Following are a few different performance objectives for different types of jobs. They were all developed by asking the hiring manager, "What does the person need to accomplish with the skills and experiences listed on the job description that would result in a Win-Win Hiring outcome?"

➤ Instead of saying the person must have three to five years of experience selling SaaS software to the Fortune 500, it's better to say, "Maximize the territory plan to achieve a quarterly run rate of $250K within 12 months."

➤ For a software developer with one to two years of experience using C# and .NET Core Angular, an aggressive KPO could be "Within six weeks, establish best practices for how the team will handle application data on the front end, using Angular with NGRX."

➤ "Complete the implementation of the updated FCPA international reporting requirements by Q2," is much more insightful than saying the person must have five years of international accounting experience, be detail oriented and have a CPA from a Big 4 accounting firm.

It's important that at least one or two of the most major KPOs are written as **SMARTe** objectives (**S**pecific task, **M**easurable, **A**ction verb, **R**esults defined, **T**ime bound, and include something about the **e**nvironment, such as pace, culture, hiring manager, unusual challenges). By putting the performance objectives into context this way, it's easier to determine how the environmental factors (i.e., the fit factors) will impact the candidate's performance. These are the factors that Todd Rose validates that drive individual performance. For example, the accounting spot above could be made SMARTe by stating that the reporting system will be an intense hands-on project with limited staff and with a very tight time frame to meet critical public reporting deadlines. During the interview you'll ask about these fit factors to ensure the candidate is capable of handling the work in the environment in which it takes place and is interested in doing it.

■ DIFFERENT TECHNIQUES TO DEVELOP PERFORMANCE-BASED JOB DESCRIPTIONS

Aside from clarifying expectations up front using a performance-based job description, which incidentally has been shown to be the number one trait of all successful managers in *First, Break All the Rules*:

What the World's Greatest Managers Do Differently,[3] this approach also ensures recruiters are screened on criteria that best predicts performance and fit. Unless recruiters understand real job needs, they'll be unable to properly screen candidates or convince top people about the career merits of the role.

This is why shifting to a performance-qualified assessment approach is the difference maker when it comes to attracting and hiring stronger talent. It's important to emphasize that making this shift does not require any compromise in ability, performance, or potential. It only requires an understanding that the skills, experiences, and generic competencies typically found on job descriptions puts a lid on the quality of people being seen and ultimately hired.

While it's best to complete these performance profiles during the intake meeting with the hiring manager when the job requisition is first opened, it's not essential. At a minimum, they should be completed before too much time is spent looking for candidates. However, in a worst-case situation, the first technique below demonstrates how one can be prepared moments before the interview starts.

Take a Tour of the Factory and Call Me in the Morning

Several years ago I was contacted by a business owner who had heard me speak at a business leader's conference. He was clearly desperate. He implored me to tell him the two questions I had said were all you needed to ask to fully assess competency for any position. He was looking for an operations VP, and being a full-time executive recruiter at the time, I told him I would be happy to reveal my "secret" assessment technique, but we needed to meet in person and discuss the actual job first. He continued to protest, demanding the questions on the spot. Sensing panic, I relented. Before proceeding though, I asked him what was so urgent that he needed the questions instantly. "The candidate is in the waiting room," he quietly confessed.

---

[3]Harter, Jim. *First, Break All the Rules: What the World's Greatest Managers Do Differently*. Gallup Press, 2016.

After getting some sense of his business and the position he was trying to fill, I told him the following instructions without compromise, and then to call me right after meeting with the candidate.

1. First, do not meet the candidate in the office. Take the candidate for a tour of the manufacturing facility instead.

2. As part of the tour, stop at each area that clearly demonstrates some of the biggest operational problems the person taking the VP job would have to address right away. These turned out to be poor factory layout, too much scrap, outdated process control measures, and excess raw material inventory.

3. After describing each problem for a few minutes, ask the candidate, "If you were to get this job, how would you fix this?" Then have a 10- to 15-minute give-and-take discussion around his ideas. The purpose of this conversation is to understand how the candidate would figure out the problem and develop a reasonable solution. Based on this, evaluate the candidate on his problem-solving skills, the quality of the questions asked, and his general approach for implementing a solution.

4. When you're done with this line of questioning, ask the candidate to describe something he has already accomplished that's most comparable to the problem needing fixing. Spend another 10–15 minutes on getting specific details about this, including names, dates, metrics, type of equipment used, how vendors were managed, how labor problems were solved, who was on the team, how these people were managed, and the results achieved. Don't be satisfied with superficial or general answers. I told him he must push to get actual details, even if painful, and especially if he already thought the person was hirable.

5. Ask the same two questions and follow up the same way for the other operational problems.

6. It should take at least 90 minutes to complete the tour. When done, tell the person you're impressed with his background, and will get back to him in a few days after seeing some other candidates. Then call me and we can discuss your reaction and figure out next steps.

The call came three hours later. The owner's insight was profound. He said the candidate aced the problem-solving questions but didn't have any evidence of achieving comparable results. Given this he concluded the candidate would make an excellent consultant but a poor operational executive. He didn't hire the person but gave us the search assignment. We placed a very talented person in about 30 days who went on to meet all of the performance objectives of the job in the first year.

> *Moral: If you know what you need done it only takes two questions to figure out if a candidate is competent and motivated to do it. If you don't know what you need done, take a tour of the factory and call me in the morning.*

Basic Techniques for Determining the Key Performance Objectives

Figures 7.4 and 7.5 highlight a number of related techniques to better understand the job and identify the objectives most critical to successful performance. During the process of preparing a performance profile you might develop 12–15 performance objectives. Once completed identify the 6–8 most important for job success and put these in priority order. You'll want to give this

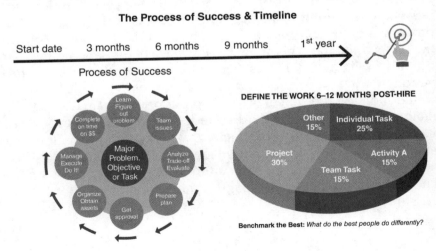

Figure 7.4 The Process of Success and the Timeline.

Given the major KPO, what does the person need to do in the first 30, 60, 90 days to ensure success?

Develop 6–8 critical subtasks and put in priority and/or time order.
Define: Task – Action – Time – Measurable Result

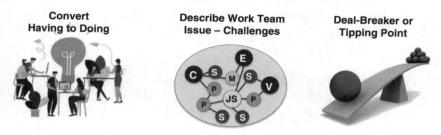

| Convert Having to Doing | Describe Work Team Issue – Challenges | Deal-Breaker or Tipping Point |

Figure 7.5   Convert Having to Doing.

version to any candidates you think are likely to become finalists. In fact, you can ask these candidates what they think of the profile and if they have any suggestions on how to improve it. Make sure you save the other performance objectives. They'll come in handy once you hire the person and are worth discussing during the onboarding process.

Whether conducting a class or just providing an overview of the Performance-based Hiring process, we suggest that the simplest way for hiring managers and recruiters to understand the process is to first prepare a draft version of the performance profile for an open job. This starts by drawing a one-year timeline like the one in Figure 7.4 and asking, "What does a person in this job need to do over the course of the first few months to one year that would indicate the person was a top performer?" This is how the major objectives are first determined. Once these are developed, it's important to break these major tasks into the most important subtasks. One way to start thinking about these subtasks is to ask, "What would a top person naturally do in the first few weeks and months to ensure the major objectives are completed successfully?"

**Use the Process of Success and the Timeline to Determine
the Key Subtasks**

All projects regardless of size can be divided into a sequence of logical steps from the beginning of the project to its completion. For any engineered product, including software development, this sequence is called the product development lifecycle. In Performance-based Hiring it's called the *process of success*. It's shown on the left portion of Figure 7.4. While there's a lot more detail involved when developing and launching a product, for our purposes the process of success is a useful approach for identifying the critical subtasks required to complete a major project.

Once you've defined the major project, like "Implement a new IT system," use the process of success wheel to identify the critical subtasks. One way is to just go around the circle and define a performance objective for each of the steps shown. You can also use the timeline to determine what the new person hired would need to do in the first 30, 60, 90 days and so on, to ensure the overall project is completed successfully as a series of interim performance objectives.

As an example, for an IT project, in the Figure Out the Problem step the task could be, "During the first 30 days, review the project status and identify any technical challenges that need to be prioritized." In a similar IT project that involved a team component, the subtask could be, "Work closely with the user group and finalize all product specs within 60 days and organize the development team." For the same project the 90-day task could be that the detailed plan had to be completed and approved and within six months the project must be ready for test and evaluation.

The purpose of the project planning-like approach is to better understand the important subtasks and roughly when they need to be completed. While all of these subtasks won't be included in the final performance profile, the most critical ones must be.

Reverse engineering the process of success is also a good interviewing approach when asking candidates to describe their most comparable accomplishments. Have them walk you through the process of success they used to complete the project, paying particular attention to the most critical subtasks. This method of interviewing incorporates the organizational, collaborative, and "soft" skills needed to successfully handle any type of project in combination with the technical or "hard" skills.

Benchmark the Best People Doing the Same Job

For jobs that are more process-focused (e.g., call center, retail, non-exempt), performance objectives can be determined by observing what the best employees do differently than average employees. Start by preparing a pie chart identifying the major activities the person works on a regular basis and what percent of the time is spent on each task. These tasks could be handling inbound calls, processing orders, writing or factoring code, or negotiating vendor contracts. Then take the most important activities or where the most time is spent and conduct the best versus average assessment.

Here's one example of how the benchmarking process works in practice. Recently I was working with a number of hiring managers for a company selling a business application managing medical and professional appointments. We were preparing the performance-based job description for a customer success manager (CSM) and I first asked what the major KPO was for the role. It turned out it was to grow sales by 50% in the first year for the total group of clients each CSM was supporting. Using the pie chart approach it turned out that most of the CSM's time was spent with new customers, but the best people spent the most time with the customers most likely to upgrade their services. Identifying these high-value customers was the tipping point for ultimate success and it turned out that the best CSMs figured out who these clients were based on the quality of the questions they asked during the initial launch meeting. Assessing the ability to separate insightful questions from the more typical ones then became a key focus of subsequent interviews. This technique was later included in the company's training program for all new CSM hires.

Here's another example using the benchmarking process for a totally different type of job. Many years ago we visited a number of YMCA camps to figure out what the best camp counselors did differently to ensure their groups of 10–12 children had a positive daily experience. It turned out those with the highest rankings on this measure planned their daily activities in great detail the night before. Those with the lowest rankings tended to be more spontaneous. To address this we created an interview guide that asked candidates to give examples of planning and prioritizing their schoolwork and extracurricular activities. This interviewing approach was very successful. Counselors hired the next year all scored well on this factor by giving examples during the interview of planning ahead of time for important tasks rather than always reacting.

Here are some other examples of benchmarking for a variety of job types:

➤ At a major fast-food restaurant, the best last-shift counter staff wouldn't leave the restaurant until the floors and tables were spotless.

➤ At a large in-bound call center for an insurance company, the best reps were able to complete the processing of orders with all team members in a very positive manner, even at the end of a long day. Endurance was the key factor here, ensuring their productivity was pretty constant all day long.

➤ For a software developer, the best went out of their way to understand their end-user's real needs before writing a line of code. This is a great example of Stephen Covey's "Begin with the end in mind" habit of highly successful people.[4]

Benchmarking the best is a great way to better understand all types of jobs, especially those that involve some type of repeatable process or series of similar steps. One or two of the performance objectives developed this way usually make the final short list, especially when consistency and work quality are important for job success.

Convert "Having" to "Doing"

There are many old-fashioned managers who cling to the notion that a person must have the exact skill set listed on the job description. Asking the hiring manager what the candidate needs to do with the skill or competency to demonstrate proficiency is a great way to

[4]Covey, Stephen. *The 7 Habits of Highly Successful People.* Simon & Schuster, 2000.

shift to a performance measurement rather than years of experience or some absolute or ambiguous factor. This technique is shown in Figure 7.5.

For example, if the job description indicates the salesperson must have five years of industry sales experience, ask the hiring manager what the person needs to do with that five years of industry sales experience to be considered successful. A typical response might be, "During the discovery call, conduct a thorough needs analysis and present the product as a solution." Then ask the hiring manager if he or she would see someone who accomplished something similar even if the candidate didn't have the exact same skill set or years of experience. Most hiring managers will agree, since they have made the mental shift to focus on a performance outcome and measurement rather than just on some arbitrary list of skills and experiences.

It's also important to reemphasize the point for hiring managers to understand that this step opens the door to strong candidates with different industry backgrounds who might see the shift to a new business and/or product line very appealing. I remember someone in the trucking industry who wanted a person to implement a complex IT logistics system. At first, he demanded someone in the same industry, until I asked which companies in the trucking industry have already implemented this type of sophisticated system. Once he realized none did at the time, he agreed to expand the candidate pool to anyone who had worked on comparable complex supply chain systems.

Here's another convert "having to doing" example for the common prerequisite "must have excellent communication skills." To covert this vague "having" into a measurable performance objective, ask the hiring manager to describe how these skills are used and how effectiveness is measured. In a search a few years ago for a financial analyst, the performance objective for strong communication skills became "Make monthly presentations to the management team covering performance to plan and be in a position to handle all questions related to variances." Getting examples from candidates of how they made similar presentations is far better than relying on gut feelings or judging a person based on his or her accent.

Converting having to doing can also be accomplished by asking the hiring manager to identify any technical skills or competencies listed on the traditional job description that were somehow missed or overlooked using the other techniques to develop performance objectives. As part of this review, also ask the hiring manager to highlight the most important "must have" deal-breaker skills that the new hire must possess. Then just ask, "How is this capability used on the job and what do the best people do differently with it?"

For example, for a technical skill for the business intelligence analyst example in Figure 7.1 shown at the beginning of this chapter, we asked the hiring manager why the person needed a CPA for the job. She said it was to ensure the reports were auditable since the company's CPA firm used this information to certify their tax and public financial reports. Preparing auditable reports then become the performance objective and the criteria for success. This opened up the talent pool to more highly qualified and interested candidates, since it was clear a CPA was not necessary to handle this job. In fact, very few CPAs would want this job since the rest of the work didn't map to what CPAs typically do.

Understanding how a skill or trait is actually used on the job is often the key to moving hiring managers away from strict reliance on some artificial, ambiguous, or some absolute and unnecessary requirement. That's why it's important for recruiters to master this "convert having to doing" technique before they conduct another intake meeting.

Use the Four Work Types to Map Performance Objectives to the Company Lifecycle

Hiring for cultural fit is important, but it's often hard to quantify and measure. One good proxy for company culture is the pace of the organization. In many cases this pace can be mapped to a company's position on the classic corporate or product lifecycle, as pictured in Figure 7.6. Each phase shown requires a different type of work and worker in order for the company to successfully move on to the next growth phase. An inability to successfully bridge these talent gaps is why many companies struggle getting past a certain size. The use of Work Types to develop performance objectives can help smooth this transition.

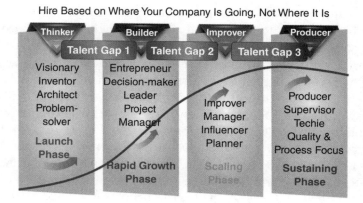

Figure 7.6   Hire Based on Where Your Company Is Going.

To incorporate this idea into the performance-based job description, just ask the hiring manager to develop one or two performance objectives for each of the Work Types defined below. Then add these to the complete list of performance objectives developed and select those that are most important for on-the-job success.

Thinkers: These people are the idea generators, strategists, and creative types. They're at the front end of the growth curve, and their work covers new products, new business ideas, and different ways of doing everyday things. An example of a performance objective for the Thinker could be, "Develop a workaround to the technical bottleneck to ensure the launch date is met."

Builders: These people take ideas from the Thinker and convert them into reality. Entrepreneurs, project managers, and turnaround executives are typical jobs that emphasize the Builder component. They thrive in rapid change situations, make decisions with incomplete information, and can create some level of order out of chaos. "Rebuild the entire product management department in 90 days to support the global launch," would be an example of a Builder performance objective.

Improvers: These are the people who take an existing project, process, or team, organize it, and make it better. Here's an example of an Improver performance objective: "Develop a detailed plan for upgrading the international reporting system over the next 18 months."

Producers: Technical skills dominate the Producer Work Type. A pure Producer is someone who executes a repeatable process on a regular basis where quality and reliability are essential. More often, the Producer Work Type is a component of the job, for example, combining problem-solving (the Thinker) with some technical process to implement a solution. Here's an example of a pure Producer performance objective: "Handle 6–7 inbound calls per day at a 90% resolution rate."

Regardless of the size or scale, most work requires a mix of different thinking, project management, process improvement, and executing skills. Getting the scale, scope, and mix right is essential for hiring the right person.

As part of the interview you can assign the candidate's most significant career accomplishments to the appropriate Work Types. Then see how they compare to the KPOs on a scope, scale, team, and complexity basis. This is a great way for translating accomplishments across different industries and work experiences.

Use the Master Checklist to Develop the KPOs

One way to get hiring managers to consider making the shift to using a performance profile is to give them a partially completed version to review and edit consisting of one or two major objectives and a few subtasks. This approach is less daunting when first presenting the performance profile concept to a hiring manager than starting from a blank sheet of paper. It also demonstrates the "doing versus having" idea in a very practical way. Once hiring managers see the performance profile started this way they normally get interested and modify it themselves. The checklist below is a great way to start this iterative process.

Checklist for Preparing a Performance-based Job Description

First Define the Major Performance Objectives. These are the things you'd tell a candidate they'd be expected to accomplish during the first 6–12 months on the job.

Examples:

1. *Project Accountant*: Upgrade the international consolidations process by Q3 to ensure the preliminary close figures are within 1–2% variance of the final close.

2. *Product Manager*: Working with engineering, sales, and operations prepare a product launch plan for the (product) within 90 days. Within ____ days identify all critical design and test issues needed to ensure an on-time product release to manufacturing.

3. *Call Center Rep*: Within 30 days be in a position to handle 4–5 simultaneous in-bound calls fully resolving 90% of all calls within 4–5 minutes.

4. *Sales Reps*: Reach quota within 120 days after satisfactory completion of the 30-day training course. Within nine months establish a hunter-based sales model for the territory with the objective of increasing the quarterly sales quota by 5% per quarter.

Now break the major objectives into subtasks. Create performance objectives describing the task, the primary action required, the expected results, and a rough time frame.

1. **What kind of work will the person be doing most of the time?** (e.g., Building, managing, and developing a team of software design engineers 50% of the time.)

   Marketing Analyst: The focus of this position is analyzing competitor sales trends by product line. This involves the preparation of weekly and monthly in-depth evaluations of major business trends and their impact on current and future product features.

   Sales Development Rep: Within 90 days be in a position to set up 2–3 onsite prequalified discovery calls per week for the sales team. This involves evaluating 8–10 potential clients every week and making contact with the key decision makers.

2. **What are the key subtasks the person would need to accomplish over the life of the project?** It's useful to describe these using a time frame (e.g., during the first month prepare a flowchart of the process), but it's only necessary to highlight the major steps.

   Production Manager: During the first month put together an assessment of the department's ability to ensure production levels remain constant during the move to the new assembly plant in Toledo.

   Project Manager: Working closely with the development team and product marketing, finalize the launch plan within 90 days. This needs to include identification of all critical resources and technical challenges.

3. **What are the biggest (technical) challenges or problems the person would need to address?**

   Software Developer: Use your JavaScript, Agile, and HTML5 background to take over a critical project developing a new breed of universal mobile storefronts. Quickly assess project status, why it's been delayed, and the feasibility of a Q4 launch.

4. **What are the team issues or challenges? Include who the person will work with regularly.**

   Program Manager: Working with the corporate finance and manufacturing engineering group teams, implement a Lean Six Sigma program for GE's robotic welding system at our primary vendor's subassembly plant.

5. **What are the key deliverables? (Include dates and details.)**

   Human Resource Generalist: Conduct a complete compliance audit of the HR practices, processes, and procedures at the Ridgefield distribution facility. Prepare a comprehensive written review for the Audit Committee and present the findings at the next quarterly session.

6. **Are there any strategic, long-term, or big-picture issues that need to be considered?**

   Supply Chain Specialist: As part of our operational excellence program, this person needs to become the company

SME for state-of-the-art distribution and supply chain management programs. Within year one benchmark our company versus industry leaders and put together a series of recommendations to ensure we're taking full advantage of new technologies and IT systems.

7. **Are there any changes or improvements that need to be made?**

Maintenance Supervisor: Figure out within a few weeks a means to make sure our painting facility is operating at no more than 2% downtime versus the current level of 6%. This is causing severe production delays that needs a short-term and long-term fix.

8. **What's a typical problem the person is likely to face?**

Procurement: Develop a dual source procurement plan for all critical components and prepare flexible production schedules with vendors. Put contingency plans in place to ensure adequate supply if the new line increases more than 20% over the production forecast.

Once completed, select the top six to eight objectives described above and put them into priority order. Alternatively, identify the critical subtasks that drive overall performance and put these at the top of the list. For example, for a product manager it could be putting together the product requirements specification within a very short time frame collaborating with engineering and marketing. Preparing creative advertising might be essential for a marketing person. For a sales rep, it might be completing up-front discovery to understand a client's root cause problems and issues. For a retail department manager, it might be keeping the team motivated throughout the day, every day. Each job has two or three factors like this that ultimately drive success. Identifying these critical drivers allows increased focus during the interview.

Job Branding: Creating the Employee Value Proposition (EVP)

While developing the performance objectives for the role is essential, just as important is that the hiring manager recognizes there's more involved in hiring the strongest and most in-demand talent than there is in hiring an average performer. Presenting the job as a career move is part of this, and this is where the EVP comes into play. One way to develop this is to ask the hiring manager these questions as part of the job requisition process:

➤ *Why would a top person who is evaluating multiple opportunities want this job for just a modest increase in compensation?*

➤ *Why is it any better or different than competing jobs?*

➤ *Is the job tied to some important project or company initiative?*

The answers need to be job-specific and customized for the ideal candidate with an emphasis on what the person will learn, do, and become if successful. The EVP can be expanded by describing the importance of the job and linking it to a major company project or initiative. This is called job branding, and when it comes to attracting more senior-level people it's much more important than generic employer branding.

Here's an example for the procurement role earlier:

This is a critical position in our international expansion supply chain management and vendor development program. This is a critical strategic program for the company driving costs to more competitive levels. The person in this role will be the primary lead for developing these long-lead procurement efforts.

The EVP will be a key part of your sourcing and advertising messaging used to first convince strong prospects to begin an exploratory evaluation of the role. During the assessment and recruiting process this message needs to be reinforced and proven. It will also be used by the candidate to generate and maintain interest in the role as the person compares opportunities. In many cases the EVP will override the need to provide the biggest compensation increase by establishing your opening as the best career move.

Prioritize the Performance Objectives

If you used all of the approaches described in this chapter, you'd wind up with a list of 12–15 performance objectives. While you might want to keep them all somewhere, you do not need them all for assessing candidates or for posting your job. In fact, there is no legal requirement to post your internal job descriptions (see the legal compliance summary in Appendix 1).

For internal purposes a good performance-based job description should include a high-level summary of the job, followed by the most important six to eight performance objectives. This is the summary I'd suggest you share with the three to four finalists for the job to ensure they're fully competent and fully onboard. For external posting and message purposes I'd shorten this to the three or four most important objectives still headlined with a short paragraph emphasizing the importance of the EVP. In the chapters on sourcing and advertising and recruiting, we'll show how this approach can be used to increase the initial response and final close rates.

While it might seem that a lot of time is spent preparing these performance-based job descriptions, it turns out there is more time wasted not preparing them. This includes hours interviewing unqualified candidates and even more hours spent every week post-hire trying to get someone who shouldn't have been hired in the first place to achieve average performance. Hiring top-tier talent on a consistent basis starts by knowing what the best people do on a consistent basis once on the job. All of this is captured in the performance profile.

■ CONVINCING HIRING MANAGERS TO USE PERFORMANCE PROFILES

While preparing a performance profile makes great sense, many hiring managers for one reason or another aren't convinced it's a worthwhile effort. In fact, "I don't have the time" is the most common excuse given by hiring managers to recruiters who just want to post the job and get it filled. So if you're a recruiter trying to convince hiring managers to clarify the performance objectives during the intake meeting, you'll need to learn some different techniques to convince them to at least give it try. Creating a draft template of the job and asking the hiring manager for comments is a great way to start, but if this doesn't work, you'll need to persist using some of these other approaches.

The "No Time" Rebuttal

To get hiring managers over the phony "no time" issue, I just ask them who they spend more time with after the person is hired, those in the top half or those in the bottom half. Not surprisingly, they'll all say the bottom half. The obvious retort is to then ask the manager, "What does the person need to do to be in the top half?" Follow this up with the point that if these criteria are used to develop a performance profile and screen candidates, then the hiring manager won't need to meet as many people during the interviewing process and the person hired will save hours per week by being self-motivated to do the work required with little direction or training.

The "When Are You Going to Tell the Candidate?" Approach

First, ask the hiring manager when he or she will be telling candidates about the job, either before the person is hired, during the onboarding process, or after starting. Hopefully, the hiring manager will instantly realize this is too late, especially if the candidate asks during the interview, "Can you tell me a little about the job and some of the performance expectations?" Follow this up by saying you'll screen candidates on these factors, so the hiring manager won't be wasting time seeing unqualified candidates.

The "Become a Top Manager" Rebuttal

Give your hiring managers a copy of *First, Break All the Rules: What the World's Greatest Managers Do Differently*, which provides the in-depth evidence that clarifying expectations up front is the number one trait of all successful managers. Then say all we're really doing is pulling our performance management process (used after the person is hired) into the hiring process.

Conduct an "A versus B" Test

For hardcore managers who demand the technical skill set, propose sending two or three people who have the skills and two or three who are performance qualified, meaning they have done comparable work. Hiring managers can then compare the two groups.

Tell Some Stories about People Who Have Been Promoted

If all else fails, just ask the hiring manager how he or she got promoted into their current role or why someone in the department or company got promoted. While the manager will pause when asked the question, the answer is often obvious. It relates to the person's track record of past performance doing comparable work, his or her work ethic, decision-making, team skills, work quality, and potential. Given this new level of open-mindedness, suggest to the hiring manager that we should try to hire people from the outside the same way we promote people from the inside. You might even want to use this convincing technique first rather than waiting until you've exhausted yourself trying all of the other techniques.

Dealing with the Diehards

Despite this commonsense approach for defining the real job, some hiring managers still protest. They justify their laundry lists for selecting candidates by saying all of the skills are needed to ensure the people hired can handle a variety of different and unknown assignments. This is just an excuse for not defining the job adequately. While hiring for potential and the unknown is a worthy objective, the worst way to achieve it is by overspecifying the requirements needed. The better way is to create a performance objective that covers the need to handle different jobs with different skills. During the interview, ask candidates how they handled comparable situations. You'll discover that the strongest people are more flexible, they learn faster, and they have the ability to successfully handle stretch assignments. This is one way to assess potential. Other techniques for measuring this critical factor are covered in the chapters on interviewing.

■ SUMMARY

There are a few examples of completed performance profiles as downloads on hirewithyourhead.com. These will help you determine the best format to use for your company and situation.

From a summary standpoint it's important to note that a performance profile or performance-based job description describes the work a person needs to do as a series of performance objectives. By focusing on what people need to do, rather than what they need to have in terms of skills and experiences, you open up the talent pool to a more diverse group of people without compromising performance. But this is just the first step in any company's hiring process. It also drives the interviewing and selection process and how job offers are positioned as career moves. This story sets the stage for redesigning your company's hiring process with an emphasis on performance rather than skills and experience as the criteria for success.

At some long ago YPO event, one CEO asked me before I spoke how much experience a senior VP of Marketing needed to have. I said, "Enough to do the work. If they have too much, the person might not be motivated to do what you need done, and if not enough there might be too much risk involved in hiring the person." During the session I then went on to describe how to prepare the performance objectives for the job and how to get examples of past comparable accomplishments to make an accurate evaluation. He agreed this was a better way to assess competency rather than using some arbitrary factor like years of experience.

At the end of the session I told the group of CEOs that the best way to embed this concept into their company's existing hiring practices was to require a performance profile be prepared before any new job requisition was approved. Then before a person was hired the interviewing team should complete the Quality of Hire Talent Scorecard (copy in Appendix 2 and hirewithyourhead.com) as a group. While they wouldn't be very effective at this process when they began, by using these two bookends to control what needs to be done they'd eventually learn the process. Since an earlier edition of Hire with Your Head was given to the attendees at the meeting, I suggested that their hiring managers should read the appropriate chapters before they interview another candidate. A number of CEOs contacted me later and thanked me for this simple, low-cost way to hire better people.

Despite the commonsense logic of using performance profiles rather than the more traditional skills-laden job descriptions, there is a lot of resistance in making the shift. Some of this is hiring managers unwilling to change how they've always done things or those in human resources concerned about compliance. In this chapter both of these issues have been shown to be untenable. This is especially true since clarifying expectations up front is essential for being an effective manager.

> **By *defining what success looks like post-hire, you'll be able to more accurately predict it pre-hire.***

Since these objectives need to be discussed formally during the onboarding process and shared with the candidates before they're hired, there is no reason they shouldn't be developed as part of the requisition process. Just starting with six to eight performance objectives roughly describing the task and some measurable result is enough to begin the hiring process. These will be expanded, clarified, and prioritized as candidates are met and a person is hired. Focusing on what a person needs to do to be successful, not what the person needs to have is the foundational first step for implementing Performance-based Hiring.

Just as important is developing the employee value proposition (EVP). By capturing the ideal candidate's intrinsic motivator into the job description and by tying the job to the company's mission or major project, you'll be able to attract a different and more motivated candidate.

By defining what success looks like post-hire, you'll be able to more accurately predict it pre-hire. Achieving these Win-Win Hiring outcomes on a consistent basis starts by replacing traditional job descriptions with performance profiles. While this is just the first step in implementing Performance-based Hiring, it is the most important step.

Chapter

8

Conducting the Exploratory Phone Screen

■ THE EXPLORATORY PHONE SCREEN DRIVES HIRING SUCCESS

Caution: The following shouldn't be a very controversial statement, but for some of your hiring managers it will be.

Hiring managers must embrace the idea of conducting an exploratory phone screen with 100% of the candidates their recruiters highly recommend.

107

If they do not, they will spend too much time trying to find a reasonably competent person. Yet if they do agree to this step, it will help them hire more outstanding people on a consistent basis and minimize the need to see more than three or four people for more in-depth interviewing to make one great Win-Win Hiring outcome. This chapter will describe how this is done.

The phone screen with the hiring manager occurs as soon as possible after a recruiter mentions to a prospect, who they believe is a possible semifinalist, that arranging a preliminary phone call with the hiring manager is the next step in the company's hiring process. This is a critical step since the strongest prospects, especially those who are passive, won't become seriously interested in the role until they speak with the hiring manager to determine for themselves the career merits of the job. While the hiring manager does need to provide this convincing information, just as important, he or she must conduct an assessment in parallel to determine if the person realistically would become a semifinalist.

The exploratory phone screen is the next step in the process of converting a small pool of 15–20 prequalified potential semifinalists into three or four true semifinalists. Most often a version of this is conducted by the recruiter to ensure only the strongest candidates are presented to the hiring manager. This does not eliminate the need for the hiring manager to get engaged in the recruiting process long before the candidate formally agrees to become a serious candidate for the role.

By conducting the assessment in phases and mapping it to the hiring funnel described in Chapter 12 on sourcing, it's possible to minimize the time spent with candidates who are unlikely to become true semifinalists. Just as important, by tracking the yield or conversion rate at each stage (i.e., the percent of candidates moved forward in the process), it's possible to identify process problems and correct them before they become too serious.

Without the tracking process, too often the lack of qualified candidates isn't apparent until the hiring manager gets desperate enough to fill the role with the person seen last, not the best person possible. For example, a big problem exists if only 10% of the people contacted out of the small pool of 15–20 at the top of the funnel agree to the first exploratory phone call. On the other hand, if 50% agree to the call but none are interested or qualified for the role, you have a bigger problem: an inability even to identify potential semifinalists.

Regardless of the problem, it's important to keep track of what's happening in real time at each stage of the funnel. Then, rather than proceeding with the process, it's best to figure out the problem and fix it before you hear the worst possible words in a recruiter's life from the hiring manager: "Do you have any more candidates?"

The Phone Screen Is the "Swiss Army Knife" of Hiring

There are other critical aspects of the phone screen that are rarely appreciated when they're conducted ad hoc that will also be addressed in this chapter. For one, they're a great tool to convert strangers into acquaintances before they're hired. For another, they minimize bias by using the interview to objectively assess the candidate's ability to do the work before the person is invited onsite. This minimizes the impact of first impressions when the candidate is met in person. It also lets the candidate fully understand the dual nature of the process to see if the role represents a true career move. At a more tactical level you'll save lots of time by minimizing the number who need to undergo the full in-depth onsite or online assessment process.

Given all of this, I contend the phone screen as described in this chapter is the single most important tool in the hiring manager's and recruiter's entire hiring toolbox. When used properly it not only determines the effectiveness of the company's entire hiring process but also controls it to ensure effectiveness. Just like in sales, if you can't get enough high probability buyers who have a need to buy your product at the top of the funnel, you won't get many closes at the bottom. That's why keeping track of what's working and what isn't needs to be done in real time, not three to six months after a person has been hired.

Consider that a lot of work has been done finding and screening candidates by the time the recruiter has presented a person to the hiring manager to be seriously considered. Then once a hiring manager talks with the prospect, it's the first time these two decision-makers have enough information to determine if it's worth proceeding or not. One part of this is if after learning about the job, the candidate wants to invest more time in seriously considering it.

On the other side of the desk are hiring managers who learn if their recruiters can source and recruit people who are realistic semifinalists. Too many noes from either hiring managers or the prospects indicates some type of problem that should be corrected before too much time is invested in the process. Here are some of the obvious big problems when either or both the hiring manager and candidate say no:

➤ If the hiring manager doesn't want to proceed after the first call, it could be a problem with the recruiter's sourcing and assessment skills. On the other hand, maybe the hiring manager isn't very good at interviewing. Regardless, when this happens after the first two or three candidates are seen, it's time to stop and figure out what's wrong.

➤ When the strongest people decide to opt out after the call with the hiring manager, it's likely a problem with the job itself or the hiring manager.

➤ If the hiring manager needs to interview more than three or four candidates onsite to hire one great candidate, there's a problem with the job, the compensation package, the assessment process, or the hiring manager's ability to attract and hire the best talent.

Regardless of the problem, by tracking the conversion rates right after the phone screen, it's possible to improve the process in real time. Once all of these issues are corrected it's time to conduct a proper phone screen. And when done properly it becomes a game-changer.

With a Phone Screen You Only Need Three or Four Semifinalists to Make One Great Hire

Following are the big benefits of a properly conducted phone screen:

➤ **Saves time.** You'll save time by only inviting three or four true semifinalists for the full onsite assessment.

➤ **Reduces the impact of first impression bias.** The phone screen interview described as follows ensures candidates are evaluated on their ability to do the work described in the performance profile. The impact of the candidate's first impression will be less pronounced when the hiring manager objectively assesses a person this way.

➤ **Forces the hiring manager to take responsibility.** Hiring outstanding people is the responsibility of the hiring manager, not the recruiter or HR department. The strongest people consider the leadership qualities of the hiring manager just as important as the job and the compensation. That's why they need to get engaged early in the hiring process.

➤ **Increases assessment accuracy.** One interview, no matter how long, is not enough to make an accurate prediction of on-the-job success. Multiple online and in-person interviews in different situations spread out over a week or two is a critical aspect of a professional assessment process.

➤ **Ensures fewer early opt-outs and higher close rate.** Not only will the assessment be more accurate, but by investing additional time in the process the candidate will also only learn more about the role. This is the best way to minimize candidates from opting-out of your process before learning about the career merits of the opportunity.

➤ **Achieves More Win-Win Hiring outcomes.** It takes extra time to ensure that both the hiring manager and the candidate have enough information to make the best long-term decision possible. The phone screen sets the stage for this to happen.

■ USE THE PHONE SCREEN TO FIND AND RECRUIT SEMIFINALISTS

Going from an unstructured interviewing process to the implementation of the Performance-based Hiring system described in this book is an important but big bridge to cross. While it's reasonably straightforward for one person trying it out one hiring project at a time, implementing it companywide is an order-of-magnitude more challenging. On top of this add in the fact that strong-willed hiring managers are reluctant to be told how to hire people by someone in HR who isn't necessarily a technical expert in the field. Making the entire process a deal-breaker by saying that throwing in a phone screen is a compulsory step just adds to their reluctance. This almost eliminates the chance for its adoption.

That's why when any hiring manager says, "I don't have the time," your response needs to be, "That's exactly why you need to do this!"

So while some persuasion is in order, I'd suggest the biggest reason for doing it is that it's not only easy to learn but it will also save hours of time before the hire and hours per week afterwards by not hiring any more 90-day wonders. These are the people who after they've been on the job for 90 days, you wonder why they were ever hired at all. If you've hired people with this type of question mark over their heads, you know they consume a hiring manager's time and energy in a failed attempt to push and coach them into achieving average performance.

As you'll discover, once the basics of the performance-based phone screen as described in this chapter are grasped – which is pretty easy – learning the rest involves just a dash of some common sense and a few modifications on a theme. As important, you'll start seeing the time-saving benefits during the first phone screen with the first candidate you interview this way.

It's important to reiterate that the purpose of the phone screen is to determine if a person is a realistic semifinalist for a specific role. If so, you'll invite the person to the next step in your hiring process. If the person isn't a likely semifinalist, you'll diplomatically terminate the process. Using the phone screen as described, you'll be able to eliminate candidates from consideration in 20–30 minutes. It will take another 15–20 minutes to determine if the strongest candidates remaining are true semifinalists.

As a refresher, here are the three factors that determine if someone is a semifinalist:

1. The person must be performance qualified. This means they can do the work described in the performance profile.

2. The person must possess the Achiever Pattern. This means they have been recognized for being at least in the top half of their peer group.

3. The person would see the role as a significant career move. This increases the likelihood the person will accept an offer if one is extended based on the opportunity it represents, not just the compensation package.

No one should be invited onsite or asked to proceed with a more in-depth assessment unless all three conditions are met. A good phone screen can assess all of these factors, which is why it's such an important step in the hiring process. The infographic in Figure 8.1 summarizes this entire process.

As long as job success is first defined as six to eight key performance objectives (KPOs), there are only three more steps involved in the phone screen. The details on how to develop these performance-based job descriptions, or performance profiles, was covered in Chapter 7. The idea behind this is that if it can be proven that a person can do the work defined, they have all of the skills and experiences necessary. This is what it means to be performance qualified. For example, something like "Develop a new user interface for the budgeting system by year end," is much more useful for assessing ability than saying the person must have a CPA or MBA, three to five years of budgeting experience, and a strong attention

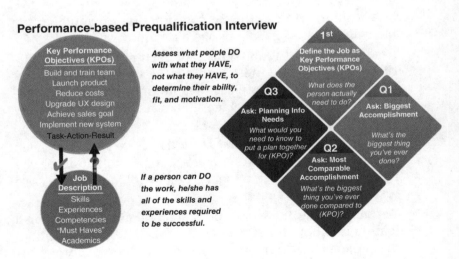

Figure 8.1   Performance-based Prequalification Interview.

to detail. You'll be able to prove they're performance qualified by digging into their major comparable accomplishments. This is the core of the performance-based phone screen. But before asking about the person's accomplishments, it's important to conduct a quick work history review.

Conducting the Phone Screen Work History Review

Conducting a preliminary work history review takes about 15–20 minutes asking about the person's past few jobs. The main purpose of this is to determine general fit for the open role on a scope of responsibility standpoint, if the person has managed teams of comparable size, and if the projects the person has handled are similar. If so, then you'll want to dig deeper to see if the person possesses the Achiever Pattern. Here are some of the obvious clues:

➤ **Look for progression and recognition.** At each company ask about promotions, special recognition, bonuses, title or job changes, and why the person was assigned to different projects. Lack of any of these, or a series of short tenures at multiple companies, should raise the caution flag.

➤ **Determine if the person is career focused.** Ask candidates why they changed jobs and if they achieved the objective as a result of the change. Be concerned when you hear too many excuses about why things didn't work out.

➤ **Assess quality of team skills.** For each major job, ask candidates to describe the teams they've been assigned to or were managing. If the teams are multifunctional and expanding in size, scope, impact, and influence, the person is likely worth more consideration.

➤ **Find out about management skills.** It's a significant clue that the person has strong management skills if he or she has been promoted into bigger jobs over bigger groups as a result of previous successes.

➤ **Deductively evaluate the person's technical skills.** You'll learn a lot about a person's core strengths by asking about the projects they were given after about three to six months on the job. Those with real talent in a specific field get assigned to handle important projects or to stretch assignments by their managers ahead of their peers.

The Phone Screen Recommendation Scorecard shown in Figure 8.2 is a good summary of what it takes to "pass" the work history review. Interviewing is not an exact science but if the person meets the criteria shown in the Work History Review section of the scorecard then it's appropriate to continue the phone screen by asking about the person's most significant career accomplishment of all time. In fact, it's probably best to ask everyone this question if they seem pretty strong, even if the person isn't a perfect fit for the current role based on the work history review.

Phone Screen Recommendation Scorecard	
Work History Review	
Threshold for Continuing Assessment	
General Fit for Open Role	Strong fit on all core factors. Brings other strengths with good track record.
Team Skills and Impact	Growing role and impact with cross-functional teams.
Achiever Pattern and Growth Trend	Positive trend with evidence of achievement and recognition for exceptional work.
Most Significant Comparable Accomplishment	
Requirements for Job-Related Accomplishment	
Comparability of Accomplishments	Accomplishment is a strong match and person had positive role in project success.
Organizational and "Soft Skills"	Strong planning and organizing skills. Logical and proactive. Meets goals.
Problem-solving and Thinking Skills	Has successfully handled problems and challenges at least consistent with needs.
Cultural Fit, Job Fit, and Recruitability	
Minimum Requirements for Moving Forward	
Culture and Environmental Fit	The person has successfully worked in similar situations at similar pace and intensity.
Job Interest, Compensation, and Likelihood of Closing	Strong candidate and worth pursuing. Job represents a good career move. Comp is within range and/or negotiable.

Figure 8.2   Phone Screen Recommendation Scorecard.

Semifinalists Must Answer These Two Questions

This scorecard has been divided into three segments. Each takes about 15 minutes to gather the necessary information to make a recommendation. Then after each segment the interviewer has the option of proceeding or not. This alone is a great time saver since you'll be able to eliminate clearly unqualified or uninterested people in 30 minutes or less.

Looking at the scorecard it's clear that there are some pretty significant factors that need to be evaluated for those who pass the work history review. Specifically, determining if the person's major accomplishments indicate the person is a top performer and if the job represents a good career move for the person. Assuming these are both positive, then you need to determine if the candidate is recruitable given the compensation package and other situations the person might be considering. Figuring this out starts by asking two questions.

The first question: *Can you tell me about your single most significant career accomplishment of all time, including when it happened?*

There's a complete section in Chapter 9 on conducting the Performance-based Interview on how to properly peel the onion to fully understand a person's major accomplishments. SMARTe is the short version of this technique. By asking about the following you'll have enough information to make the phone screen recommendation on whether to proceed.

- ➤ **S:** Specific details. Ask about the biggest problem and how it was solved.
- ➤ **M:** Measurable facts. Push for details.
- ➤ **A:** Actions taken. Get examples of initiative and the candidate's actual role.
- ➤ **R:** Results and metrics. Ask about the planning process and how results were achieved.
- ➤ **T:** Time and team. Find out when the project took place, how long it took to complete, and who was on the team.
- ➤ **e:** Environment and context. Ask about the pace, the depth of resources, and the company culture.

It will take about 10–15 minutes of SMARTe fact-finding to determine if this accomplishment is directly comparable to the needs of the job. If the person's most significant accomplishment of all time isn't even in the ballpark, you can stop the interview. However, if it is, you'll then ask this next question.

The second question: *The biggest accomplishment required for success in this job is (describe one of the major required performance objectives). Given this, can you tell me about something you've achieved that's most comparable, including when it happened?*

Based on the candidate's answers, you'll be able to compare the two accomplishments to the required performance objectives on the job to see if there's a reasonable fit. Given this, here's how to determine if the person should be considered a serious candidate for your job and worth trying to recruit.

Assess the Comparability of the Accomplishments to the KPOs

Some of the SMARTe fact-finding necessary to fully understand the candidate's accomplishments involves understanding the scope and scale of the role, the person's organizational responsibility, if it was a team or individual accomplishment, how the person planned and managed the task, the underlying environment (i.e., pace, depth of resources, company culture, the person's manager's role, etc.), and specific details about the results achieved. Most of these factors should match the needs of the open job. Be concerned if the accomplishments weren't recent or if they were much bigger or smaller than needed.

Connect the Two Accomplishments to See the Trend of Performance over Time

It's concerning when the biggest accomplishment was long ago and the most comparable accomplishment is a lot smaller in terms of scope and scale, even if more recent. On the other hand, if the person is currently doing outstanding work related to the job and it's work he or she finds intrinsically motivating, the candidate should be seriously considered.

Determine If the Person Is Recruitable

While there is enough information to determine if the candidate is a possible semifinalist for the job, it's now necessary to determine if the person is likely to accept an offer if one were extended and if a Win-Win Hiring outcome is likely. There's no reason to pursue the person if neither of these conditions are possible. But if the possibility is yes on both fronts, it's important to start the recruiting process in earnest.

In order for a job to represent a true career move and lead to a Win-Win Hiring outcome, it needs to offer a realistic 30% nonmonetary increase in the first year. This is the 30% Solution described in Chapter 13 on recruiting and how to drive the Big Red Tour Bus. Some of the factors comprising this include a more important job, one that offers stretch and learning, and one where continuing multiyear growth is realistic. It's important to proactively look for these things as part of the phone screen SMARTe fact-finding process. If these nonmonetary factors are minimal, it's unlikely you'll be able to recruit and hire the person within budget. More important, you likely wouldn't want to hire the person unless you can make the job bigger in some way. In these cases, or if the person is too light for the job, connect on LinkedIn and proactively ask for referrals as described in the sourcing and networking chapter.

Assuming the job does represent a career move, describe the factors consisting of this and suggest moving to the next step in your process. For example, for an engineering role you might want to emphasize the technical challenges the person will be handling, some of the teams the person will likely be on, and the fact that these products represent the core of the company's future growth plans. The idea behind this is to give the person a positive view of the potential of the role and why this should be the focus of making any career decision, whether it's with your company or not. This is very important, particularly if the compensation increase that might be offered is likely to be modest. How to handle this is fully covered in Chapter 13 on recruiting and negotiating offers.

At a minimum, though, it's important to suggest that the reason for moving forward is for the career opportunity the role represents, not the compensation package received on the start date. Conclude with a description of the importance of achieving a Win-Win Hiring outcome. Then go on to say the purpose of the next round will be for both the candidates and the company to gather the information needed to ensure this is possible.

■ SUMMARY: USE THE PHONE SCREEN TO CONTROL YOUR ENTIRE HIRING PROCESS

This chapter came about when one of our clients asked if we could develop a short version of Performance-based Hiring that hiring managers could learn quickly and would actually use. The challenge when implementing any HR initiative is getting hiring manager adoption. When it comes to interviewing, most hiring managers learn it on their own or they hire people just like them. In many ways this problem is the root cause of why many companies have watered down their interviewing process to meet some minimal compliance standards or to get hiring managers to at least give token lip service to using it.

One example illustrates this point. We were working with a big insurance company when the third edition of *Hire with Your Head* was published. The head of HR wanted to convert from their traditional behavioral interviewing program when they learned that their hiring managers only used the process to exclude candidates. For candidates they wanted to hire they used their own personal process and pet questions. The company did make the conversion to Performance-based Hiring using this short-form approach. Afterwards one director of sales told me it worked as advertised: 75% of the first 20 people they hired this way made quota in six months, versus less than 25% using the previous mish-mash approach. As a result the company adopted the complete process and embedded it into their standard operating procedures. But getting full hiring manager adoption started with the phone screen version described in this chapter and then running a small pilot program to prove that it's effective.

The information gathered in the phone screen provides enough information to determine whether the hiring process should be continued. However, it is certainly not enough to decide to hire someone. This requires a number of additional and in-depth interviewing sessions. They all start by mastering the complete Performance-based Interviewing process described in the next chapter.

It's important to note that the phone screen is much more than a very effective assessment tool. Used properly, it's a great way to get strong referrals, to highlight sourcing and recruiting problems, and to ensure candidates proceed on the basis that you'll be offering the best career move, not necessarily the biggest compensation package. In the end, that's how you hire for success and satisfaction rather than speed and cost.

Chapter 9

Conducting the Performance-based Interview

This chapter will provide a comprehensive summary of the eight-step Performance-based Interviewing process. To fully understand the techniques covered, it will be helpful if you download the basic Performance-based Interview guide and talent scorecard from the link in Appendix 2 to follow as you read through this chapter. Figure 9.1 offers a high-level graphical summary of the factors in the scorecard and how they relate to the Hiring Formula for Success. You'll use the Performance-based Interview described in this chapter to gather the evidence needed to rank each of the factors on the 1–5 scale shown. The combined score from all of the interviewers is a good measure of Quality of Hire. In fact, this same scorecard can

Figure 9.1   Quality of Hire Talent Scorecard.

be used post-hire to track the accuracy of this prediction. This is a great process control feedback system to understand what factors drive on-the-job success and how the interviewing process can be improved to assess these more accurately.

The eight-step Performance-based Interview brings all of the job analysis, recruiting and assessment techniques covered in this book into a practical all-purpose interview guide. All of the other interviewing approaches described in other chapters in this book are modifications of this basic interview. These variations are used for different purposes, such as assessing a subset of the fit factors, ensuring other interviewers conduct evidence-based assessments, using it for conducting a phone screen, or leading or participating in a panel interview.

When conducted as described in this chapter, this Performance-based Interview will provide enough objective and bias-free information to properly assess a candidate on all of the factors shown on the Quality of Hire Talent Scorecard. However, one interview or one interviewer is not enough to make a final decision to make a candidate an offer. To make the most accurate decision possible, the following step-by-step interviewing checklist should be used.

■ CHECKLIST: THE PERFORMANCE-BASED HIRING INTERVIEWING PROCESS

❑ **Conduct an exploratory phone screen before ever meeting candidates onsite.** This process uses a condensed version of the full Performance-based Interview. It is described in detail in Chapter 8. The big win in conducting a phone screen is that only semifinalists will be invited onsite, saving time, money, and effort. Another benefit is that first impression bias is neutralized when first meeting the candidate in person due to the professional and business-like nature of the phone screen.

❑ **Conduct an onsite formal interview.** The hiring manager should conduct a complete Performance-based Interview onsite with the candidate using all of the techniques and tools covered in this chapter. This first full interview with a hiring manager should be at least 60–75 minutes.

❑ **Get other interviewers involved.** As part of the first formal onsite interview, it's advisable to have two or three other people interview the candidate separately. These secondary interviews should be at least 45–60 minutes each. Under no circumstances have the candidate endure a series of 30-minute short interviews, which are, at best, invitations to use bias and first impressions to decide yes or no. While the interview questions will be the same type of accomplishment-based questions, the focus of the interview will be more in-depth on other factors in the talent scorecard. For example, one interviewer could focus on team skills while another could conduct a deep dive on job-related technical competency.

❑ **Complete the talent scorecard.** While each interviewer should complete the talent scorecard on their own after the interview, it's best for the entire interviewing team to meet and share their evidence in an open discussion. This is a great learning experience since the difference between insightful and biased evidence is readily apparent.

❑ **Conduct at least one panel interview with three or four interviewers.** A well-organized panel interview as described later in this chapter is a great technique to increase assessment accuracy, reduce bias, and train new interviewers. The key is to have one leader who asks about major accomplishments and the others peeling the onion and asking for additional details. Eliminate the pet questions and the interruptions. Unorganized panel interviews are worse than anarchy and from the candidate's perspective are considered unprofessional.

❑ **Second round and subsequent interviews.** For critical positions hiring managers should conduct at least two in-depth, one-on-one interviews and be part of a panel interview, but not the leader. In addition, the hiring manager should meet the person outside the office in a more casual setting like for lunch or coffee. Spending three or four hours or more with the final candidate over multiple interviews helps convert a stranger into an acquaintance before the person is hired.

❑ **Problem-solving session.** One of the questions in the interview is to ask the candidate how he or she would organize a solution to a job-related problem. This can be formalized in a final panel interview with the candidate describing the approach taken and getting into a give-and-take session with the panelists. This technique not only reveals critical thinking and planning skills but also how the person interacts with the team.

❑ **Finalize the Quality of Hire Talent Scorecard.** It's important to get group agreement on any critical new hire in order to ensure a Win-Win Hiring outcome. But this agreement needs to be evidence-based. It's relatively easy to separate fact from fiction, bias, and emotions when each of the interviewers shares what they learned during their interview with the candidate going step-by-step through each of the factors on the scorecard. Most interviewers will adjust their rankings when they hear strong objective evidence. Regardless, be concerned when there is still a wide variance on any of the factors. This indicates an interview process that's too loose. When there is reasonable agreement on these same factors after the evidence is shared (ideally no more than plus or minus half a point on the five-point scale), you can be more confident the group assessment is correct, whether it's positive or negative.

Subsequent chapters will go into more depth on all of these steps, including alternative interviewing techniques for assessing each of the factors on the talent scorecard. This chapter will cover the core eight steps of the Performance-based Interview in sufficient detail to begin using it right away.

It's important to emphasize that one purpose of the interview is to assess a candidate's ability and motivation to do the work defined in the performance profile in the environment or context in which this work takes places. These are the fit factors. But this is not the only purpose.

The other purpose of the interview is to recruit the candidate being interviewed. Recognize that only the strongest and most interested candidates will undergo the complete series of steps shown above. As you'll find out in the chapters on recruiting and negotiating offers, portions of the final offer package should be negotiated in small steps to gain concessions by the candidate in order to move to the next step in the process. For example, if your benefits package is subpar, this should be revealed before the final round of interviews. If the candidate agrees to move forward knowing this, the person has essentially agreed to this component of a final offer.

By gaining concessions this way, by the time an offer is made there will be few surprises on either side. Given this dual purpose of the interview it's important that each interview is professional, that all the interviewers are prepared and on time, and that everyone has seen the performance profile for the job and has reviewed the candidate's resume or LinkedIn profile. Collectively, this is how a company can demonstrate with actions – not just talk – that it has high standards and wants to attract the strongest talent.

Figure 9.2 summarizes the eight-step Performance-based Interview. Its purpose is to determine if the person can handle the KPOs defined in the performance profile shown in the top circle on the left and if this work represents a career move. If it can be proven beyond a reasonable doubt that the person can do this work, he

Conducting the Performance-based Interview

Compare Past Performance to the Key Performance Objectives

Figure 9.2 Conducting the Performance-based Interview.

or she will have all of the required skills, experiences, and competencies necessary to achieve a Win-Win Hiring outcome. But these will rarely be the same as what was initially included in the more traditional job description.

■ THE EIGHT-STEP PERFORMANCE-BASED INTERVIEW GUIDE

There is an abridged version of this full interview guide in Appendix 2, including a link to download the PDF. This interview and talent scorecard is based on the performance profile for the job. It's important to review the candidate's background ahead of time to develop some of the fact-finding probes.

Step 1: Introduction, Review Job, and Discover Motivation for Looking

Use the Opening to Control the Interview and Set the Standards of Performance

Let me give you a short overview of this job. (Provide one-minute summary.) Given this, can you give me a quick overview of how your background relates to this job?

This type of preface prevents the candidate from giving their rehearsed version of "Tell my about yourself" by requiring the person to describe their background in context with the job.

What are you looking for now in a new job? (Pause.) Why is having _____ and _____ important to you now and what would you need to find out to see if this job meets your criteria?

Fact-Finding and Advice

Ask for clarifying details to understand how the candidate's background, trend line, and current role fits with the current job requirements.

(Continued)

Asking the "Why?" follow-up question gets at the true source of motivation. Determine if the person wants any job, or if he or she wants this job.

The purpose of the introduction is to understand the candidate's motivation for looking for another job and how active or passive the person is. Part of this includes taking control of the conversation and starting to understand what the person considers a good career move and if a Win-Win Hiring outcome is possible.

Begin the interview with a one- to two-minute overview of the job. Then ask the candidate to give you a quick overview of what he or she has done that's most comparable. This is a good way to force the candidate to "tell me about yourself" in a more focused and non-rehearsed way.

Follow up with questions about how active the person is job hunting, how he or she found out about your opening, and what the person wants in their next role. Asking why these factors are important reveals the person's short- versus long-term needs. For example, if the person says they're looking for a better career opportunity, ask why this is important. They'll likely say there's a problem with their current job. This will offer clues to the candidate's true motivation for looking and allow you to position your job as the best among other alternatives being considered.

If the candidate has met other people in your company before conducting this interview, just ask the person what was discussed and the focus of these earlier interviews. Then ask if the person has any questions related to these prior interviews. Just as important, based on this you'll know what wasn't discussed. These "missing" factors can then be the updated focus of the current interview. For example, if organization and management skills haven't been evaluated, you'll ask about this as part of the major accomplishment question in step 4. This is a great means to self-organize the interview process as long as everyone on the interviewing team is using the Quality of Hire Talent Scorecard to make their assessment. Each subsequent interviewer can learn what was discussed earlier and fill in the scorecard blanks, knowing they'll all meet later to discuss this candidate.

Step 2: Put Your Biases in the Parking Lot by Measuring the Impact of First Impression

Exposing Your Instant Emotional Reaction to the Candidate Increases Objectivity

Be aware of your biases. Write down your immediate emotional reaction to the candidate – relaxed, uptight, or neutral. Write down the specific cause whether it's the person's appearance, age, accent, personality, or communication skills. At the end of the interview you'll measure your first impression of the candidate again, when you're less affected by it. More important, you'll assess how the candidate's actual first impression will impact their job performance. If you have a concern about this, make sure you get evidence to support or contradict your instant assumption.

Fact-Finding and Advice

➤ Wait 30 minutes before making any yes or no decision.

➤ Use the interview to collect the evidence to make a decision; don't make it during the interview.

➤ Force yourself to do the opposite of your normal reaction (i.e., don't look for facts to support your instant judgment; look for facts to disprove them).

➤ For those who make a positive first impression: initially be more critical, seek out proof of every statement.

➤ For those who make a less positive first impression: assume they're competent; give them the benefit of the doubt.

➤ Script the interview questions at the beginning and ask everyone the same questions.

➤ Be cynical, seek out evidence, get proof, examples, facts.

More errors are made in the first 30 minutes of an interview than any other time due to bias. Chapter 4 was devoted to this topic and covered a number of techniques the interviewer could use to increase objectivity. The most important: use the interview to collect the evidence to make a hiring decision – do not make the actual decision during the interview. At a minimum wait at least 30 minutes before reaching any hint of a yes/no decision. Just conduct a work history review (step 3, following) and ask about the person's major career accomplishment first (step 4). If you think first impressions are important to job success, measure it at the end of the interview when you're less affected by it (step 8).

Some examples will help clarify the difference between a biased and an evidence-based assessment. Many times an interviewer who doesn't like a candidate will use phrases like, "I have a bad feeling," "The person didn't seem too assertive," or "Just won't fit." All of these types of comments need to be challenged. Good evidence of not fitting would be something like, "Given the fact that she is always assigned to work on purely technical teams with peers, I'm concerned she would have trouble working with product marketing and our executive teams preparing product launch plans." A challenge to a superficial "not fitting" phrase for the same job could be, "I don't agree. At her last two companies she was asked to be the technical lead on a similar launch program by the marketing team. In fact, she received a personal letter from the VP of Marketing for her efforts."

Step 3: Conduct a Work History Review

The Work History Review Adds Structure to the Candidate's Accomplishments

Spend 20 minutes as part of a one-hour interview reviewing the candidate's resume or LinkedIn profile. Focus on general fit on a scope, scale, and pace standpoint. Use this to develop the structure behind the person's experience and accomplishments. As part of this, look for the Achiever Pattern indicating the person is in the top half or better of their peer group.

Please tell me about your most recent job. What was your position, the company, your duties, and any recognition you received?

Fact-Finding and Advice

For the past few jobs, focus on titles, promotions, basic duties, have the person draw a 360-degree team chart, and find out how the team was built if the person is a manager. Highlight the big changes and impact made; ask about challenges faced and the recognition received. Go back five to ten years looking for an upward trend of growth. Ask why the person changed jobs and if the new job achieved the primary reason for changing. Evaluate if excuses are based on the person's lack of due diligence.

Achiever Pattern: Evidence Person Is a Top Performer

➤ Seek out all forms of recognition, including raises, promotions, special awards, and commendations.

➤ Find out if assigned to stretch and/or important projects and frequency.

➤ Ask about special training.

➤ Ask about peer rankings and supporting evidence.

Recruiting Tips: Look for Opportunity Gaps to See if Person Is Recruitable

➤ Project size and span of control

➤ Influence and exposure

➤ Impact and growth rate

➤ Mix of more satisfying work

The work history review is the most important part of the entire interview. Based on this step you'll be able to determine if the candidate is a possible fit for the role, if the person is in the top half or better of his or her peer group, and if the person can be recruited within the compensation budget while offering a better career move.

Start the work history review by going through the person's background in reverse chronological order, starting with the most recent position. You'll get a quick sense of general fit comparing the person's scope of responsibility, the size of the teams the person has been on and managed, who was on the team, the person's role, and the impact they made. To assess cultural fit ask about the pace of the organization, how decisions were made, and the resources available. Get into their manager's leadership style and how this impacted their job performance. This information will help you determine if the person can work in different cultures and with different managers and how these factors impacted their performance, either good or bad.

The Achiever Pattern indicates the person is in the top half or better in their peer group. You'll be able to get evidence of this by looking for recognition the person received at each company. This could be promotions, special awards, bonuses, being assigned to important projects ahead of their peers, being asked to train coworkers, and if the person was ever involved in working with senior management. For sales, find out how often the person made quota and what sales awards they received. The best people get recognized for being the best, so seek this evidence out.

Be sure to ask why the person changed jobs, how they found the new job, and if the job change achieved its purpose. Be careful if the person exhibits a pattern of changing jobs for short-term reasons – typically more money – even though the stated reason is more career growth that never occurs. Frequently people use this as an excuse for changing jobs when in fact the fault is theirs: they didn't conduct the due diligence needed to make a thorough evaluation of the new job. I call this Job-Hopping Syndrome.

Sometimes job hopping can be turned around to your advantage by describing how a Win-Win Hiring decision should be made. The details of this technique are covered in more depth in Chapter 13 on recruiting where I explain how to position your job as the superior long-term move even if it's not the best in terms of compensation, title, or location. Changing jobs is an important decision, so understanding how and why these decisions are made provides a strong clue into the person's career motivation. I give character kudos to those who focus more on learning, growth, and making an impact over short-term convenience and monetary considerations.

Step 4: Assess Two to Three Major Accomplishments

Past Performance Doing Comparable Work Is the Best Predictor of Future Performance

Dig into a candidate's major accomplishments most comparable to real job needs. Assign different projects to other interviewers. Review the trend line of performance over time as a measure of rate of growth. A plateau is fine if work quality is outstanding.

Ask the most significant accomplishment (MSA) question:

Can you please tell me about your most significant accomplishment at [company]? Or consider a project or event that you're quite proud of or where you excelled.

One major project we're now working on is [describe KPO/OKR]. Please tell me about something comparable you've led.

Spend 12–15 minutes (each) on two or three different major accomplishments in order to determine comparable fit and to develop a trend line of accomplishments over time. Pay specific notice to the type of work where the person excelled and/or was highly motivated and the circumstances involved.

Other interviewers can use this modified form of the MSA question focusing on different attributes on the talent scorecard like project management skills or technical skills.

I'd like to focus on (skill, attribute, or competency). Can you tell me about a major accomplishment that best demonstrates this?

Fact-Finding and Advice
- ➤ Obtain overview of job, company, and situation.
- ➤ Get dates and time frames; when, how long did it take?
- ➤ Get a snapshot of the beginning and the end to understand major changes.

(Continued)

➤ Ask how and why the person got assigned the project.

➤ Define team, role, and organizational structure.

➤ Understand the environment: pace, resources, culture, decision-making.

➤ What results were expected?

➤ How did you plan the project or task?

➤ Obtain two or three examples of initiative.

➤ What did you change/improve?

➤ Describe big challenges or conflict faced and how it was resolved.

➤ What did you learn about yourself and improve as a result?

➤ What (technical) skills were needed and how were these used on the job?

➤ What other (technical) skills were learned and how were these used on the job?

➤ Describe likes and dislikes.

➤ Where did you exceed expectations? Where did you fall short? Why?

➤ How did you improve yourself?

➤ What would you do differently?

➤ What formal and informal recognition did you receive?

Long ago I discovered that hiring managers weren't as good at interviewing as they thought they were. My contention was that they couldn't all be accurate when there was so much disagreement among members of the hiring team after interviewing the same candidate.

Through years of trial and error I learned that this didn't matter, at least from a recruiter's perspective. I could never convince hiring managers of the errors of their ways without providing detailed evidence of a candidate's ability to do the work. This led to the development of the most important interview question of all time, now referred to as the most significant accomplishment (or MSA) question. I wrote a version of this question when I first started posting on LinkedIn around 2012. In a few months it had 1.3 million views.

It still is the most important question of all time since it describes a rational way to make a gut decision.

Due to the question's importance in measuring all of the factors listed on the talent scorecard in the Hiring Formula for Success, there are a few other chapters describing how to ensure the hiring team gets all of the evidence needed to determine competency, fit, and motivation to excel. This section will provide a good starting point, though.

The basic MSA question involves first describing one of the performance objectives in the job and then asking the candidate to provide a detailed example of something he or she accomplished that is most comparable. Fact-finding is the key to fully understanding the candidate's accomplishment and if it's comparable to the requirements of the job.

The MSA question can also be considered the universal interview question since with minor modification it can be asked for different technical and team accomplishments, specific soft skills, and every competency and management skill required for job success. The modification takes this form:

> One of the critical aspects of this role is [describe the factor, like organizational skills] to accomplish this critical objective [describe, like manage a project]. Can you please describe something you've accomplished that's most related?

It takes about 12–15 minutes of fact-finding and peeling the onion (i.e., asking the who, how, when, and why questions) to fully understand the accomplishment and if it's comparable to what's needed. This is also a good interviewing technique since by just changing the factor being assessed, other interviewers can use the same MSA question without the candidate thinking everyone's asking the same repetitive questions.

This segmented approach provides another huge benefit: by giving other interviewers responsibility for assessing a subset of the factors rather than giving them a full yes/no hiring decision, they tend to spend extra time getting more detailed evidence about their assigned factors. This richer evidence is also given more credibility due to its depth when it's shared in the formal debriefing session.

There's another subtle but important reason why organizing the interview by factors increases assessment accuracy. Typically whenever a secondary interviewer is given full yes/no voting rights there is a tendency to vote "no" more often than "yes," since it's a safer decision. Worse, when a "yes" is given it's often based on some emotional reason or some narrow skill set, rather than on past performance doing comparable work.

Step 4a: Assess One or Two Major Team Accomplishments

Team and Organizational Skills Are Revealed by the Role the Person Played on Major Projects

Spend 12–15 minutes each on one or two team accomplishments. Observe trend line and changes in scope and makeup of team. Make note of the types of people on the team, variety of functions worked with, and how influential the person was in moving the team forward and/or changing the direction of the team.

Can you please tell me about a major team accomplishment? Consider one where you either led the team or one where you were a key member of the team.

Fact-Finding and Advice

➤ Have the person draw an org chart, including titles.
➤ Ask about the person's role on team and why he or she was chosen to be on the team.
➤ Find out if the role changed while the person was on the team.
➤ If team leader or manager, ask how the team was selected.
➤ If a manager, have the person rank the quality of the people on the team.
➤ If a manager, have the person describe how he or she developed and coached team members.

➤ Ask about mentoring others or being mentored.

➤ Walk through the plan, how it was managed, and if the results were met.

➤ Ask about biggest team problems and the person's role in resolving them.

➤ Get specific examples of how the person impacted team decisions.

➤ Get two or three examples of initiative helping or coaching others.

➤ Get examples of being influenced, how, who, and why.

➤ Have the person describe how they could have been a better team player.

➤ Get proof of major team strength.

➤ Describe biggest conflict faced and how it was resolved.

➤ Ask about team recognition, like being asked to be on other teams.

In most cases, when candidates describe their major accomplishments without prompting, they choose one that best represents their individual contributor skills. That's why it's important to proactively ask the person about their major team accomplishments. In this case, notice that the fact-finding probes all relate to team issues and how the person collaborates with others, including the need to identify who these people are at least by title.

Here's a story about the importance of assessing team skills in order to avoid making hiring mistakes. Around 2015 I was asked by a very young CEO leading a VC-based start-up if I could recommend an interviewing technique he could use to make sure he didn't hire any jerks. He was concerned that everyone he met seemed likeable enough, but since they were all older than he was he wasn't sure he could work with them. To address this I told him to have the candidates describe each of the major teams they were on or led over the past few years. As part of this have them describe why they were assigned to the team and if they were later assigned to other teams with some of the same people. I went on to say that jerks are never consistently assigned to more important teams or asked to lead important teams by previous team members or asked to be on a team by a former leader.

However, he should be concerned if the candidate makes excuses about why the teams he or she worked on were comprised of a narrow group of similar people, especially if these never grow in size or importance or the person's role never changed. This is a sign the person could have some interpersonal challenges.

As far as I'm concerned, the ability to work with others, especially those in other functions, is an essential skill. For managers, building and developing teams of strong people should be embedded into one of the top three performance objectives. You'll be able to get a good sense of the quality of the person's team skills and how they compare to the requirements of the job, observing the growth and makeup of these teams over time.

Step 5: Assess Critical Thinking and Job-Related Problem-Solving Skills

Assess the Process of Problem-Solving, Not the Solution

In the first full interview with a candidate, it's important to have a back-and-forth discussion around one major job-related problem the person is likely to face. The purpose of this approach is to assess critical thinking, strategic planning, problem-solving skills, and upside potential. Make this assessment based on the questions and process the person uses to figure out how the problem would be solved, not the actual solution. This question is part of the Anchor and Visualization Pattern used to assess overall competency and the likelihood of achieving a Win-Win Hiring outcome.

One major problem we're now facing is _____. How would you go about addressing this? What would you need to know and how would you plan it out?

What have you done that's most similar? (This is an anchor to ensure that the candidate doesn't just talk a good game. The answer to this question might have been previously covered as part of the MSA questions.

Fact-Finding and Advice

Some questions and ideas on how to frame the conversation:

- ➤ What would you need to know to get started?
- ➤ What big questions would you need answered?
- ➤ How would you get these answers?
- ➤ What would you do first, why?
- ➤ Who else would you involve to get some insight?
- ➤ What would you need to know to organize the project to implement a solution?
- ➤ How would you figure out the root cause?
- ➤ How would you prioritize tasks, why?
- ➤ How would you find out critical issues?
- ➤ What resources do you think you'd need to implement a solution?
- ➤ How long do you think it would take, and why?
- ➤ What would be some of the implications involved with taking this course of action (describe a different approach)?
- ➤ How would you make the business case for making a tradeoff between option A versus B?

While the MSA is the most important question, the job-related problem-solving question is my favorite. Regardless, some behavioral interviewing "experts" will take instant exception to the entire idea of any type of problem-solving question before they even know what it is or how it's used. While there is merit in not asking hypothetical problem-solving questions that are brainteasers or not related to the job, that's not the issue here. Instead, I'll explain the critical importance of this question in assessing planning skills, strategic and critical thinking skills, and the candidate's current knowledge of the job. So if these "experts" don't want to use it, they'll be conducting an incomplete assessment.

The problem-solving question goes something like this: "If you were to get this job, how would you go about handling (one of the KPOs in the performance profile)?" For example, if you're hiring a sales manager, the form of the question might be, "How would you go about ensuring that the team met quota every month?" For an engineer, it might be, "How would you design and qualify this product to ensure it's in production by next March?"

A few years ago I asked this problem-solving question for a senior director of tax search I was conducting: "Given the new U.S. tax rules on inversions, how would you modify the company's current global tax strategy?"

I am no tax expert, so I told the candidate to answer the question as if she were describing this approach to an HR business partner. I then spent the next 15 minutes in a give-and-take discussion making sure the candidate understood the problem and had a logical approach for developing a solution. The person not only answered the question properly, but she spent extra time to describe the business impact of these tax rules in a way that was understandable to a layperson.

This question uncovers a critical ability of all top performers: job-related problem-solving skills. The best candidates I've met in my 40-plus years in executive search, regardless of job level or function, all have the ability to anticipate the needs of the job before starting it. This includes 16-year-old camp counselors at the YMCA who were asked how they would handle a situation if one of the 10-year-olds in their group was being shunned or bullied. It also includes accountants who know what to look for to improve the closing process, as well as mold makers who know how to begin fixing design flaws in injected molded parts.

The point here is that competent people can describe the steps needed to solve a problem, put a plan together to implement a solution, and figure out what resources are needed to do it, how long it would likely take, and who needs to be involved. Even better, they "see" the problem, the solution, and the steps needed to get there. They also know what they don't know and are confident enough to tell you how they'll get this information.

As part of the give-and-take process, the best candidates will naturally begin peppering the interviewer with questions. This demonstrates their problem-solving techniques in action. "What's the budget, the time frame, the staff, the resources?" are all great questions. The quality of these questions provides the interviewer another dimension for assessing the candidate's competency and fit for the role.

When you ask this problem-solving question it's important to turn off the spotlight and shift the conversation into a more natural give-and-take discussion about real job needs. This way the meeting is no longer an interview, but a business-like discussion with a team member trying to work together to figure out a solution to a real problem.

What's being assessed with this question is the process the person uses to figure out the cause of the problem and the planning involved to implement a solution. What's not being assessed is the solution itself. Be concerned when this thinking is shallow or vague, when the planning lacks judgment or the person doesn't even know how to get started. Be just as concerned when the person instantly comes up with a solution without understanding the problem first.

There is a caveat to this type of questioning: to ensure the person isn't just a good talker, thinker, and planner, but can also deliver results, follow up with the MSA question by asking, "Now can you tell me about something you've accomplished that's most related to solving a comparable problem like the one just discussed?"

I refer to this two-question combination as the Anchor and Visualize approach. A track record of past performance and the ability to visualize the future is a great indicator of ability. When combined with a clear understanding of real job needs using a performance-based job description, the problem-solving question might soon become your favorite question, too.

Step 6: Delay the Candidate's Questions Until the End of the Interview

The Quality of the Candidate's Questions Reveals Insight and Interest

Questions asked at the beginning of the interview are typically rehearsed. That's why it's important to delay candidate questions until the end. Meaningful questions at the end of the interview are insightful when they incorporate some of the information covered during the interview.

Based on what we've discussed so far, do you have any questions?

Fact-Finding and Advice

➤ Evaluate if the questions were meaningful, appropriate, and relevant.

➤ Determine if the candidate is focusing on the long-term career opportunity or just short-term issues.

Candidate questions asked early in the interview are typically rehearsed. Spontaneous questions asked after the candidate knows the requirements of the job are better indicators of insight, ability, and interest.

Many candidates who have gone to "interviewing prep school" are taught that they should ask a lot of questions at the beginning of the interview to "control the interview." While questions about real job needs are perfectly appropriate, it's better if they're asked later in the interview when they have more context about the role and what's been discussed. One way to delay the questions until later in the interview when confronted with a barrage of questions too soon is to simply say to the candidate that they'll have a chance later to ask any and all questions needed in order to make a proper decision. Then say that since you're conducting an interview with specific time limits, you'll need to defer these questions to later in the interview.

Another important reason for this delay is that the quality of the candidate's questions is more meaningful since they're based on what has been discussed up to that point. When the questions do come, be concerned if they're too self-serving or too short-term if the candidate hasn't been told he or she is a finalist for the role. Be very concerned if the candidate asks questions that don't lack context with what has been discussed up to that point in the interview.

Good questions relate to the person trying to understand the role in more depth, the team and resources available, and the connection of the job to some important project, strategy, or company mission. The questions themselves reveal a lot about the candidate's thinking skills and understanding of the role as well as interest in the job itself. This is critical in figuring out if the candidate can be recruited and hired.

Step 7: Determine Candidate Interest and Recruiting Opportunity

Recruit by Establishing a Win-Win Hiring Opportunity

Part of the interview is to look for gaps in the candidate's background in order to determine if the open job represents a clear career opportunity. The statement/question below is relatively neutral but appropriate after the first interview.

While I've seen a few other very strong candidates, I'm also impressed with some of the work you've done. What are your thoughts now about this job? Is this something you'd like to consider further? Why? Why not?

Ask the following if the candidate seems a realistic semifinalist:

If you're interested, it might make sense to have another discussion to see if the role has the potential to lead to a Win-Win Hiring outcome. [Explain this if necessary.] Some of the areas of potential growth could be [highlight

(Continued)

two or three factors]. One area of concern would be [define a gap like size of team or rate of growth] that I'd also like to explore if you decide to move forward.

Only the hiring manager and recruiter need to ask these questions. Others can ask a softer variation (e.g., "What are your thoughts about the job?")

Describe next steps and the person's availability given other roles he or she is considering.

Fact-Finding and Advice

➤ State sincere interest but don't overstate your interest.

➤ Mentioning other good candidates makes the job more appealing.

➤ Link job to some big company projects to make it more impactful and interesting.

➤ Make candidate earn the job by describing some of the stretch opportunities.

➤ Listen four times more than you talk; don't sell.

➤ Describe concerns to create gap.

➤ Ask the candidate how the job relates to others he or she is considering.

➤ Ask what the candidate would need to know to move forward.

➤ Discuss broad compensation needs and availability.

It's important to recognize that the interview is more than about assessing competency, fit, and motivation. Just as important, especially if all of these ability issues appear to be positive, is the idea that the candidate needs to be recruited for the role within the compensation budget available. You'll rarely be able to hire the strongest talent unless your compensation is at least competitive. By assuming this, the parallel role of the interview is also to demonstrate that your opening offers the candidate the best career move among other situations the person is considering.

As you conduct the interview, it's important to recognize that the overriding objective of the entire Performance-based Hiring process is to achieve consistent Win-Win Hiring outcomes. Getting enough information before an offer is made and accepted requires a dual discovery process. This increases the chances that the hiring manager and the new hire both agree the decision was the right one after working together for one year.

In many ways this type of interview is equivalent to solution selling where the sales team needs to first understand the client's needs and then the company must offer a customized solution within the client's budget. When it comes to hiring a top person, who will either get a counteroffer or other offers to change companies, this discovery process takes place during the interview.

For the prospect to accept your offer, he or she must see the job as a worthy career move. That's why early in the process, including in the job posting, outbound messages, and the phone screen, the idea of a 30% nonmonetary increase needs to be established as the decision criteria to compare and accept an offer. This 30% – described in more depth in Chapter 13 on recruiting and closing – is called the "30% Solution." The 30% consists of some combination of job stretch, faster growth, a role with more impact, a mix of more satisfying work, and better work/life balance. The purpose of the interview is to find this gap if it exists, explain it, and use this as the condition for moving forward in the process and accepting an offer if one is made. For example, if it seems like the opening offers the chance for the candidate to manage a bigger team or work on a more important project, just ask the candidate if this is of interest, and if so, suggest that more information will be provided in the next round of interviews.

This is not a one-sided decision. While the candidate needs to decide if it's worth giving up some short-term benefits like a bigger compensation package, the hiring manager needs to make a tough decision, too: determining if the gap is too wide to confidently make the candidate an offer. This is comparable to offering a skilled and experienced person what amounts to a lateral transfer or offering someone in the top half or better a true career move. I tell hiring managers all the time that if they want to consistently hire the strongest people and raise their department's talent bar, hire external people the same way they promote someone they've worked with before: based on their past performance and their potential to take on stretch roles and succeed.

It's important to point out that the decision after the first interview is not to make the candidate an offer or not, but simply if it's worth gathering additional information to confidently make this decision. And in this case, both the hiring manager and the candidate jointly need to make the decision to move forward.

Step 8: Measure First Impression Again, Last, and Compare

Determine Impact of First Impression on You and Actual Job Performance

After the candidate leaves the interview, objectively assess the candidate's first impression, appearance, personality, communication skills, and level of nervousness. Then ask yourself these questions:

First, did the factors affecting your initial reaction to the candidate change by the end of the interview?

Second, did you put these factors – whether negative or positive – aside while you conducted the assessment of the candidate?

Third, how will the candidate's actual first impression affect the person's on-the-job performance based on the people he or she will be working with.

Fourth, did you get evidence that the person has been successful working with people just like those he or she will be working with on the job? This is an important way to make an objective assessment of first impression.

Fact-Finding and Advice

➤ Make sure you bring your biases to the conscious level and do the opposite of your natural reaction.

➤ Did the candidate's first impression get better or worse over the course of the interview?

➤ Did the person become more/less nervous during the fact-finding?

➤ Observe quiet people becoming more talkative when asked follow-up questions; this is a good sign.

➤ Observe outgoing people becoming vague when pressed for details; this is a bad sign.

➤ Try to understand how person's personality and style impacted their accomplishments.

➤ Did assessing first impression and personality at the end of the interview change your decision?

➤ Is the candidate's true personality consistent with job needs?

Recently I was giving an overview of the Performance-based Hiring program to a UK company selling cloud software used in big industrial design projects. The company needed to rapidly expand their sales force with experienced representatives who could handle the complexity of their sales process. We created a performance profile for the sales rep with one of the performance objectives focused on conducting the discovery and solution selling process involved in any complex and customized sale.

The VP of Sales loved how the job was defined and how the interview was conducted but didn't agree at all with the idea that first impressions don't matter. She contended that if a sales rep didn't make a good first impression there would never be a second meeting with a client. I then asked if all people who make a good first impression turn out to be great sales reps. She said without hesitation, "Of course not." I then asked if she ever hired a sales rep who made a good first impression but underperformed. She said with some hesitation, "Sadly, yes." So I said why not wait until the end of the interview to determine how the person's first impression helped or hindered the person's sales success, rather than being seduced by it during the interview?

The point, that she quickly understood through personal experience, was that even if first impressions are important to job success, don't let them affect your judgment while you're interviewing the candidate. Keep an open mind at the start of the interview whether the person's first impression is strong or weak. With this forced delay, you'll discover that about a third of the people aren't nearly as good as you first thought, and another third aren't as bad. This simple idea is how you avoid hiring people based on first impressions, personality, and presentation skills, and instead hire people on their past performance and future potential.

You Can Never Out-Yell a Hiring Manager, But You Can Out-Fact Them

Too many hiring decisions are based on opinions, feelings, biases, emotions, and short-term needs rather than on evidence and facts. While you'll never have all of the information needed to be 100% sure you're making the right decision to hire someone, the Performance-based Interview covered in this chapter will help minimize the gap between a gut decision and a rational one.

I learned an important lesson about the fact versus feelings decision-making long ago when I had just started my recruiting career. But it was my prior 10 years of industry experience in manufacturing, engineering, financial planning, and accounting that provided the background for me to fully appreciate it. At the time I was hoping to land a new and important client. I had a candidate I was representing for a cost manager position who was considered the sole finalist for the role by the hiring manager, other members of the accounting function, and the VP of manufacturing, but one interview remained. This was with the CFO of the company, who was considered a dominating and highly opinionated brute force.

The interview with him did not go well. While extremely disappointing and seeing my fee and long-term possibility of getting a new and important client disappearing quickly, it took me a full day to have the courage to contact the CFO and see if I could convince him of his mistake. This call did not go well either.

At least at the start.

During his five-minute opening profanity-laced diatribe he accused me and the entire recruiting profession of malfeasance and time-wasting ignorance. He then went on to say his 16-year-old son had stronger cost accounting skills than my candidate. This is when my frustration boiled over and I said without hesitation, "If your 16-year-old son has such great cost accounting skills, please send me his resume, because I realize that I have a better job for him than the one you're offering."

Silence.

Then a laugh.

Then something like, "Well, Adler, you're a pretty funny guy. But you still don't know anything about cost accounting." Then I said, "No, that's not true. It's you who doesn't know much about cost accounting." Now in this particular case I *was* a subject matter expert in cost accounting, and I wouldn't suggest anyone else use this frank, in-your-face Bronx rebuttal (that's where I was born), but all of this was less important than how I described my candidate's role in implementing a state-of-the-art cost accounting system on a new enterprise-wide IT platform at a huge union-controlled automotive manufacturing facility in the Midwest.

After the detailed summary of my candidate's role in this project, I said that as a result of his success, he was asked to lead a similar worldwide implementation of the same cost system covering over 15 manufacturing sites. While the candidate wanted the job, his wife was getting her medical degree at a local major university and he decided to put his career on hold and relocate to Southern California.

After my evidence-packed rebuttal, I suggested to the CFO he meet my candidate again for a real in-depth interview focusing on the same accomplishment. He agreed. He called me later the next day after the interview and apologized. He said the candidate's soft-spoken nature turned him off right away and he ended the initial interview too soon. He realized the candidate was an exceptional person who could lead a comparable effort at his firm – an international medical products and supplies manufacturing company. Not only did he hire the person for the cost manager spot, but he also used my search firm to hire another half-dozen senior managers in finance, accounting, and manufacturing over the next three years. The lesson: you can never out-yell a hiring manager, but you can out-fact them.

Of course, many of these problems can be avoided before the fact by eliminating the use of short interviews of 30 minutes or less. These types of "get to know you" interviews reward first impressions, bias, and superficial assessments. Replacing them with well-organized panel interviews is an ideal solution.

■ WELL-ORGANIZED PANEL INTERVIEWS INCREASE ASSESSMENT ACCURACY

When I first became a recruiter, I thought panel interviews were not only too intimidating but also too unorganized to be useful. It made no sense to me to interview anyone when everyone was interrupting everyone else before the candidate could even finish his or her answer. As a result, I asked my clients to avoid them to the degree possible. While this attempt was partially successful, I had one major client – a well-known quick-service restaurant chain in the western U.S. – who used them as their primary assessment process. In fact, the CEO told me he wouldn't use my search firm unless I agreed to their approach. There was no arguing with this demand and after sitting in on a few interviews with the company, I became a true believer and forceful advocate.

I also discovered that interviewing someone one-on-one was different than interviewing the same person as part of a panel interview. In the one-on-one the interviewer has little time to assess the candidate's answers, thinking more about when to interrupt and what to ask next. In a well-organized panel interview as described below, the panelists have a chance to observe the candidate's reaction to the questions and better evaluate their responses. In addition, there are some other important but less obvious benefits.

The Big Reasons Candidates Should Be Interviewed by a Panel

1. **The impact of first impressions and personality biases are minimized.** Biases of any type tend to lead the interviewer down a path of asking questions designed to confirm the bias. A structured panel interview with a preplanned set of questions is self-correcting, preventing any one person from going off track.

2. **Interviewing accuracy is improved while avoiding mistakes.** The entire team is collectively discovering if the candidate is competent to do the actual work, motivated to do it, and a fit with the team and company culture. This is possible using the basic Performance-based Interview as the core of the panel interview, emphasizing the work history review and fully understanding two or three of the person's major accomplishments.

3. **It gives weaker interviewers and potential subordinates a means to voice their opinion in a controlled setting.** While it's often important for a subordinate to meet a potential boss, one-on-one interviews are often awkward, with personality and hidden agendas usually dominating the assessment. Participating in a panel also gives weaker interviewers a chance to learn how to properly conduct a Performance-based Interview and understand the difference between objective and biased evidence.

4. **It changes the focus from yes/no voting to a more nuanced and deliberative evidence-based assessment.** Since everyone is hearing the same information, the assessment is much more about how to interpret the evidence, not about generic competencies and whether the person was smart, likeable, and assertive enough.

5. **Candidates get a chance to better understand the job and how potential future coworkers interact.** The best people want to work with liked-minded professionals. A well-organized, professional panel interview provides this added benefit.

Over the years I discovered that when it comes to intimidating a candidate, it doesn't seem to matter for more senior level executives. Despite this exception, it still seems best to not start off first thing with the panel interview. This delay allows the candidate to get more comfortable with the situation and offers the person a chance to meet some of the people on the panel before the session starts.

As part of using more panel interviews, you should discard the time-consuming and less than useless 30-minute series of one-on-one interviews. Having the same two to four people in a panel session for 60–75 minutes will allow them to more accurately assess performance and fit instead of making some superficial judgment based on personality, appearance, and presentation skills.

Steps for Organizing a Panel Interview

Whenever there are more than five people in a panel interview, things can become unwieldy very quickly as everyone starts competing to ask questions. Any size panel fewer than five is fine. The following guidelines describe how to organize a panel interview for maximum effectiveness given these size constraints.

Have all interviewers on the panel review the performance-based job description and the talent scorecard before the interview session starts.

It's important to conduct a short pre-meeting with the panel to review the job and the candidate's resume or LinkedIn profile. As part of this session, highlight the two to three critical performance objectives the panel will focus on during the interview and their corresponding factors on the talent scorecard. It's also a good idea to read out loud the specific 1–5 ranking guidance on the scorecard for these factors ahead of time so everyone understands what evidence is required to accurately assess the candidate. In general one of the accomplishment-based questions should focus on the person's major individual achievement to assess the depth of the person's technical skills and the other on the person's most comparable major team accomplishment.

Script the Performance-based Interview to use as an organizing tool.

The first 30 minutes of a 90-minute panel session should include some time for introductions, giving the person a short (three or four minutes at most!) overview of the job and then conducting a work-history review to help everyone learn about the candidate's background. Use the balance of the session to dig into one major team and one major individual accomplishment. If there's enough time, you might want to ask the problem-solving question to find out how the candidate would handle a major challenge likely to be faced on the job. Then ask the candidate to describe a problem they handled that's most comparable.

It's vital that there is only one leader in a panel interview with everyone else acting as fact-finders only.

Organization and the assigning of roles is essential for a proper panel interview. Rather than competing, interrupting, and asking "favorite" questions, in an organized panel interview the participants support each other. In this case, there is one leader who asks the most significant accomplishment question (e.g., "Can you tell us about your most significant accomplishment related to [describe major performance objective]?)." with the fact-finders peeling the onion to understand the person's actual role and getting lots of details. The best fact-finding question of them all is, "Can you give me an example of what you mean?" Ask this whenever a candidate makes some type of general comment or a vague statement. By getting lots of examples, candidates quickly learn that the purpose of the interview is to provide specific facts, dates, and figures.

Leaders can be fact-finders, but fact-finders can't be leaders.

Only leaders can change the focus of the accomplishment question being discussed. In order to make an accurate assessment, it's better to go narrow and deep, fully understanding a candidate's major accomplishments, rather than broad, shallow, and superficial. Leaders need to be part of the fact-finding involved in this, but fact-finders can't change the focus of the accomplishment-based question. Once a hiring team gets comfortable with this approach, the back-and-forth fact-finding questioning becomes very natural. It's certainly okay to change the leader if desired to ask the different accomplishment questions. For example, as part of a recent panel session for a COO for a major charity, I asked the CEO to focus on the fundraising objective while I led the questioning around systems implementation. In this series of panel interviews, all of the candidates found the process professional and invaluable. In fact, the person who got the job told us later that she thought it was the most challenging yet positive interviewing experience she had ever had. As a result, she then implemented the panel interview step as a core component of the organization's hiring process.

Capture everyone's insight right after the interview.

Once the interview is completed, review the talent scorecard right away. Since everyone heard the same information, the rankings should be pretty similar, especially once the evidence is shared. When there is a wide variance, it's usually due to some emotional reaction to the candidate, either extremely positive or negative. These types of out-of-the-ordinary situations should be challenged on the spot using evidence to back up any superficial claims. I remember one situation where a candidate for a sales management position was initially ruled out by the VP, who suggested he didn't seem assertive enough. The VP quickly changed his mind when one of the sales managers on the panel disagreed, reminding everyone how the candidate landed and closed a major account. The VP agreed he had reached the wrong conclusion. These instant turnarounds are not surprising. In this situation it clearly demonstrated the value of gathering and sharing evidence and challenging those who are making superficial assessments.

When organized properly, panel interviews are a great tool for saving time, giving weak interviewers an opportunity to participate, avoiding hiring mistakes (including hiring someone who normally would have been excluded), and increasing assessment accuracy. Poorly organized panel interviews are a waste of time. The key is to know the job and recognize the different roles leaders and fact-finders play. Panel interviews are truly a team sport, but in too many cases they resemble the first AYSO soccer game played by a bunch of five-year-olds.

■ KEY HIGHLIGHTS OF THE PERFORMANCE-BASED INTERVIEW PROCESS

There was a lot covered in this chapter. Here are some of the major points that are worth reviewing before conducting an interview. This will help drive home the key ideas, especially about using the interview to collect the evidence needed to make the hiring decision and not to make it during the interview. While this is easy to say, it is hard to do, but it is necessary to do in order to achieve a Win-Win Hiring outcome.

❑ An organized multistep interviewing process is required to gather all of the evidence needed to make an accurate hiring decision. The Performance-based Interview described in this chapter can be used at each of these steps with only minor modification to gather this evidence.

❏ The purpose of the interview is to assess competency, fit, and motivation to do the work required, as defined in the performance-based job description *and* to demonstrate that this job offers the candidate the best career move compared to other opportunities the candidate is considering.

❏ In order to achieve a Win-Win Hiring outcome, the candidate needs to balance the short-term compensation package with a 30% nonmonetary increase. This consists of a combination of a bigger job, more satisfying work, and continuing growth and learning.

❏ When conducted as described, the Performance-based Interview provides the evidence needed to accurately assess all of the factors predicting on-the-job success. These factors are included in the Quality of Hire Talent Scorecard.

❏ Only three basic interviewing techniques need to be mastered before interviewing a candidate: how to properly conduct a work history review, how to ask the most significant accomplishment question, and how to get into a back-and-forth dialog around a realistic job-related problem the candidate is likely to face. The other steps in the interview are needed to set up these questions, to avoid common mistakes due to bias, and to recruit the candidate.

❏ Well-organized panel interviews provide additional insight and added objectivity that's not possible with any type of one-on-one interview. At a minimum they should be used 100% of the time to replace the series of 30-minute interviews that reward bias, first impressions, and personality over performance and potential.

❏ This same Performance-based Interview can be used by other interviewers and in the other steps involved in fully assessing a candidate by changing the focus of the accomplishment and problem-solving questions.

❏ By measuring the impact of first impressions on job performance at the end of the interview, common hiring mistakes due to interviewing bias can be minimized.

Chapter 10

Making the Assessment Using the Quality of Hire Talent Scorecard

The Performance-based Interview covered in Chapter 9 was designed to capture the evidence needed to assess all of the factors in the Hiring Formula for Success introduced in Chapter 6. The overall summary of how these tools and ideas are integrated is shown in Figure 10.1.

There is a more detailed version of the Quality of Hire Talent Scorecard in Appendix 2. It will be useful to download this as you review this chapter to fully understand what evidence to look for during the interview that best predicts on-the-job performance. Following are some important points to consider as you get started interviewing and assessing candidates using the scorecard.

■ KEYS FOR CONDUCTING AN EVIDENCE-BASED CANDIDATE ASSESSMENT

1. Eliminate the 30-minute series of one-on-one interviews. Not only are they unprofessional, but they also reward bias and superficial interviewing. Conducting a well-organized panel interview with two or three people for 75 minutes not only saves time but increases assessment accuracy. (See Chapter 9 on how to conduct these types of panel interviews.)

2. Use evidence, not emotions, to rank the candidate on the 1–5 scale for each of the factors. Evidence means details and facts, not feelings and emotions.

3. While all interviewers will ask similar questions using the Performance-based Interview process, their focus will be narrowed to two or three specific factors on the talent scorecard. By assigning interviewers a subset of the factors, there is a tendency for them to "own" these factors and dig deeper to find more useful evidence.

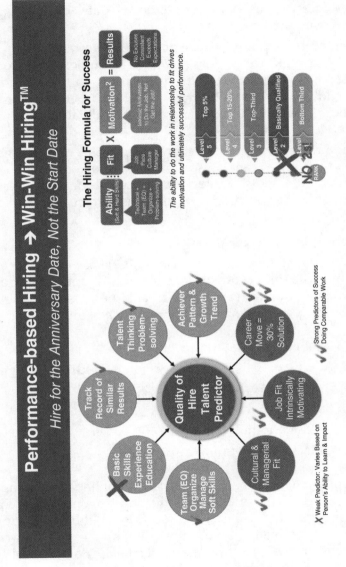

Figure 10.1 Quality of Hire Talent Scorecard.

4. It's important to share each interviewer's evidence before the final ranking for each specific ranking. This sharing is a great way to expose bias at its source and also to train new interviewers on the differences between strong and weak evidence.

5. Assume the evidence is suspect when the rankings for any one factor are too widely spread. This indicates a process that's a bit out of control. In these cases no final judgment should be made and more information, like reference checks, needs to be obtained or the candidate needs to be interviewed again.

6. When the group rankings are tight (i.e., plus or minus half a point in the 1–5 ranking scale), after the evidence is shared you can assume the interview is accurate and the assessment, whether positive or negative, is correct.

Understanding the 1–5 Ranking System

The complete talent scorecard (see Appendix 2) has one row for each of the factors in the Hiring Formula for Success, with specific guidance on what type of evidence is needed to rank the person on the 1–5 scale. Following is the general definition of each of these rankings.

Level 1: Minimal Skill Set (unqualified)

Level 2: Adequate Skill Set (marginally qualified)

Level 2.5: Average Performer

Level 3: Strong Performer (top third)

Level 4: Great Performer (top 10–20%)

Level 5: Outstanding Performer (top 10%)

It's important to note that this 1–5 scale is nonlinear, meaning it's not split in even groups of 20% each. Instead, anyone with a Level 3 ranking or better would be in the top third of their peer group. Although not specifically shown as a column, a Level 2.5 would be considered an average performer and a Level 1 and 2 would be in the bottom half of their peer group. Unfortunately, many of these people get hired due to faulty interviewing techniques.

These mistakes cover the gamut from bias, limited understanding of the actual job needs, weak interviewing skills, desperation to fill the job, and overvaluing a candidate's presentation skills rather than their past performance. These errors will be minimized by using the complete talent scorecard in combination with the Performance-based Interview. Both of these forms are included in Appendix 2.

It's important to note than anyone who ranks a Level 3 or better on any of these factors is an outstanding performer. Some hiring managers think everyone should be a Level 5 in order to be hirable. Aside from the fact it's not possible, it's not how a great team needs to be built. It's important to note that much of the rankings shown here are based on the context of the job and the people on the team. Given this reality, a person's performance can vary based on the mix of these factors over time. To handle these types of situations a great team needs to be comprised of a mix of people who are all at least Level 2.5 or better. But most importantly, NO 2s! By sharing evidence and getting everyone's point of view, many of these variables will be taken into consideration as the person is interviewed and assessed.

Share Evidence in a Live Formal Debriefing Session

It's important that the hiring team gets together, and each person shares what they've learned. This requires that some type of formal debriefing be part of the assessment as well as some up-front organization and planning. The key is to assign specific roles to everyone on the interviewing team, where everyone shares their evidence for each of the factors. One way to do this is to assign each interviewer a few of the factors in the hiring formula for success. By preventing anyone from having a full yes/no vote, you increase the need for every interviewer to be more responsible and objective. In this approach the entire hiring team makes the yes/no decision together. This collective type of focused interview in combination with a formal debriefing is a great way to minimize the impact of emotions, biases, feelings, and weak interviewing skills during the final evaluation.

Using the 1–5 ranking scale can also help minimize the impact of feelings and emotions. Under no circumstances should you allow the interviewing team to add up individual yes/no votes to make this decision. In most debriefing sessions, the hiring team gets together and shares their opinions in some informal way. The range of these rankings varies across the board, with those with more authority having more influence. Most likely these people also conducted shorter interviews, just to see if the person "fits." These short interviews are useless and should be banned! There's not enough time in 30 minutes to determine anything substantive. Reviewing all of the factors in the hiring formula as a team using the 1–5 ranking scale is how the debriefing should be conducted.

Invoke the NO 2s! Rule to Raise the Talent Bar

There are two big rules to follow to avoid most common hiring mistakes. The first one is to "Wait 30 Minutes" before even making a mental yes or no decision. This was fully covered in Chapter 4 on how to minimize the impact of bias and first impressions on the assessment. By using a semi-scripted Performance-based Interview, asking everyone the same questions, this problem is largely avoided. The NO 2s! rule is another and even more powerful technique to increase assessment accuracy, especially when it comes to achieving more Win-Win Hiring outcomes. It basically says spend most of your time avoiding hiring anyone who is not a Level 2.5 or better. These are people who are not intrinsically motivated to do the work that needs to be done – despite the fact that they all say they'll do it during the interview – or don't fit the culture or company in some other way.

It's important to note that a Level 3, 4, or 5 ranking on any of the factors indicates the person is a top-third performer. This is someone who is both motivated and competent to do the actual work as described in the performance profile. These are all outstanding people and are great hires. Someone lower than a Level 2.5 ranking is somewhere in the top of the bottom half or worse among their peer group. The problem with interviewing is that it's often difficult to determine the difference between a person who is a Level 2 and someone who is a Level 3, 4, or 5. However, the on-the-job difference is striking. It's the difference in being motivated to do the work and not being motivated to do it.

That's why the NO 2s! advisory is so important. During the first round of interviews you'll determine if the person is generally competent to do the work. Use the second round to ensure the person is not a 2 on any of the critical factors in the table. The following table offers the evidence you need to seek out to avoid hiring people who will lower the talent bar.

The NO 2s! Warning Signs for Each Factor

Factor	The NO 2s! Caution Flags: Look for evidence the candidate is not a Level 2 on any of these factors.
Motivation	No pattern of taking initiative in critical needs areas. Hard to pull out examples of going the extra mile. Inconsistent.
Talent	No evidence of person doing exceptional work, influencing others on technical matters, or understanding how to solve basic tech problems.
Management	Makes excuses for tasks not being met. Does not have a track record of consistently committing and delivering. Planning is haphazard.
Team	Lack of 360° growth, no evidence of coaching others or being asked to participate in or lead a team project.
Thinking	Lack of clarity around problem-solving approach and little evidence of handling similar issues successfully.
Job Fit	Competent, but few examples of being truly motivated to do the majority of the actual work required.
Manager Fit	Hasn't excelled under a variety of different managers, or where did excel, style was different than hiring manager.
Culture, Environment	Person's best work was different from pace, resources, decision-making process of company culture.

While the NO 2s! rule is a good one to follow, some rules are made to be broken. In certain cases you might want to still move forward with a person who is exceptional in some areas but weak in a few others. For example, someone who has shown an ability to learn and apply new skills quickly might be a reasonable offset to Level 2 on their current depth of technical skills. On the other hand, you might find someone who is technically brilliant but not the best organizer. In this case you need to figure how to shore up this deficiency if you want to hire the person.

However, under no circumstances should you ever violate the NO 2s! rule for motivation. If a person is not motivated to do the actual work required in the environment in which the work takes place the person is guaranteed to underperform. Assessing this requires a great deal of cynicism to gather the specific and recent evidence to evaluate this factor. For example, I remember many years ago when a candidate with a PhD in chemistry told me he was fully competent to handle a hands-on laboratory project. Since he had been managing senior staff doing this work for the past 10 years, I told him he was overqualified for the job. He proved it to himself when he realized he could not come up with a single example of taking the initiative, volunteering for a project, or going the extra mile doing the work required to be successful in the role. His interest in the job was purely economic and once the economic need was fulfilled his motivation would be gone. Check out Maslow's Hierarchy of Needs[1] if you want a bit more understanding on how motivation impacts job performance and for some other clues on how to assess it accurately.

■ STEP-BY-STEP COMPLETING THE QUALITY OF HIRE TALENT SCORECARD

Following is a short summary of each of the factors in the talent scorecard and some ideas on how to gather the evidence needed to make an accurate assessment. Good evidence needs to support the guidance in the scorecard. For example, for someone to rank high on organizational skills the evidence should describe a project that's comparable to the required work with specific details on how the person managed the project, tracked performance to schedule, and overcame setbacks. Weak evidence would be superficial, emotional, or clearly biased. For example, something like, "I didn't like the person, she was too soft-spoken to manage the group and I don't think anyone would respect her," should be instantly discarded. However, saying something like, "I ranked her a Level 2 because the biggest project she managed was half the size in terms of team size

[1]https://www.simplypsychology.org/maslow.html.

and budget in comparison to the one she'd be handling in this role. Despite this she did a great job and maybe she should be considered for another more suitable role," would be valid evidence.

Basic Competencies
Core Skills

When first preparing the job requisition it's important to ask the hiring manager what the essential or most important skills are the person must possess on the start date. These are the deal-breaker or "must have" skills in order for the person to even be considered a viable candidate. Often these are higher-level skills with the assumption that the person couldn't have mastered these without learning some of the other less important ones first. By asking how these skills are used on the job, it's possible to quantify these skills based on real job needs. For example, if someone needs to have three to five years of SQL and Tableau preparing complex database reports extracted from the company's financial system, the performance objective might describe how this needs to be developed, tested, and used. Getting candidates to describe the most complex projects they worked on using these skills would be enough to determine if the person is qualified or not. A high ranking would be justified if the person brings another dimension to the role that wasn't previously considered.

Overall Experience

On one director-level search the VP asked me how much experience a person needed to have. I said something glib like, "Just enough to do the job." If the person had too much, they might not be motivated to do the work required, and if too little, likely unable to do it. The more serious answer is less than typically on the job description but enough doing comparable work. More important than the absolute number of years is having enough time to demonstrate a level of mastery in their previous roles that the company is comfortable with hiring the person. To me, meeting this minimum threshold of experience would be enough to seriously consider the person for the job. Given this point of view, even a high ranking on the "years of experience" factor wouldn't offset the need for the person to score very high on all of the other factors in order for the person to be considered the number one finalist.

For example, on this director of accounting search the candidate hired for the role had the least amount of public reporting experience but had enough to demonstrate mastery when asked to handle the role when his boss became ill. This same person went on to handle multiple roles that appeared over his head when measured on years of experience but not when assessed on ability and motivation to excel.

Achiever Pattern and Trend of Growth

One of the three factors involved in determining if a candidate is a semi-finalist for the role is if the person possesses the Achiever Pattern. This indicates the person is in the top half or better in their peer group. During the interview it's important to validate this by asking the person to describe the type of recognition they received for each major accomplishment. This could range from a pat on the back, a formal commendation, a promotion of some type, or a monetary award. The following are some of things you'll need to use as evidence to justify the person should be ranked a Level 3 or better on this factor.

Upward trend of growth. Those with the Achiever Pattern generally get promoted more rapidly than others. Aside from a bigger title and job, this could be in the form of being assigned to lead larger or more important teams or handling more important and more complex projects.

Asked to handle challenging technical projects. The best hiring managers tend to push their most promising subordinates, giving them stretch roles, assigning them to difficult projects, providing early exposure to senior managers and influential executives, and giving them advanced training opportunities. Look for this pattern at the candidate's last few jobs. As part of this, ask how the person got assigned to the project and why. The pattern typically reveals the person's core strengths, learning ability, and potential. A brilliant technical person would clearly rank high on the Achiever Pattern even if the person's growth rate seems to have plateaued. This is comparable to a manager who develops great teams or to a salesperson who always meets their goals or is assigned to the toughest clients. In this case the quality of the work is what matters, not the rate of change.

Being assigned to more important teams. During the interview, ask candidates to describe the people on the teams they've been on and the role they played. Those with the Achiever Pattern show a pattern of consistently being assigned to important cross-functional teams with exposure to important business leaders on a continuing basis. Ask how they got assigned to the team, the reason they were assigned (this reveals the person's core strengths), the success of the team project, and what happened after the team project was complete. The best people are asked by former team members to be on subsequent team projects.

Rehired or referred by former coworkers. Ask how the person got the job to begin with. Those with the Achiever Pattern are typically promoted into the role but if not, they're often referred by a former coworker or hired by a former boss.

Staff development. When hiring people for management positions it's essential that they possess the hiring manager Achiever Pattern. Clues for this include low turnover, a formal approach to staff development, hiring former coworkers, and hiring other top achievers validated by a major portion of their previous staff members getting promoted into bigger roles. These are the managers that everyone in the company wants to work with and for.

Formal recognition. It's a good idea to ask candidates what type of formal recognition they received at each job. This could include special or bigger bonuses, letters of praise, public awards, some type of prize, or some type of recognition at a company event.

If the hiring team needs to struggle finding evidence of the Achiever Pattern, it's pretty obvious the person doesn't have it. In my mind this is a deal-breaker in terms of hiring the person unless the person has limited work experience.

■ ESSENTIAL CORE COMPETENCES

Talent and Overall Technical Ability

Focus on what was accomplished with the person's technical skills rather than their absolute amount. Compare these accomplishments to their peer group to see if they're in the top or bottom half.

Asking about the projects the person was assigned soon after starting and regularly thereafter offers a clue to what the person's managers thought of the person's ability. Top performers tend to volunteer for atypical projects to stretch themselves. So seek this out. The best people get some type of formal recognition, and without this it's hard to get a Level 5 ranking.

Management and Organization Ability

Organizing and planning and getting work done on time and on budget might be considered soft skills, but whatever you call them, they're vital for successful performance. To rank high on this factor it's important to get evidence that the candidate has successfully managed projects of comparable size and scope to what's required for the job. As part of this, understand the complexity of the projects, who was on the team, the person's role, and the pace and intensity required to meet deadlines. Get specific details about the plans the person put together and how they were used to manage the project. Recognition for exceptional performance on this factor would be being asked to lead complex comparable projects and/or volunteering for them.

This is an important factor to assess for individual contributors, too. While much of the evidence required is similar, it's important also to understand how reliable and committed the person was as part of a project team.

Team Skills (EQ), Staff Development, and Leadership

One great way to assess this factor is to have the person prepare a 360-degree work chart during the work history review and for each major accomplishment showing the names and titles of the people the candidate worked with on a regular basis. Rank the candidate high on this factor when the teams are comparable in scope to the actual needs of the job and when the person's team role is growing in responsibility. Be concerned if the makeup of the teams is static over time and narrow functionally. Rank the person very high if those on the team ask the person to lead or be on other teams, especially if they're cross-functional in nature and comprised of more senior level executives.

When hiring people who will be managers, ask about the people on the teams, how they were hired and developed, and how many of their people were promoted into bigger roles.

Thinking and Job-Related Problem-Solving

There are two good ways to assess this critical factor. One way is to ask candidates to describe the biggest problem they've handled most comparable to one they're likely to face on the job. The other way is using the problem-solving question and engaging with the candidate on how they would go about solving the same problem. In this case you're assessing the process used to solve the problem, not the solution itself. The quality of the questions asked indicates the person has some sense of how the problem could be solved. Those who rank very high on problem-solving and thinking have a track record of solving comparable problems and who can visualize potential solutions by understanding how to figure out and eliminate their root cause.

Situational Fit Factors

The ability to do the work in relationship to fit drives motivation to excel. That's why you should use the first series of interviews to objectively determine overall competency and the second series to focus in-depth on the fit factors and motivation to excel in the job. Much of this involves getting to know the person as more than just a candidate for a job, but also someone you can work with on a regular basis on different teams and on critical projects. Separating these two critical parts of the assessment will help get past all of the biases we have when interviewing the person for the first time.

Job Fit and Recent Comparable Results

When you come to this factor during the formal debriefing, headline it with this statement:

The purpose of this factor will be to rank the person on their competency and motivation to do the work we've defined in the performance profile and in our actual environment.

Given the importance of this goal, I wouldn't compromise on the Level 3 or better requirement. You'll be able to rank the person by asking about the person's major accomplishments related to the performance objectives of the job, the trend of these accomplishments over time, the quality of this work, the teams the person has been on and led, and the person's intrinsic motivation to do this work. Be most concerned when this work isn't in the recent past, if the job doesn't seem to be a worthy career move, or if the role doesn't leverage the person's critical strengths and interests.

Keep on sharing evidence until everyone on the hiring team is in close agreement on this factor. If getting this tight agreement isn't possible, get more evidence.

Managerial Fit

After 1,500 placements over 20 years, it became pretty clear to me that unless the hiring manager can support, develop, and mentor the new hire during the onboarding process and throughout the first year a Win-Win Hiring outcome is unlikely. Just as important is for the new hire to be able to mesh with the hiring manager's style of management rather than putting the entire burden on the hiring manager. We figured out how to accomplish this after one of my clients asked me to incorporate Hersey and Blanchard's *Situational Leadership*[2] model into our hiring manager's interviewing training course. It turned out that by mapping a manager's approach to leadership and development to the new hire's need for direction and coaching, we could accurately predict "Managerial Fit." The concept is shown in Figure 10.2, with the explanation of how to figure it out during the interview described below.

How to Accurately Predict Managerial Fit and Ensure a Great Hire

As part of the intake meeting, ask the hiring manager to describe how much coaching, training, and direction he or she likes to provide to new hires. Then get some examples of some recent good and

[2]Management of Organizational Behavior: Leading Human Resources, Ken Blanchard, Paul Hersey, Dewey Johnson, Pearson College Div; 8th edition (October 1, 2000).

Managerial Fit: The Driver of Engagement & Satisfaction

MANAGER'S LEADERSHIP AND DEVELOPMENT STYLE
Degree of Involvement in Subordinate Tasks

Controller	Supervisor	Trainer	Coach	Delegator	Hands-off

100% ●━━━━━━━━━━━━━━━━━━━━━━━━━━━━━━━━● 0%

Dependent	Structured	Trainable	Coachable	Manageable	Self-directed

SUBORDINATE'S COACHING AND DEVELOPMENT NEEDS
Degree of Direction Needed/Wanted

Performance-based Hiring

Figure 10.2   Assessing Managerial Fit.
© 2019 All Rights Reserved. Performancebasedhiring.com

not-so-good hires. Based on this, assign the hiring manager into one or two of the categories on the top scale in the graphic. As part of the fact-finding during the work history review and digging into major accomplishments, ask candidates to describe their best and least-best managers. The objective is to find out how the candidate's managers affected the person's performance. Some candidates can work with all types of managers and some can't. Just as important, some candidates thrive under different types of managers and underperform with others. This is a critical aspect of assessing managerial fit.

To ensure NO 2s! make sure there is some flexibility across the styles and some vertical alignment between them. This would be a Level 3. An extreme example of poor managerial fit (that's quite personal for me since this is why I quit a job I liked as a business unit manager over a manufacturing division) is when the employee doesn't want much management and the hiring manager – in my case the group president – wants everything done his way, which in my mind was pretty dumb. A more common example is a hiring manager who would rather hire experienced people since they have little interest in coaching and training their new hires even if they have lots of upside potential.

To get a level 4 or 5 on managerial fit, both the manager and the candidate need to be flexible.

Culture and Environmental Fit

Practically speaking, a Level 2 on any of the fit factors would justify a "No Hire" decision. While everyone describes the importance of cultural fit, few people can actually describe what it is and how to measure it. Defining cultural fit was described in Chapter 7 on preparing the performance profile and in Chapter 6 on using the Hiring Formula for Success to guide the assessment process. The big idea covered was to use the pace and intensity of the organization and the decision-making process as proxies for assessing cultural fit since both of these factors impact the company culture and capture many of its values. For example, if someone has done well in a large slow-paced company, they're unlikely to be a strong cultural fit when the depth of resources is far less and the decision-making needs to be quicker. As part of the assessment, have the candidate go step-by-step through the biggest and most recent decision they ever made and map this to how your company handles similar decisions. But dig deeper if it seems like there is a fit.

Much of a company's culture is also driven by its financial performance, the industry it's in, and how the company is financed. If you've ever worked for a company that is struggling, you know it has a culture all its own. In a similar vein companies backed by private equity or venture capital have their culture defined for them, at least with respect to the strategy, the budget, the intensity, and the high expectations. When hiring someone for these types of companies you need to make sure the person can succeed in an environment of limited resources and where failure is not an option. Just as important in making these hiring decisions is to recognize that many of these companies are founded by entrepreneurs who tend to overmanage people when in charge and who struggle mightily once they're funded by outside investors.

All of these factors impact cultural fit and whether a new person will succeed. Don't take the hiring risk when you see a big gap on any of these dimensions.

Motivation to Excel

Part of the fact-finding involved in asking the accomplishment questions is to find out how the person got assigned the project being described. In some cases they were given the project by their manager, while in other cases they volunteered for it. In either case, make sure you ask why and under what circumstances the person got the project. If they were assigned it reveals the person's technical, team, and organizational strengths. Volunteering for it reveals the person's intrinsic motivators. The stretch in the project also reveals a lot about the candidate's confidence level and aspirations since the strongest people are willing to take on projects over their heads.

These are all good clues to share as evidence when assessing intrinsic motivation. You'll get additional insight by asking candidates during each accomplishment question where they took the initiative or went the extra mile. The pattern that emerges over multiple projects reveals intrinsic motivation as well as commitment, reliability, and character. For example, you know you found a highly motivated and remarkable person if he or she naturally puts in extra effort on work they find satisfying but will also still put in the same extra effort when necessary to meet deadlines or to help their colleagues meet theirs. Rank the person a Level 4 or Level 5 on motivation in the later situation when it seems to happen frequently, and all of the other fit factors are at least Level 3.

■ ADDRESSING THE BALANCING ACT BETWEEN RECRUITABILITY AND COMPETENCY

While the determination of whether the person is recruitable is made in parallel with the final assessment, some people making the assessment tend to forget this part. Too often hiring managers and their bosses want people who can "hit the ground running" on Day One, oblivious to the fact that these people won't take an offer without a substantial salary premium. As far as I'm concerned, in the long run it's far better to hire people who can handle most of the job but who need some training, coaching, and support to handle it all. These gaps make the job more appealing and more likely you'll hire the person based on the size of the growth opportunity, not the size of the compensation increase. On the other hand, everyone on the hiring team and those who will work with the person post-hire need to understand and support this balancing act. The 30% Solution described in Chapter 13 on recruiting is the right balance here. By providing enough stretch and growth with a mix of more satisfying work, a Win-Win Hiring situation is both realistic and likely.

With this recruitability component in mind, it's important to review the scores on all of the other factors to see if anything would change as a result. For example, someone who is a great team leader might find managing a smaller staff less motivating than someone who sees managing the same team an important step in their personal development.

■ ORGANIZING THE INTERVIEW TO MAXIMIZE ASSESSMENT ACCURACY

During our interviewing training courses we're often asked if everyone asks the same questions. The answer is yes and no. While the bulk of the interview involves asking about the person's major accomplishments in comparison to real job needs, the fact-finding can be modified to assess the different factors on the talent scorecard. Assigning two or three different factors to each interviewer allows everyone on the hiring team to ask similar questions but obtain different insight about the candidate to share during the formal debriefing session.

One common example of how this can be done is to have someone in HR ask about the person's major team accomplishments, the hiring manager's boss ask about how the person organized and managed a complex multifunctional project, and having the hiring manager fully understand the person's overall talent and problem-solving ability. This type of organizational approach is shown in Figure 10.3. It shows how each of the factors are assigned to the different interviewers.

The basic Performance-based Interview guide in Appendix 2 has many of these modifications for team and individual accomplishments already incorporated to get started. Here's an example of how the same basic accomplishment questions can be modified even further.

Basic Major Accomplishment Question

One of the major projects the person hired for this role will be handling is [describe the performance objective]. Can you tell me about something you handled that is most comparable?

Organize the Interview by Objectives and Factors

Interviewer Roles	Hiring Manager	Recruiter	Technical	Team	Panel	Fit Factors	HR
BASIC COMPETENCIES – Work History Review							
Skills			✓				
Experience	✓	✓			✓		
Achiever Pattern & Growth Trend	✓	✓		✓	✓		
CORE COMPETENCIES – MSA and Problem-Solving							
Talent and Basic Technical Ability	✓	✓					
Management & Organizational	✓	✓		✓	✓		✓
Team Skills	✓	✓		✓			✓
Thinking & Problem-Solving	✓		✓	✓			
SITUATIONAL FIT FACTORS							
Job Fit, Trend of Performance & Results	✓	✓	✓		✓	✓	
Managerial Fit	✓			✓		✓	✓
Culture & Environment				✓	✓	✓	✓
Motivation²	✓	✓	✓		✓	✓	

Assign Roles

Narrow vs Broad. Use Performance-based Interview with role-based fact-finding

Formal Debrief

No Yes/No. Share evidence to reach consensus.

Figure 10.3 Organize the Interview by Objectives and Factors.
© 2017 All Rights Reserved. The Adler Group, Inc.

Modification for Problem-Solving

One of the major projects the person hired for this role will be handling is [describe the performance objective]. Before we can even begin, there are a number of core process problems that need to be addressed and resolved first. Can you describe something you've handled that's comparable and how you handled these types of problems?

Modification for Team Skills

There are a number of team challenges involved with [describe the performance objective]. Some of these include hiring a few critical people and working with other functions that aren't supporting the project. Can you describe a comparable multifunctional project you've handled and how you handled these types of team challenges?

Surprisingly, when interviewers are assigned a subset of the factors to assess rather than having a full yes/no vote, there is a tendency for them to conduct a more in-depth assessment. Realistically speaking, it's not possible to make a confident yes decision in a one-hour interview. This is one reason why people vote no more often than yes since it's a safer decision. Just as bad, saying yes is generally based on emotion, need, bias, and first impressions.

By organizing the interview as described in this chapter, all of these self-induced problems are eliminated.

While it takes some preparation to organize the interview this way the first time, once it's been done a few times everyone pretty much knows their own roles. In fact, after a few debriefing sessions it's possible to self-organize the interview with minimal up-front discussion. For example, after the first interview has been conducted with a candidate, every interviewer who follows just needs to ask the candidate what was discussed in the previous interviews. Then they just need to ask accomplishment questions selecting factors from the scorecard that hadn't yet been assessed.

■ SUMMARY

Based on over one thousand different interviewing situations I'm confident in concluding that a well-organized interviewing process is as important as the quality of the interview being conducted. This is truer if the objective of a company's hiring process is to improve diversity hiring, raise the talent bar, reduce turnover, avoid hiring mistakes, increase job satisfaction, and achieve consistent Win-Win Hiring outcomes year after year. None of these important objectives can be achieved in a haphazard fashion, letting hiring managers use their own pet questions and decide if someone should be hired or not based on bias, emotions, lack of job knowledge, and who has the biggest thumb.

Regardless of how you organize it, the interviewing process must be organized and professionally conducted. As suggested earlier, the first round of interviews should be used to assess overall ability and general fit with the job on a scope and scale basis. This can be achieved using the Performance-based Interviewing process described in Chapter 9. The second round of interviews and all subsequent reference checking should focus on the fit factors. The NO 2s! rule should be strictly enforced when it comes to each of these without compromise. In Chapter 14 on recruiting I suggest that a few days before making a candidate an offer you ask the person if they want the job, putting money aside. All will say yes, but then you need to ask why. Those who can explain it properly will describe these fit factors in superb detail. If not, don't make the offer until they can. The hiring manager and the new hire will appreciate the persistence.

Chapter 11

Comparing Performance-based Hiring and Behavioral Event Interviewing

We're often asked if Performance-based Hiring is different than behavioral event interviewing (BEI).

The short answer is that Performance-based Hiring is BEI on steroids.

Here's why.

As I was preparing this chapter, I spoke with one of our clients – a director of talent at a midsize international financial services company – who had just become Performance-based Hiring certified. She was a perfect choice to get some insight from since she was also a certified BEI trainer and before she took our course, she told me she was skeptical that Performance-based Hiring was even worth taking. Despite her reluctance to proceed, she had no choice since her company began rolling out Performance-based Hiring before she was hired. Upon completing the course and after interviewing a number of candidates, she wholeheartedly and quickly agreed with the "BEI on steroids" conclusion. If you're familiar with BEI and have read the book up to this point, you know why she agreed. In case you jumped to this chapter to see if the whole book was worth reading, following are the big differences.

■ LACK OF JOB ANALYSIS IS THE BIG GAP IN BEI

Practically speaking, no book about hiring and interviewing would be complete if it didn't discuss behavioral event interviewing[1] and the Situation-Task-Action-Result (STAR) questioning approach. BEI involves asking candidates to give an example of how a critical competency or behavior was used on the job using this format: "Can you tell me about a time you had to (e.g., confront a colleague on a difficult problem)?" This is followed up by the interviewer using the STAR questioning pattern to better understand the significance of the example chosen.

An essential component – but one that's often ignored or minimized – of the BEI-STAR process is the requirement to compare the candidate's examples to a thorough job analysis conducted before the requisition was opened. Without this job analysis it's not possible to make an accurate assessment. It seems mind-boggling that people who use and advocate BEI disregard this critical part.

Without the job analysis the process has limited value since every candidate you'll ever meet has multiple examples of every competency imaginable. In fact, if you search on "behavioral interview questions" you'll find millions of examples of how to practice answering these BEI questions. Given the lack of a job analysis and the overly rehearsed nature of the examples provided, everything

---

[1]"A Guide to Conducting Behavioral Interviews with Early Career Job Candidates," Society for Human Resource Management, https://www.shrm.org/LearningAndCareer/learning/Documents/Behavioral%20Interviewing%20Guide%20for%20Early%20Career%20Candidates.pdf

is then left up to the interviewer to decide if the example chosen is relevant.

This reality alone should eliminate using traditional BEI methodology as a valid interviewing process, yet some vendors argue that there is still some positive correlation between predicted and actual on-the-job performance despite this glaring weakness. Without getting into the statistical weeds, I contend the reason there is some slight correlation has to do with the fact that the interview is structured, not with the behavioral questions asked. The big benefit of any structured interview is that it helps minimize mistakes due to bias where interviewers quickly go off course and look for facts to justify their initial reaction to the candidate. While the use of a structured interview is not an insignificant benefit, the statistics used to validate it shouldn't be used to demonstrate improved accuracy due to behavioral interviewing when that's simply not the case.

Aside from the faked and overprepped answers, another rarely mentioned problem with BEI relates to the relevancy of the accomplishment from a time perspective. Describing an accomplishment from five to ten years ago or more to validate a current need has little value, especially if the person is no longer motivated to handle what could be a reduced role. For example, a person who's currently a director managing managers might not still be motivated to coach and develop individual contributors despite being great at it 10 years ago and having great examples to prove it.

■ BEHAVIORAL FACT-FINDING IS THE KEY TO AN ACCURATE ASSESSMENT

Despite these misgivings, BEI has value when used properly. In the case of Performance-based Interviewing this means first developing a list of major performance objectives and subtasks as the replacement for the job analysis. Then, rather than asking for an open-ended example of a specific behavior, ask it as part of the fact-finding involved in understanding each of the candidate's comparable accomplishments. For example, when asking a candidate to describe one of their major accomplishments related to a critical job need, find out what behaviors and competencies were required to successfully complete the task, whether it was taking the initiative, team building, dealing with conflict, or lack of resources. This approach is called behavioral fact-finding and it's where BEI and Performance-based Hiring overlap.

Since it takes a mix of behaviors and competencies to achieve any objective, it's better to put these under the umbrella of an accomplishment to see how they interact. As part of this you'll be able to view the growth trend of these accomplishments and how the mix of these critical behaviors changed over time. This concept is graphically shown in Figure 11.1. This approach is called the behavioral consistency model[2] and is considered one of the most accurate interview methods for predicting on-the-job success.

Seeking the Advice and Counsel of Sherlock Holmes Himself

This approach becomes even more accurate when combined with the Sherlock Holmes deductive interviewing technique. The idea behind this is to look for recognition and supporting evidence that what the candidate describes is corroborated by other data. A few examples will help clarify how this confirming information can be

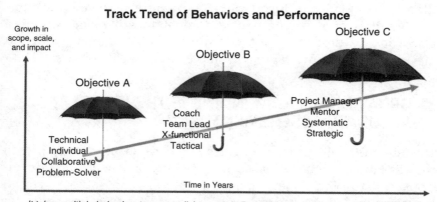

It takes multiple behaviors to accomplish any task. By putting the behaviors under the umbrella of specific accomplishments it's possible to accurately assess fit, growth, and potential.

Figure 11.1 Track Trend of Behaviors and Performance.

[2]Schmidt, F. L., and Hunter, J. E. (1998). The validity and utility of selection methods in personnel psychology: Practical and theoretical implications of 85 years of research findings. *Psychological Bulletin* 124(2): 262–274. https://doi.org/10.1037/0033-2909.124.2.262.

found during the interview. Let's start with the assumption that a candidate demonstrates a multiyear pattern of taking the initiative to improve some technical process. Based on this alone an interviewer could conclude that the person would rank high on technical competency and intrinsic motivation if the process improvements were related to real job needs.

But for those cynics among us this might not be enough. So imagine the following scenario playing out during the debriefing session, when one of the other interviewers suggested it wasn't conclusive for one reason or another. In this case, Sherlock Holmes can help by providing deductive proof that the candidate's claims were valid.

As a counter to the original cynic, one of the interviewers on the team pushes back and says that based on her interview she discovered that the person was assigned most of these stretch roles soon after starting the job and in each case met the critical technical goals assigned. She further goes on to say that in her department we always assign our best technical people to stretch jobs early in their careers with us and then once experienced enough they handle our most critical projects since we're confident they can be completed properly. Then another manager chimes in and mentions someone everyone knows, Ankita, and said that's exactly what happened with her. Everyone on the team nods in agreement that she is extremely talented. With all of this extra evidence, the original cynic becomes fully convinced. In fact, he says the Ankita story was the tipping point for him since he just asked her to be on his next product launch team.

This type of evidence, including examples of others who got ahead the same way, would earn a high five from Sherlock himself. This is what proof and deductive evidence looks like: it's the result of what happened as a result of someone being successful. Some people get a letter, an award, a promotion, assigned to some other critical project, or put on some type of fast-track program. Regardless of what it is, you'll be able to start figuring it out by asking every candidate this question as part of the behavioral fact-finding under the umbrella of each accomplishment:

"What kind of recognition did you receive for this work?"

Of course, with this information you still need to figure out if the expertise being recognized is appropriate for your open job. When it comes to individual contributor roles, recognition involves finding out why and how a person got assigned to different technical projects and what happened once the project was completed. Behind this is the idea as described in the above scenario that those with the strongest technical skills get assigned to stretch and important projects once they've proven themselves, with the pattern continuing as long as the person hones these skills. It's pretty obvious that the projects a person is regularly assigned is an accurate assessment of their competency since it's made by those who work with the person.

Assess Team Skills by Finding Deductive Evidence

The same concept can be used to find deductive evidence of recognition for team skills. Start during the interview and ask to what types of teams the person has been assigned. Find out their roles on these teams and how this role changed on subsequent teams. You'll quickly discover that the strongest team players have a pattern of getting assigned to important cross-functional teams, which increase in importance over time. The graphic in Figure 11.2 is another version of the team-based behavioral fact-finding first mentioned in Chapter 9 on how to conduct the Performance-based Interview. A copy of the complete interview is in Appendix 2.

You'll need to ask these team accomplishment questions for the person's past few jobs to fully understand the types of teams the person has been on, how the person's role has changed, and the types of people the candidate tends to work with most often. In addition, you'll also have a strong sense of the person's technical skills by fully understanding why the person was assigned to each of these teams. The above scenario demonstrates this concept since Ankita was assigned to the product launch team for her overall product knowledge.

Rank the candidate high on team skills if the types of teams the person has been assigned are reasonably comparable to the types of teams the person will likely be working on in the new role. This will be uncovered in the job analysis conducted before the

---

The MSA Team Question

Paint "word pictures" of 2–3 major
team accomplishments. Observe
growth in scope and person's role.

*Can you please describe your
biggest team accomplishment?*
Clarify using these fact-finding tips:

◆ Describe team, purpose, and role
◆ Draw team chart with titles
◆ Ask how got assigned to team
◆ Find out team objectives
◆ Biggest team challenge
◆ Role played achieving goals
◆ Get examples coaching others
◆ Examples of dealing w/conflict
◆ Ask about x-functional impact
◆ Describe recognition received
◆ Ask if improved in team role
◆ Ask about likes, dislikes & who
◆ Describe interpersonal problems
◆ Ask about team recognition

Figure 11.2 Team-Based Fact-Finding.

requisition is approved by asking the hiring manager what types of teams the person will be on and what they'll be expected to contribute.

A Simple Hack to Ensure an Accurate and Unbiased Assessment

Despite the overwhelming logic of this deductive approach and the use of evidence to counter a hiring manager's claim of incompetence, it's just as important to avoid the problem before it becomes one. Start by convincing the hiring manager to conduct a phone screen by presenting the evidence of outstanding performance emphasizing the recognition the person received. With this agreement it's important that the hiring manager interviews the candidate properly since most will revert back to form, focusing on the depth of the person's technical skills and his or her ability to cleverly answer some unrelated technical problem-solving question. Sadly, this happens frequently. It's how fully qualified candidates get excluded due to improper interviewing. Even Sherlock Holmes needs help in these situations. This is when I suggest using another one of my favorite assessment techniques, inspired by Charlie Rich's epic song "Behind Closed Doors."[3]

To get started with this, and as a supplement to the resume, have the candidate summarize in writing two significant accomplishments most closely related to the requirements of the job before the interview. One should clearly relate to some major technical achievement and the other focused on the person's team or project management skills. Each write-up should be short and sweet: no more than two or three paragraphs long, including a high-level summary, some specific details of what was actually accomplished, why the person was assigned the role, and the recognition the person received for the effort. Make sure you review this with the candidate ahead of time. Then send the write-ups to the hiring manager as the reason why the candidate should be phone-screened for the role.

As a setup for the phone-screen interview, ask the hiring manager to first review the two accomplishments with the candidate, asking for clarification and additional details as part of the conversation. Assuming the hiring manager agrees these are worthy accomplishments, suggest he or she conducts a short work history review (the method is described in Chapter 9 on how to conduct a Performance-based Interview) to see if there's a fit on a scope and scale basis. If so, have the hiring manager describe the job in more detail and invite the candidate to the next step in the interviewing process.

Preparing and reviewing these write-ups is a great self-preparation process for the candidate to get ready for the interview. Since the person knows what will be discussed at the beginning of the phone interview, it will reduce nervousness on their part. More important from the hiring manager's point of view, the impact of first impressions will be neutralized if the person is ultimately invited onsite since the focus of this interview will be

---

[3] Rich, Charlie. "Behind Closed Doors." American Originals, CBS Records, 1989, track 4. YouTube, youtu.be/uCUU0pklhcc

on the accomplishments themselves, not the person's appearance, personality, or communication skills.

■ SUMMARY: PERFORMANCE-BASED INTERVIEWING IS BEI ON STEROIDS

When it comes to interviewing, it's important to ensure that what goes on "Behind Closed Doors" is an accurate and objective assessment of the person's technical ability to handle the actual requirements of the job. The approach described here doesn't require any training either. The idea is to force the interviewer to focus on understanding how the candidate used their technical and team skills to accomplish objectives most comparable to the actual performance requirements of the job. Having the hiring manager review the candidate's write-ups at the beginning of the interview leaves much less to chance. This is how to proactively minimize the chance that a good candidate will be excluded for the wrong reasons. Without any extra effort, intervening this way ensures the hiring manager and the candidate are both fully prepared to discuss what really matters: the person's ability and motivation to do the work that's required. After you've tried this approach a few times and seen its impact, go ahead and thank Holmes and Rich for providing you some additional ideas on how to ensure candidates are interviewed objectively and accurately.

While a structured behavioral interview is somewhat useful for minimizing bias, it is far less effective for assessing actual on-the-job performance, fit, and motivation without a detailed job analysis supporting the assessment. However, none of this is necessary as long as you have a performance profile in hand and an understanding of how to use behavioral fact-finding while asking about the candidate's major accomplishments. Once these are firmly in place, turn on Charlie Rich for some background music and put on your Sherlock Holmes hat to reconfirm everything the candidate says, by gathering some deductive evidence for proof.

Chapter 12

Sourcing Outstanding Talent: Blending High Touch with High Tech

Sourcing great candidates is much more than hoping someone applies to your job posting or responds to an email sent to a long list of skills- and experience-qualified people.

As far as I'm concerned, sourcing great candidates is a high-touch process that starts by preparing a performance profile as described in Chapter 7. You'll use a few of the major performance objectives and the employee value proposition developed in this process to create Boolean strings to identify some outstanding people, to prepare compelling messages and job postings, and to generate referrals. This chapter will cover how to use these tools to develop a short list of outstanding candidates who hiring managers will want to meet and who are highly likely to want to talk to you and discuss what you have to offer.

When it comes to sourcing, this high-touch idea means spending more time with fewer, but only prequalified, candidates. These prequalified candidates are called potential semifinalists. As you'll discover in this chapter, identifying these extremely talented people is actually quite easy. Recruiting them is what's hard. But let's start with the identification part and the definition of semifinalists.

■ SEMIFINALIST CRITERIA FOR PREQUALIFYING CANDIDATES

➤ **The Person Must Be Performance Qualified.** This means the person can do the work described in the performance profile.

Sourcing people who are performance qualified opens the talent pool to all diverse, nontraditional, and high-potential talent who have a different mix of the skills and experiences than typically found on most job descriptions.

➤ **The Person Must Possess the Achiever Pattern.** This indicates the person is in the top half or better of his or her peer group. This could be due to rapid progression or some type of special award, certification, or recognition of outstanding performance.

➤ **The Person Needs to See the Role as a Likely Career Move.** This could be working on a more important project or a job with a better title or with a company with more obvious upside opportunity.

All three conditions need to be met in order for the person to be considered a potential semifinalist. By working only with prospects who have been prequalified this way, you won't need as many people at the top of the funnel to consider. Here's the rationale behind this. If the first two conditions are met, hiring managers will be more likely to meet with the person. In parallel, if the job seems worth considering, it's more likely the person will respond to your outreach messages. The probability is also higher that when all of these conditions are met, an offer will be extended and accepted based on the career opportunity the job represents. Building a talent pool of potential semifinalists this way is comparable to sales reps using online research to prequalify customers before making contact. This is a very common sales process. Few sales reps are willing to make random cold calls to potential customers in the hope that someone wants to buy their products and services. By doing the prequalifying research before making contact, there's no need to spend time with unlikely buyers. The same is true when sourcing candidates.

Small Batch, High Touch

However, managing the entire sourcing and recruiting funnel using this "small-batch, high-touch" approach requires that sourcing and recruiting be fully integrated and seamless. As far as I'm concerned, separating the two functions – with sourcers giving supposedly qualified candidates to a recruiter in a talent scarce situation – is an inefficient process that will not yield the desired results. In fact, each party will then blame the other as the source of the problem.

The need for an integrated sourcing and recruiting process is obvious when you consider that the best people, whether active or passive, always have multiple opportunities, and convincing them your opportunity is worth considering involves just as much recruiting as sourcing. Chapter 13 uses the metaphor of driving the "Big Red Tour Bus" to describe the recruiting techniques required to get these semifinalists interested in what you have to offer and then how to keep them engaged throughout the process. What's important, though, is that as soon as these potential semifinalists are identified, the recruiting process must begin.

Hiring managers will typically need to play a big role in this recruiting effort, too. Frequently this outreach needs to happen within a few days after the performance profile is written and once candidates have indicated a willingness to discuss the opportunity.

■ UNDERSTANDING THE SOURCING AND RECRUITING FUNNEL

It's important to recognize that sourcing and recruiting the strongest talent in a talent scarce market, whether these candidates are active or passive, involves a coordinated series of steps. This is comparable to selling an intangible product to two very sophisticated buyers. When it comes to hiring, one of these buyers is the hiring manager and the other is the top person. This type of selling process is referred to as discovery or needs-based selling,[1] where the sales rep first uncovers the buyer's needs, and the company puts together a customized offer. Having two buyers makes this process even more challenging.

Two Buyers: The Hiring Manager and the Top Person

But these buyers differ in a number of ways. From a motivation to buy standpoint, the hiring manager has an immediate need to

[1]Spin Selling, Neil Rackham, McGraw-Hill; 1st edition (May 1, 1988).

complete the process and wants to use a rigid approach to select the "right" person. On the other hand, the best candidates for this role are either not looking or have multiple opportunities to consider. This alone requires the sourcer/recruiter to manage the timing differences, with one party wanting to go as fast as possible, and the other not wanting to move at all or having less pressure to move quickly. On top of this, the hiring manager always has a number of people "advising" the manager on how and whom to hire, each one having a different perspective on what makes a great hire. On the other side of the table the candidate has a bunch of equally opinionated advisors, including family, friends, and coworkers who care more about the money and location rather than the content of the job.

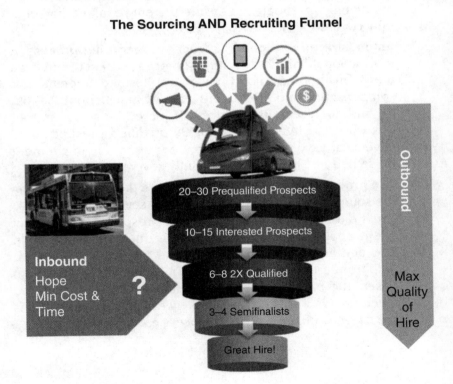

Figure 12.1 The Sourcing and Recruiting Funnel.

Most of these differences can be minimized by sourcing people who are likely to be semifinalists before first contact is even made. That's why such a big point is made of implementing a prequalification sourcing process. The infographic in Figure 12.1 describes the recruiting funnel for this approach and the steps and metrics involved in converting a small talent pool of potential semifinalists into one great hire.

Working through the recruiting and sourcing funnel will be covered in this chapter and the next two on recruiting. To get started it's important to appreciate these points:

➤ **Only reach out to prequalified prospects**. This is the top of the funnel. These are people who are performance qualified, possess the Achiever Pattern, and would see the role as a career move. In some cases we'll also specifically target diverse candidates to ensure the entire talent market in fully covered.

➤ **Emphasize an outbound "attract in" recruiting process**. A transactional, inbound recruiting process is akin to driving a metro bus hoping a good person applies and agrees to the compensation and title before learning much about the job. An outbound recruiting process is more like a custom tour bus where we reach out to highly qualified prospects and have a career discussion to see if our open role might meet those needs. This technique is fully covered in Chapter 13.

➤ **Use process control metrics to manage the funnel**. By using the sourcing and recruiting techniques covered in this book, you'll only need 20–30 prequalified prospects in the initial talent pool to generate three or four true semifinalists and hire one great person. However, the metrics shown in the graphic need to be tracked daily. Then, whenever a problem arises, the process must be revisited and fixed before too much time is wasted pursuing the wrong candidates. This is the essence of any feedback process control system.

■ MAKE IT PERSONAL: LET'S GO FOR A CAREER RIDE

To better appreciate the effectiveness of a small-batch, high-touch sourcing and recruiting process, it's important to consider the idea from a personal point of view. In this case we're going to make the assumption that you're the ideal candidate we're trying to find for a very important job and someone we want to invite to ride on our Big Red Tour Bus. This is a job that could put you on a better career trajectory. However, finding you and getting you to hear our pitch will be the big challenge since you don't have the traditional background as defined in the original job description, nor are you looking for another job.

This assumption alone eliminates the possibility of using traditional Boolean skills-based searching and filtering to find you. Despite these shortcomings, the reason you're the ideal candidate is that you've been recognized for doing outstanding work in your field and the hiring manager has already agreed to talk with people who are performance qualified this way.

Using a series of performance-qualified filters as a means to expand the talent pool to include more diverse, high-potential, and nontraditional candidates is a great way to begin. But when it comes to you, we have another problem: you're employed, you're satisfied with your current job, and you're not even thinking of changing jobs. The only hope we have is that you might take a call from a recruiter you know or one who has been given your name from someone you trust, like a former hiring manager. With this connection you're likely at least to take the call out of courtesy, and there's a good chance you'll say yes to having a preliminary conversation if you were asked this question: "Would you be open to exploring a possible career opportunity if it were clearly superior to your current situation?"

In this chapter we'll describe step-by-step a number of different ways to find people just like you. It starts by developing a sourcing program designed to attract the best people. This checklist will help us get started.

■ SOURCING CHECKLIST

❑ **Implement a "Scarcity of Talent" sourcing strategy.** Develop a sourcing strategy to attract the strongest and most diverse active and passive people for the role.

❑ **Fish where the big fish hang out.** Spend more time with fewer people, but make sure they're the right people. In this case the right people are potential semifinalists or people who can refer these people to you.

❑ **Define your ideal candidate.** Prepare a candidate persona defining the "ideal" candidate, including the nontraditional terms you'll need to use to search for the person.

❑ **Conduct a supply versus demand analysis.** Compare the total talent pool to the demand for these people to determine what sourcing channels are most appropriate to reach these ideal candidates. This includes some mix of job postings, emails to direct-sourced candidates, and getting referrals.

❑ **Use "clever" Boolean to identify semifinalists.** You don't need to be a Boolean expert to find outstanding talent, but you need to be good enough to be clever using the right terms to prequalify the big fish.

❑ **Prepare compelling job posts and messages.** By capturing the candidate's intrinsic motivator, you'll be able to get someone interested enough to respond to your outreach messages and get on the tour bus to discuss the opportunity.

❑ **Implement a two-step application process.** Use the two-step process for job postings to have candidates self-select in and out. This is a great way to have candidates do the heavy lifting rather than your ATS.

❑ **Learn how to drive the Big Red Tour Bus.** Many top candidates opt out before learning about the career merits of the role. It's possible to minimize this by selling the career discussion rather than the job itself.

❑ **Engage the hiring manager in the recruiting process.** The strongest people generally won't become serious prospects without a preliminary discussion with the hiring manager first.

■ IMPLEMENTING A SCARCITY OF TALENT SOURCING PROGRAM

When the demand for talent exceeds the supply, you need to proactively attract the best people rather than hoping a good person applies to a job posting that's not only boring but hard to find. It's pretty easy to recognize that you are using a surplus of talent approach if you spend most of your time weeding out unqualified candidates. The hope with this approach is that a few good candidates will remain standing at the end. Even if your company has a strong employer brand and you are seeing strong candidates for your open roles, you'll discover that you'll see even stronger and more diverse people by implementing a multipronged "attract the best" sourcing program as described in this chapter.

■ THINK SMALL-BATCH, HIGH-TOUCH: SOURCE SEMIFINALISTS

The key to improving Quality of Hire without it taking longer to fill roles is to spend more time with fewer people. This is a high-touch process that leverages existing high tech but is not subservient to it. Of course, these have to be the right people who meet the definition of a semifinalist, as described above and shown in Figure 12.2. The idea underlying the "Fish Where the Big Fish Hang Out" message is to avoid spending time reviewing resumes or talking with

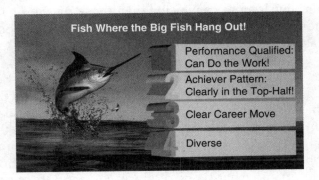

Figure 12.2 Fish Where the Big Fish Hang Out.

people who are unlikely ever to become semifinalists or with those who are unlikely to provide a referral for a semifinalist. Implementing this idea requires a recruiter/sourcer not just to identify these semifinalists but also to get them on the phone, prequalify them if possible, and get referrals of other potential semifinalists if the person is inappropriate for the role for one reason or another. This is how you keep the "Big Red Tour Bus" filled with enough strong talent to achieve your hiring objectives.

One way to start building a talent rich pool of semifinalists is by using a process called Career Zone Analysis. This approach allows a recruiter/sourcer to understand how the best people look for jobs, when they look for jobs, and what they need to know before they get too serious in the process. Knowing this allows you to spend the most time and effort in areas where you'll find the most big fish.

Conduct a Career Zone Analysis to Find Out Where to Fish

The Career Zone model shown in Figure 12.3 tracks changes in employee satisfaction over time from high growth on the left, flattening in the middle, and declining on the right. By figuring out where on the Career Zone curve your ideal candidate is likely to fall, a recruiter is in a stronger position to offer a more attractive opportunity. This includes figuring out what you'll need to do to find the person, what messages would work best, and what you'll need to do to demonstrate that your open role will put the person on a more promising career trajectory. It's pretty obvious, graphically speaking at least, that candidates on the left who are highly satisfied will require much more convincing than those on the right who are seeing their career opportunities declining. A big part of positioning your job as the best career move needs to consider how satisfied or how desperate the person currently is.

You might want to select a job that will likely need to be filled in the short term as you review these descriptions of each of the Career Zones. This will help you figure out what you'll need to do to source and recruit the person. In order to better understand how the Career Zone Analysis works, use yourself as an example by figuring where you are on the curve based on your current job satisfaction. Based on this, determine what types of messages and job opportunities would be required to get you interested enough to discuss them.

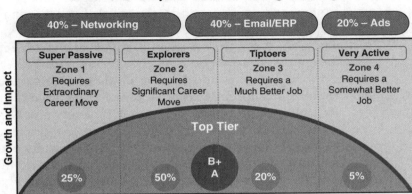

Figure 12.3   Career Zone Analysis.

Note: The percentages shown on the infographic are based on work conducted with LinkedIn in the period 2015–2017 and updated in 2019 using our own survey data of over 3,000 responses.

These are the same types of messages and job opportunities you need to present to the candidates you're targeting.

➤ **Zone 1 is comprised of Super Passive candidates**. These people are highly satisfied, currently making a significant impact, and not looking to make a job change. In normal economic times about 25% of the people responding to our surveys categorized themselves as Super Passive. The flipside of this is these are the people who are highly satisfied and fully engaged with their jobs. This is consistent with the Gallup studies on employee engagement.[2] Hiring these people is unlikely unless it's for an extraordinary career move. However, even in our survey work about 50% of these people will at least explore the idea of a possible career move just to keep their options open. These people are great to network with and get referrals, but you typically need a referral from a trusted source to first get their attention.

[2]Harter, J., 2016. *First, Break All the Rules*. New York: Gallup Press.

➤ **Zone 2 is the domain of Explorers**. People who aren't actively looking but are open to the idea of considering a possible career move are referred to as Explorers. While declining a bit, these people are still satisfied enough with their current roles and their future prospects that they have no need to put energy into finding another job. However, they will take a call from a credible recruiter to discuss the idea. That said, all credibility will be lost if the recruiter goes into instant high-pressure sales mode once the prospect agrees to a preliminary discussion. Our survey results over the years indicate that about 50% of the fully employed talent market considers themselves Explorers. You'll be able to identify the names of these people using the clever Boolean techniques described in this chapter. Regardless, you'll need some compelling messages and lots of persistence to get them to respond. Then once you have them on the phone, you'll need to convince them to at least discuss the possibility of the long-term career merits of the job rather than talking too much about the compensation, title, and location. How to conduct this discovery-based recruiting process is fully covered in the next chapter about driving the Big Red Tour Bus.

➤ **Zone 3 represents the Tiptoers**. Once a person sees their current career prospects dimming for whatever reason, they tend to start quietly looking, for another job. This is typically a low-key affair, and while not announcing to the world they're ready to leave their current job, they first contact their close personal network to discuss potential next moves. This includes recruiters they have worked with in the past. If these people are top performers, it's highly likely they'll find a better job this way pretty quickly. Our surveys indicate that about 20% of the talent market would classify themselves as Tiptoers. In addition to using recruiters who already have a deep network, the second best way to reach Tiptoers is via a proactive employee referral program. In this approach company employees invite their best former coworkers to first contact them whenever they're ready to look for another job. If these people are top performers, you'll still need to offer them a better job with some longevity prospects along with it, but just as important is the need to move fast since if they're top performers they'll quickly be off the market

➤ **Zone 4 represents the Very Active job seekers.** Very few top performers in critical high-demand positions need to ever become active job seekers. While many of these people will look at job postings to see what's available, most of the time they'll contact someone they know at the company to get referred in. We found that only about 5% of the talent market for professional staff and mid-management positions will use job boards exclusively to find another job. To attract the attention of the best, make sure your job postings are compelling and easy to find. In fact, you should include a link to these career-focused job postings in your outreach emails to people you've identified as semifinalists. This way the job posting becomes one part of your marketing campaign, not the primary means to find someone.

Given these definitions, where would you categorize yourself on the Career Zone satisfaction curve and where do you think you'll find your ideal candidates for the role you're trying to fill? Figuring this out needs to be your first step before you begin posting jobs or conducting some type of clever Boolean search.

Use Supply versus Demand to Implement a Targeted Multichannel Sourcing Plan

The sweet spot for most important senior staff and management roles is typically at the top of the Career Zone where it just begins to flatten or just starts declining. If you can get to Explorers before they become Tiptoers, you'll have a significant first-mover advantage. Just as important is to get to Tiptoers before they've found any other opportunities through their own networking efforts. Achieving this and being successful requires doing everything covered in this chapter. A great way to start is by developing a 40-40-20 sourcing plan.

This means spending 40% of your time networking and generating referrals, 40% direct sourcing and leveraging your employee referral program, and 20% on writing compelling job descriptions and posting them on the most appropriate job boards. For example, Dice .com might be a better way to find techies and Ladders.com is better for management level positions.

While this 40-40-20 sourcing plan is a good starting point for most professional roles, you'll need to adjust this mix based on the actual supply versus demand market conditions in your target market. For example, if there are a lot of companies looking for the same type of candidates, you'll need to emphasize more networking and direct sourcing. LinkedIn Recruiter is a great tool for conducting this assessment. To do this, first find out how many total candidates meet your basic requirements and then compare this to the number of open jobs listed. For example, in a search for the business intelligence analyst role described in Chapter 7 on preparing performance profiles, it turned out there were 1,455 open jobs with this same title in the San Francisco Bay area compared to 1,705 candidates who had a similar job title. This roughly 1:1 ratio of available candidates per open job indicates a very tight labor market. Making it even tighter is that only 258 of these people indicated they were open to explore other opportunities.

Also note that 258 represents only 15% of the 1,705 in this specific talent market versus the 25% (the sum of the Tiptoers and the Very Active) shown in the Career Zone Analysis graphic for the overall talent market. Given this very tight talent market, I'd suggest a 45-45-10 sourcing plan would be a more appropriate allocation of efforts. This simple analysis suggests the need to spend more time networking and direct sourcing to find and recruit the right person and essentially zero time hoping someone applies directly.

■ DEVELOP AN "IDEAL CANDIDATE PERSONA"

Once you've conducted a supply versus demand analysis, it's important to prepare an "Ideal Candidate Persona." This is equivalent to a marketing plan used to identify an ideal customer. In the case of sourcing it will identify the terms you'll use to search for the best prospects and the message content required to get them to become interested in what you have to offer. The table shown here is a shortened version of the complete candidate persona available in Appendix 2. The persona summarizes the key factors that need to be considered before starting to look for candidates.

The Basics, Job Branding, the Employee Value Proposition (EVP), and Messaging	
Identify the core components of the 30% Solution	The 30% nonmonetary increase (i.e., stretch, growth, impact, and satisfaction) needs to be the foundation for the career and one the prospects need to understand in the first email and conversation.
Candidate's intrinsic motivator	Determine what motivates a person to excel at this type of work. Once this is understood, messaging can be created to leverage this idea. Consider internal versus external and team versus individual motivators.
Determine the Employee Value Proposition (EVP)	Why would a top person want this job if he or she is not looking and if the person has other offers that are paying more? Then prove it with specifics and examples. What would the logical next step be?
Create a customized "Job Brand"	Tie the job to a bigger mission. This could be an important project or company strategy or value. This needs to be customized by job, not generic boilerplate. Job branding is more important than employer branding for attracting passive candidates.
Survey people currently in the role	Ask people in this role what they find most satisfying about the job. Use this to prepare the EVP and related messages.
Tagline	Add a short, clever tagline to the job title for emails and job postings. For example: "Prepare whitepapers in any color you want."
Prepare email to drive person to the job post and your LinkedIn profile	Sell the discussion, not the job! Mention multiple positions. Take off the time pressure. Mention the hiring manager viewed the person's profile and was impressed.
Sourcing: Defining, Understanding, and Finding the Ideal Candidate	
Understand the typical progression of someone in the role who is a top performer	Understand where the person went to school or the area of specialized training received. What types of jobs would the person have held previous to your current opening? You'll use this to search for the candidate.

The Basics, Job Branding, the Employee Value Proposition (EVP), and Messaging	
Find out ideal candidate's job-hunting status. What is the candidate looking for in a new job?	Use Career Zone Analysis to find out the job-hunting status of your ideal candidate. The four types are Passive, Explorer, Tiptoer, and Active. On the Maslow scale, does the person want a career move or a lateral transfer?
Types of jobs previously held	Consider comparable positions in other industries or vendors and consultants servicing the industry.
Direct and functional competitors	Consider industries or companies where the person would obtain similar experience.
Comparative titles	Consider all types of titles including those that are more generic.
"Cherry Pick" the ideal candidate as part of a "Small-Batch, High-Touch" sourcing approach. These all must be potential semifinalists.	Determine the demographics of a person who would quickly see your opening as a possible career move. For example, this could be a senior manager at a big company who would see being a director at a small company as a good career move if it had more impact.

For most professional staff (i.e., those with more than two or three years of experience) and mid-management positions, it's best to start with a 40-40-20 sourcing plan adjusted based on a supply versus demand analysis. As the search process begins it's important to keep track of the sources of the best candidates and modify the overall plan as necessary, spending more time where it will do the most good.

Prepare Customized and Targeted Messaging

Understanding your ideal candidate starts by figuring out how the best people for the jobs you're trying to fill actually look for new jobs and what they're looking for in order to move. Some people are looking for career moves, others just a job to earn a regular paycheck. The Career Zone Analysis will help figure out where to allocate your efforts, but the messaging (emails, job postings, voice mails, tweets, and texts) needs to reflect the candidates' intrinsic motivators. For example, techies tend to be more internally motivated and/or want to play an important role in creating or using new technology. The best managers want to build teams and handle big projects. One way to figure out what these motivators are is to ask people already in the role why they like their job. Then capture this information in your messages. Understanding your candidates' motivators for looking for a new job is the first step in finding candidates to fill it. For example, we found that sales reps for a pharmaceutical company were mostly concerned about the breadth and quality of the new product pipeline since they felt this was the best way to develop more long-term customers. As a result, this internal motivator was captured in the first line of the job posting and carried through the entire recruiting process.

Job Branding and the EVP

A job can be made more important by tying it to some major company project, initiative, or mission. Some examples will help describe this important messaging technique for attracting stronger talent:

➤ For an inbound call center rep position for an insurance company, the job branding statement related to the fact that the reps talked to their best customers every day.

➤ It was clear in the job posting for a software maintenance role that keeping the company's main legacy program functioning was vital to the success of the company while a major upgrade was taking place.

➤ In one marketing support role the position was described as being part of a team that was leading the launch of a series of critical products that would impact the company's future direction.

You'll quickly gain more interest when statements like these are at the top of your job postings and email messages. Similar results can be achieved by highlighting the employee value proposition (EVP) in the title as a tagline or in the first line of the message or tweet. For someone technical, advancing the state of the art might be the information needed to get the person's attention. For an entry-level sales position one company described the role as the first step in a six-figure sales career. For an HR VP position a few years ago, we described converting the HR function into a strategic asset as the key to job success. We identified about 15 people for the role on LinkedIn and put this in the subject of the email. Within two days just about everyone responded.

If you need help figuring out why your best performers find a job appealing, just ask them. Then make sure you capture this information where it can be easily found.

Job Postings, Job Boards, and Reverse Engineering

While many companies emphasize job postings as their primary means to find candidates, this is the least efficient of all of the sourcing techniques for filling critical roles. They are also the least effective in terms of improving Quality of Hire. That's why no more than 20% of your sourcing budget and time should be spent here other than as part of a multichannel program. In this case you'll need to make your jobs more compelling and story-like and then push your direct-sourced candidates to these postings as part of an email marketing campaign to gain interest.

One way to assess the quality of your job postings is to reverse engineer the process. In this approach assume you're a candidate trying to find a job you now have posted. Then use the standard search fields available on the job board to see if your job even turns up and on what page. Whether or not you paid for a higher ranking, compare your summary description to other similar jobs to see if it stands out and is compelling enough to get a candidate even to click the short summary and read the full posting. Sadly, most won't, with the only differentiator being the name of the company and its logo.

Making your titles easy to find using a common title rather than some internal company name and a tagline is sometimes all you need to do to attract stronger people and get better response rates. For example, just changing the title to "Flight Nurses – Saving Lives Everyday" helped a West Coast hospital chain fill these critical positions within days after the job was posted. Before adding the tagline the same job had been posted for months without any qualified candidates applying. This was during a period of an acute nurse shortage, too, making the results even more impressive.

Taglines that Speak the Language of the Ideal Prospect

Following are a few examples that highlight the need to be creative in order to stand out from the crowd. These could be taglines in the job title, subheadings in the email or job posting, or the first line of the first paragraph. Regardless of where you put these compelling statements, they need to be not just different but also personalized to such a degree that the person reading it is more likely to respond since you're speaking directly to their needs. This approach is also a great way to turn a "must-have" qualification into a positive and appealing attribute. Some examples:

➤ For a controller with lots of travel requirements: *Use your CPA and see the world.*

➤ For a creative marketing intern: *Prepare whitepapers in any color you want.*

➤ For someone who must be very analytical and detail oriented: *Your attention to detail drives our corporate profitability.*

➤ For a bus driver: *Spend your time driving the nicest people in the world through its most beautiful city.*

These specific examples were successfully used to attract the right type of people who found the message speaking directly to their internal motivators. Of course, if your job postings are never found, it doesn't matter how compelling they are since they won't be read anyway. So if you are going to post jobs, make sure they're on the right job boards, they're pushed to the right people, and they stand out from the crowd.

Use Emails as the First Step in a High-Touch Process

The sample email below was used to get a number of engineering leaders to contact the recruiter to discuss some current and future job openings. The original email, sent to the same target list of about 20 people, had only one response since it was too specific, too pushy, and only discussed one opening. By taking off the time pressure and giving the person a chance to discuss a variety of different positions, the response was overwhelming: almost 75% of the people contacted the recruiter to set up a short preliminary discussion. The lesson here is that every email that's sent out should invite a person to the top of the recruiting funnel, not somewhere down in the middle of it.

> Dear _____,
>
> You might be aware that we just received Series C funding to expand NewCo globally. This will open up a number of senior staff and management BI and UX positions. We're now doing our workforce planning for Q1 and Q2 for next year and your background looks like it could be a possible fit for a number of different positions we're considering.
>
> Very little is defined yet, but I'd like to reach out to see if you'd be open to having a very preliminary conversation to determine if one of these roles could represent a significant career move for you. This would be a very short exploratory conversation to share ideas and determine if it makes sense to have a more in-depth conversation as these roles become more defined.
>
> Feel free to contact me when you have the chance. At a minimum we can stay in touch and network as the roles at NewCo become more clarified.

Using emails as part of an outreach program to a small group of potential semifinalists is a critical step in sourcing and recruiting outstanding talent. But the quality of these emails matters a lot, especially since you're starting with just a small pool of about 15–20 people. Given this small pool you need to get about 50–75% of these people to respond to the message. Once you get them on the phone and chat, you'll need to further qualify these people and convert them into interested prospects. But it's essential to remember that the point of the email is just to get the person on the phone to talk about some potential career opportunity. Nothing more. You'll know the initial prequalification process has been done properly if at least half of the people who do call you back are worth serious consideration or can give you referrals to those who are better suited for the role.

You'll need to rework your prequalification process if the people contacting you aren't strong enough to be considered potential semifinalists. The following section on direct sourcing will help you with this effort. As part of this you might want to expand the candidate pool a little, but in my opinion, this is not the best way to proceed. Too many recruiters and sourcers fall into this trap, worried more about the number of people applying rather than the quality of the people who respond.

Once you've identified some outstanding people it's better to modify the email until the response rate is at least 50%. This often takes a lot of persistence and multiple messages, including texts, tweets, and voice mails, but it's worth it. Mentioning the hiring manager often helps. In fact, you might want the hiring manager to reach out directly in some cases. This alone will increase the response rate, especially if it's prefaced with some positive compliment about the person, why the job is important, and an offer to have a short exploratory chat. Just as important for the recruiter is driving the person to your LinkedIn profile with a parallel offer to connect for networking purposes. If your LinkedIn profile indicates you're someone worth knowing, you'll get an instant connection and another way to make contact with the person.

■ DIRECT SOURCING AND NETWORKING

We now have to find some candidates who will receive our creative and compelling messages and who will respond with an instant "Yes, let's talk about the career opportunity you've described in your recent email."

Finding these candidates is referred to as direct sourcing and it can be done by using search strings on Google looking for resumes or going to LinkedIn directly and using their built-in search fields. In my opinion you don't have to be a Boolean expert to find outstanding talent either way, but you do need to be good enough to be clever using it. That's what will be covered now. It starts by completing the remaining sections on the candidate persona.

Direct Sourcing: Searching Directly for the Ideal Candidate	
Define typical places the ideal candidate would use to find another job, including job boards, associations, and networking groups	Reverse engineer some ideal candidates' profiles to find groups (consider online and LinkedIn) or create one that you develop. Figure out where these people "meet up" and then join the group.
Achiever and recognition terms that indicate the person is a top 25% person	An achiever term indicates the person is in the top of their peer group and indicates remarkable progress. As you search for candidates, review their awards and honors for other achiever terms. Then search on these terms.
Professional societies and specialty groups the person would join	Include honor societies, professional groups, and LinkedIn groups. If possible, join them or start one. Use the important terms in your Boolean search.
Two to three most critical skills	Highlight the essential few. Consider all-inclusive "master" terms.
Demographic or diversity terms	Consider groups, pronouns, programs, organizations, colleges.
PRP: Proactive Networking: Who Knows the Ideal Candidate?	
Ask, "Who would know this person?" Build a 360° network of the ideal candidate's likely coworkers to get referrals	Describe the types of people the person would work and interface with. You'll be able to connect with these "nodes" and search on their first-degree connections for referrals. Consider vendors, consultants, and customers.
Implement a Proactive Employee Referral program (PERP) at your company	Connect with people in your company who are likely to know or who are connected to your "ideal" candidate. Then search on their connections using clever Boolean and ask if the person is strong. Have your coworkers reach out to the person.

A quick way to get started with clever Boolean using some of the search criteria developed when preparing the ideal candidate persona is to copy the following Boolean string and paste it into a Google search bar. We'll then walk through what the string means. The assumption behind the explanation is that you know enough Boolean that it's not necessary to explain the "AND," "OR," parenthesis, and quote functions, but rather what's contained in them. If you're a bit rusty with this process, search "Boolean search terms" for some introductory lessons. As part of standard Boolean searching, note that each of the separate logic phrases in a search string are evaluated separately and all must be "true" in order for any results to be returned. Basically this means that there's an invisible "AND" between all of the separate phrases.

A Clever Boolean Search to Learn the Basics of Direct Sourcing for Semifinalists

> site:linkedin.com/in "Business Intelligence Analyst" (SQL AND Tableau)
>   (DynamoDB OR S3 OR Redshift OR Athena) (San Francisco OR 415 OR 408)
>   (opportunities OR relocate) (teach OR train OR coach OR mentor OR tutor)
>   (award OR honor OR society OR prize OR patent OR white-paper OR speaker)

Figure 12.4 is the short list of what came back.

Google — site:linkedin.com/in "Business Intelligence Analyst" (SQL AND Tableau) (Dy

Business Intelligence Analyst

Business Intelligence Analyst @ Mercari ... San Francisco Bay Area500+ connections ... BI Tools: BigQuery, Microsoft SQL, Looker, Tableau, Qlik, AWS ... Identified potential investment opportunities through research, due diligence, ... Activities and Societies: Japanese Honor Society, Key Club, Ensemble Band, Dance ...

- Phoenix, Arizona, United States | Professiona...

Strong technical skills including SQL (SSIS, Management Studio), Access and ... Train and verify data entry batches of new employees. ... job opportunities | Data Analyst | Business Intelligence | SQL | Python | Tableau ... Analyst | Business Intelligence Analyst | Product Manager | SQL Developer ... San Francisco Bay Area.

- Business Intelligence Analyst - Amazon Web ...

Advanced Tableau Developer, providing BI solutions, critical performance ... Dynamo DB, AWS Athena (Amazon s3), SQL Server management (Microsoft), Snowflake, PostgreSQL ... of students of various colleges who take pride in reviving the society. ... Data Science | Big data | BI

- Senior Business Intelligence Analyst ...

Sr. Business Intelligence Analyst @ PlayStation | Assistant Instructor @ USC | Data Engineer | Public Speaker ... Lead the extract, transform, and load (ETL) process on Redshift, Teradata, Box, and various excel sheets using SQL, Tableau Prep and ... Mentor students Data Science topics along with job search, resume, and ...

Business Intelligence Analyst - Datto, Inc ...

-SQL: MYSQL, Oracle, Redshift, HiveQL. -Databases: Snowflake, BigQuery -Data Visualization/Dashboarding: Tableau, Looker, Domo, Google Data Studio. New York City Metropolitan Area · Sr. Business Intelligence Analyst · Datto, Inc.

Figure 12.4

As you review the explanations below, substitute any terms that are more appropriate for a critical professional position you're trying to fill. Then redo the search. In the process you'll find some great candidates. By the time you're done with this chapter you'll have completed most of the fields on the candidate persona and have developed a short list of people you can contact using the email concepts described earlier.

If you need more than what's covered in this sourcing chapter when it comes to using more advanced Boolean search, I urge you get a copy of Jan Tegze's *Full Stack Recruiter*.[3] Jan is an expert in this field and someone worth following.

X-raying. The term "site:linkedin.com/in" tells the search engine to only look at the website named. In this case it's the site for all LinkedIn public profiles.

You don't need to be a Boolean expert to find outstanding talent, but you do need to be clever. That's the purpose of the rest of the terms in the string: identifying 15–20 outstanding people who all have the potential to become true semifinalists. For this sample job the title "Business Intelligence Analyst" is in quotes. This ensures that every profile returned will have this exact term somewhere on the person's LinkedIn page.

The "(SQL AND Tableau)" term indicates that both of these critical skills are required to meet the minimum requirements of the job with the "(DynamoDB OR S3 OR Redshirt OR Athena)" indicating that only one of the four is required. On the original job posting all were required, but practically speaking if a person has any one of these, he or she is fully qualified to handle the others. A good sourcer/recruiter needs to be able to push the hiring manager during the intake meeting to determine what are the fewest and most essential skills that are needed to generate a small pool of top talent. Otherwise the search becomes never ending. As part of refining these search strings, it's important to review the preliminary list of potential semifinalists with the hiring manager to make sure you're on the right track.

---

[3] Tegze, Jan. *Full Stack Recruiter: The Ultimate Edition*. Jan Tagze, 2020.

The search terms "(opportunities OR relocate)" and "("San Francisco" OR 415 OR 408)" help narrow the list to those in the local geographic area who have indicated on their LinkedIn profile that they're ready to move.

Now it's important to narrow the list down to only outstanding talent. To be considered outstanding the people identified must possess the Achiever Pattern. This is evidence indicating they're in the top half or better within their peer group. Possessing the Achiever Pattern is essential for the hiring manager to agree to have an exploratory call with the person. Just as important, you'll lose a lot of strong prospects if the hiring manager is unwilling to do this. It's important to note that few outstanding people will agree to become serious candidates for the job without first talking with the hiring manager. That's why this extra step can't be short-circuited.

These two terms in the sample string are a good starting point for identifying those with the Achiever Pattern from those who are just basically qualified:

➤ (teach OR train OR coach OR mentor OR tutor)
➤ (award OR honor OR society OR prize OR patent OR whitepaper OR speaker)

Teaching others is a common attribute of those who have been recognized as subject matter experts (SME) in their field. That's the purpose of the first string. In the second string this SME idea is carried further by searching for people who have been formally recognized for their technical achievements in some way. While there are other ways to do this, in this search we're looking for someone who has written a whitepaper, has been awarded a patent, spoke at some industry conference, or has been honored by some professional group.

Once you start searching on these types of terms, you'll discover others that might be better suited or will help narrow the search to the strongest of these highly qualified people. For example, on one search project I found a remarkable tax director by reviewing the list of speakers at a previously unknown industry conference. You'll also find that people often put the specific names of honor societies like Tau Beta Pi for engineers or an award like the Turing Award for computer scientists that can be added to the search. In addition, you'll be able to find more achiever terms by function just by searching for them on Google or going to the sponsoring site. In fact, you might find the award winners listed there that you can contact and add to your short list of potential semifinalists.

Diversity Matters

This search string below was used to find a marketing VP for a mid-size U.S.-based company. While the pattern of the search terms is similar to the previous string, this one includes two big differences. The first one is the two diversity strings "(woman OR women OR female OR sorority OR she OR her)" and "(Black OR Hispanic)." The second one is the title string "(Vice OR VP OR Director)."

> site:linkedin.com/in (Consumer AND Marketing AND demand AND channel) (Portland OR Seattle) (Vice OR VP OR Director) (MBA OR Masters OR MS) (teach OR train OR coach OR mentor OR tutor) (award OR honor OR society OR prize OR laude OR expert) (woman OR women OR female OR sorority OR she OR her) (Black OR Hispanic)

Rather than belaboring the point, identifying diversity candidates doesn't take any more effort than adding the appropriate terms into your search strings. Adding the names of specific diversity groups or societies is also effective for narrowing your search to the appropriate audience. Searching on the term "NSBE" returns members of the "National Society of Black Engineers." For example, this Google search, "site:LinkedIn.com/in "Tau Beta Pi" (NBSE OR "National Society of Black Engineers")" returned over 1,700 Black engineers who are also members of this prestigious engineering honor society.

What's important to note in all of this clever Boolean searching is the need to eliminate the long laundry list of skills and specific criteria as requirements that only limit the quality and diversity of the talent pool being built. Generally speaking, including the most critical two or three skills will be enough from a performance-qualified standpoint. The logic here is that the person probably has experience with the related but less important skills or can learn them. By shifting to a performance-qualified criterion, the target talent pool is then not only totally diverse but also filled with outstanding technically qualified people. In the marketing string above you'll notice that there are no skills listed at all, just some industry background. If you try using this string yourself, you'll discover it brings back some remarkable women who can handle just about any marketing challenge presented to them.

The title phrase in the marketing string is written for a different purpose. While we were looking for a VP of Marketing, the company recognized that a person who is currently a director at a somewhat bigger company might find the offer an attractive career move. Offering a bigger or more important job is one way to attract potential semifinalists. Another way is to look for people at large companies who want to make a bigger impact at a smaller company.

Another step in completing the candidate persona is to ask some of the outstanding people who were hired in the past year at your company what caused them to switch. Whatever it is – the title, the special project, or something unique about your company – it might reveal some other search terms or message ideas that need to be captured in your direct sourcing approach.

Part of understanding your ideal candidate is to figure out the person's likely career path, what jobs the person held, some alternative titles, and the companies and industries the person worked in. You'll be able to use these terms to search for candidates directly using LinkedIn and search engines like Google.

Using LinkedIn Filters to Find More Achievers

Finding candidates using Boolean search techniques and the filters on LinkedIn are the most common ways recruiters use to identify possible candidates. LinkedIn's premium product called Recruiter offers a number of additional filters you can also use to find potential semifinalists very quickly. From a practical standpoint, searching on no more than two or three critical technical skills in combination with a few achiever terms and a professional society is generally more than enough to identify an initial group of outstanding people to consider. Then narrow the search down by years of experience (a filter in LinkedIn Recruiter) to find candidates who have achieved greater success in less time than expected. This is a clear indication of the Achiever Pattern. You can also narrow down the original list by title and company size or industry to find people who would more likely quickly see the job as a good career move. This is especially true if your industry and future prospects are more appealing.

For example, in one search for a controller for a midsize company, we used LinkedIn Recruiter to first find candidates who had a CPA from one the major accounting firms, who had less than 10 years total experience, and who were currently accounting directors for a bigger company; in this case it was in the same industry. There were half a dozen names that stood out, all in the local LA area. One person in particular had her cell phone number listed with one of her favorite leisure activities shown. We quickly sent her a personal text mentioning the hobby and suggested she check out the job posting if she was interested in "A chance to get out of the numbers and make a difference." She responded instantly and became one of the three finalists.

■ INDIRECT SOURCING AND NETWORKING

Getting Referrals Is Still the Best Way to Find Outstanding Talent Quickly

As far as I'm concerned, the most efficient and most effective way to find outstanding talent for any role is through networking. In fact, using one of the premium LinkedIn products like Recruiter, getting referrals is relatively easy. This is especially true when LinkedIn is considered a network of over 700 million people rather than just an independent database of them. While you'll be able to find the names of potential semifinalists using the clever Boolean searching techniques described above, in my opinion it's better to ask someone connected to you this question: "Who's the best person you've ever worked with doing (describe the job), why do you consider the person outstanding, and would the person call me back if I mentioned your name?"

Let's get personal again so you can appreciate this more direct approach. Given the assumptions about you as a top-performing passive candidate made at the beginning of this chapter, would you respond positively to a message from a recruiter who named a former and highly regarded hiring manager to discuss a possible career move? Most likely you would, just out of courtesy, even if you weren't looking for another job. This idea of getting referrals this way is why LinkedIn is such a valuable tool in the hands of someone who sees it as network of the world's greatest talent.

Convert Strangers into Acquaintances Before They Become Candidates

Reid Hoffman, one of the founders of LinkedIn, wrote a post about the value of weak connections in 2012.[4] This prompted some other research on my part trying to better understand why referrals always seem to be the source of the strongest candidates. This was then confirmed by a number of surveys we conducted over the next several years. Appreciating this starts by understanding the enormous value of your weak connections. These are all of the people who are connected to your first-degree LinkedIn connections.

The big sourcing idea here is that in a structured social network like LinkedIn you're only two degrees of connection away from an outstanding person if you have a big enough group of first-degree connections. These second-degree weak connections are represented by the lighter colored circle in Figure 12.5.

From a practical standpoint, it takes too much effort to find outstanding people by reaching out indiscriminately to a bunch of strangers whose only qualifications are the list of skills and experiences listed on a job description. These are the strangers in the outer circle. There is no research that supports this approach as a recipe for hiring stronger talent. Yet the promise of advanced AI

---

[4] Hoffman, Reid "Allies and Acquaintances: Two Key Types of Professional Relationships." LinkedIn, www.linkedin.com/pulse/20121126205355-1213-allies-and-acquaintances-two-key-types-of-professional-relationships/.

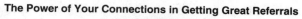

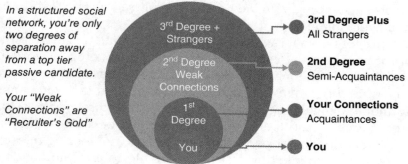

Figure 12.5   The Power of Connections.

and HR tech is that this can be done effectively and more efficiently and at scale. As far as I'm concerned, it can't be. In this case, technology is being used to solve the wrong problem. This is like going to Costco trying to find the finest evening wear and wondering why it was a fruitless effort despite the hours invested. That's why I contend that this sourcing approach should be avoided for all but high-volume entry-level requirements.

A better way to find outstanding people is to leverage your first-degree connections on LinkedIn and tap into their best first-degree connections. Optimizing this approach starts by answering this question as soon as you start looking for candidates: "Who knows my ideal candidate?" These people are referred to as "nodes" in a social network. Then connect with these people and ask for a referral of someone they know who's outstanding and perfect for your open job. Even better, by also searching on their connections you can identify some potential semifinalists using the clever Boolean techniques described earlier and ask specifically about the strongest people uncovered.

Weak Connections Are Recruiter's Gold

These second-degree weak connections are "Recruiter's Gold" since these people call you back almost 100% of the time. They're also superbly qualified. You wouldn't have called them otherwise.

Assuming you have a deep enough network, it's then possible to find some outstanding potential semifinalists within days of starting a search project. That's why I believe building a deep network should represent the bulk of the effort of any recruiter handling critical professional and management positions. Given this prequalified list of outstanding people at the top of the recruiting funnel, all you now have to do is recruit them. Doing that is the subject of the next chapter on learning how to drive the Big Red Tour Bus.

Of course, while these types of referrals are truly Recruiter's Gold, the problem in some cases is figuring out who the best first-degree connections are to get the spectacular referrals from. Aside from those you're already connected to, these network nodes can be vendors, customers, advisors, project team members, and everyone in your company, especially those you don't know, who likely worked with your ideal candidate. Before describing how to leverage your employee referral program using this "weak connections" networking concept, let me give a few examples of how to develop networking nodes from scratch.

A few years ago a former client asked me to help prepare a performance profile for a CEO position for a new, well-funded start-up. After a one-hour conversation it was clear that the ideal candidate needed to have built and run a company of about $100–200 million or be a COO at a company with multiple locations doing something similar. There are a number of business groups that cater to CEOs of these types of companies, including the Young Presidents Organization (YPO), which has thousands of CEO members around the world. I found a number of the executives in YPO listed on LinkedIn and connected with one and described the hiring challenge. I then sent a link to the hiring company's very compelling website and asked if he knew anyone who might be interested in this new role. He mentioned two. One got hired.

Here are a few other examples of how to leverage the networking power of LinkedIn.

➤ On a search for HVAC engineers I first connected with the head of the local professional group and told him I had a number of search projects under way for a well-known construction company. I then searched on his connections and asked about three outstanding people who were on the society's regulatory committees. This led to even more referrals of outstanding people. I then turned the list over to a staffing firm that turned it into a number of placements.

➤ For a controller search I connected with a partner at one of the major CPA firms in Los Angeles and quickly got referrals. It's pretty well known that this is a service CPA firms provide their alumni.

➤ I found one candidate for a software development manager role who only returned my call after I mentioned a common acquaintance we had on LinkedIn. In fact, I never called the acquaintance to ask her to intervene, but that would have been my next step.

While persistence is often the secret to getting third-degree connections to call you back, it's much better to first convert these people into weak connections. Hiring strangers is a very impersonal affair, but by first converting these strangers into acquaintances by the weak connections route, the people are more likely to call you back and the conversations are more open and honest. Then if the job is one worth pursuing, it's done naturally, without the hustle and pressure that comes when dealing with strangers. If the job is not a good fit for some reason, then the relationship built through the open discussion can be leveraged to get other and more appropriate referrals. This is a great way to build a deep network of highly connected nodes in a matter of a few weeks.

Leverage Your Employee Referral Program: Create a PERP

It's hard to believe that any company with more than a few thousand people ever needs to go outside of its own employees' first-degree connections to find outstanding talent for any critical role. This could be the untapped solution for all of its hiring needs. Of course, there are a few twists and turns that need to be taken in order to tap into this goldmine of talent properly. Here's how to get started:

➤ Make sure all of your employees connect with all of the best people they've ever worked with in the past.

➤ Have your employees reach out to a subset of the best of the best and invite them to explore career opportunities with your company whenever they believe their current jobs aren't as satisfying as desired. This way you'll get them first as Tiptoers when they begin to consider leaving their current jobs.

➤ Whenever you open a new search project on LinkedIn, first look for possible network nodes in your company who likely worked with your ideal candidate in the past. One way to figure this out is to build a 360-degree work chart showing the types of projects and teams the candidate would likely have worked on in the recent past. For example, engineers typically work with product marketing people on developing specifications, sales reps work with inbound customer support and clients, and people in procurement work with vendors.

➤ Connect with your coworkers (search on LinkedIn to find them) and mention the role you're trying to fill. In addition to asking, "Who is the best person you've ever worked with in the past who would see this job as a good career move?" also make sure the coworkers' connections are visible. This is a critical step that must be taken in order for you to be able to search on their connections. (This change can be made in the person's settings page.)

➤ Search on your coworkers' connections using the clever Boolean techniques described earlier in the chapter for some semifinalists. Then ask if these people are worthy of serious consideration.

➤ Make sure you connect with every person you talk to, including those who aren't likely semifinalists for your open position. Then search on their connections and ask about the best potential semifinalists you've found. Then contact these "weak connections," mentioning the person who referred them. You'll only have to do this iterative process once or twice to find more than enough outstanding semifinalists to make one great hire.

Of course, this two-degrees-of-separation networking technique can be expanded beyond just your own company's coworkers, but if you have a big enough company it should be sufficient to find great referrals for just about any job. This is called PERP, a proactive employee referral program. You'll find out how to recruit and move these people forward in the process in the next chapter on driving the Big Red Tour Bus.

■ SUMMARY: NETWORKING RULES!

In early 2018 an undergrad at Harvard asked if she could get the results of an old survey we conducted describing how recently hired people found their jobs. With limited data she concluded that those who found their jobs via networking were far more satisfied with their jobs and were far more likely to still be on the job one year later. The info she had at the time wasn't precise enough to determine the specific drivers of job satisfaction, but there was enough to suggest that source of hire is a critical factor in affecting Quality of Hire. One thing was clear then, just as it is today: hiring strangers is less likely to produce consistent Win-Win Hiring outcomes than hiring acquaintances. Since then we've conducted a number of comparable surveys that reinforce that point that networking – especially mining your "weak connections" – is the best way for companies to find great candidates. This is how you find and first convert strangers into acquaintances before they become great hires.

The graphic in Figure 12.6, based on a survey conducted a few years ago with 3,100 responses, indicated that over 40% of active candidates, whether employed or unemployed, still found their jobs via networking. For Tiptoers and the Super Passive, this networking figure was over 60%. The question we asked in the survey was how the person found his or her most recent job. For the Super Passives, almost 25% got their most recent job via an internal move. This is not unusual since the best people tend to be promoted more often and tend to be the most satisfied.

As I was writing this chapter, I spoke with a VP of Technology for a rapidly growing consumer services company who confirmed this commonsense idea. Just like other managers, regardless of function, he told me he always assigns his strongest team members to the most critical projects since he knows they'll consistently deliver high-quality results. That's why getting these types of referrals is the single best way to quickly find outstanding semifinalists.

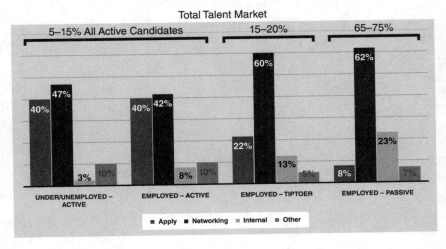

Figure 12.6 How People Get Jobs.

Some would argue that this networking process perpetuates hiring clones. I suggest the opposite is achieved. But this requires a proactive approach of searching on someone's connections and specifically looking for the most diverse and talented people possible, and then connecting with and recruiting these people. By leaving the process to chance or asking, "Who do you know who's looking?" you'll only surface active candidates with hiring success and diversity problems.

While beginning with a 40-40-20 sourcing plan is a good starting point, it's important to recognize that it's just a starting point to find some outstanding semifinalists at the top of the recruiting funnel. But once you start contacting these people, the effort should switch to getting more referrals from them, not searching for more people regardless of how clever you are at using Boolean. It all comes down to agreeing with this fact: networking is the single most important factor affecting the quality of people your company sees and hires.

Chapter 13

Start the Recruiting Process with a Career Discussion, Not a Sales Pitch

Chapter 2 introduced the Performance-based Hiring process and mentioned that recruiting a top-tier person needs to be conducted in parallel with the assessment process, rather than afterwards. The idea here is that by waiting until the end of the interview to decide if you like the person, it's often too late, since the candidate will likely feel disrespected or slighted. This is truer if the interviewer is unprofessional or unprepared.

A similar situation exists when it comes to sourcing and recruiting. Now that you're starting to reach out to semifinalists and getting responses, it's necessary to immediately convert these names into serious prospects or into nodes to get additional referrals. This is why sourcing and recruiting needs to be a tightly integrated process rather than considered separate functions.

This is especially important when working with a small pool of highly qualified prospects. Recognize that the people you'll be contacting will either be potential candidates for your current role, or they'll be able to provide outstanding referrals for it. You wouldn't reach out to them otherwise. Just as important, talking with top people and building relationships is how you build a deep network to fill future jobs with outstanding talent quickly and efficiently.

■ CONDUCT CAREER DISCOVERY ON YOUR FIRST CALL

This combined process becomes clear when using a Big Red Tour Bus, as shown in Figure 13.1, as a metaphor for fully understanding this approach. The tour bus idea was mentioned earlier in Chapter 12 on sourcing as a means to differentiate the high touch Win-Win Hiring process from the more common high-volume transactional process. Being able to apply it in your everyday recruiting activities starts by getting your Big Red Tour Bus recruiter's driving license and learning the rules of the road.

In the case of recruiting, this requires some insight into human nature and behavioral economics.[1] Since we're targeting outstanding people who have not applied to the job, they start out in the driver's seat, and rightly so, especially if they are not actively looking for another job. While this same approach can be used when

[1]https://www.behavioraleconomics.com/resources/introduction-behavioral-economics/.

Getting Your Recruiter's Driving License

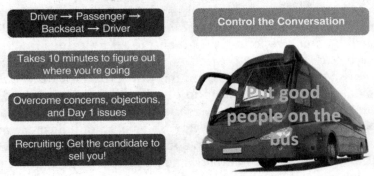

Driver → Passenger → Backseat → Driver

Control the Conversation

Takes 10 minutes to figure out where you're going

Overcome concerns, objections, and Day 1 issues

Recruiting: Get the candidate to sell you!

Put good people on the bus

Figure 13.1   Getting Your Recruiter's Driving License for the Big Red Tour Bus.

talking with candidates who have applied for the job directly, the more difficult situation is dealing with people who aren't even looking, so it's best to begin with that toughest-case assumption. Driving this bus with these types of discriminating passengers involves the most challenging route and the most skilled recruiters. Once these techniques are mastered, recruiting everyone else is easier by comparison.

The first step in getting people on the bus is convincing them the role represents a possible career move. This is equivalent to putting them in the passenger seat alongside the driver, not the driver's seat. During the ride, you'll need to nudge the person back a little in an attempt to demonstrate that the role being discussed represents a career opportunity worthy of serious consideration. You'll know you've arrived at your destination when the person is so excited that he or she won't get off the bus until you get back to the company's headquarters.

It's critical to note that none of this persuading is achieved by overselling the job; it's achieved by fully understanding the role you're trying to fill and by over-listening and asking in-depth and insightful questions to see if there's a fit. This is similar to the discovery process sales representatives use when developing custom solutions for their clients by first understanding their needs. That's why this recruiting process is referred to as "career-based discovery."

Bottom line, when it comes to recruiting outstanding talent, including those who are truly passive, being successful involves getting the person interested enough that they begin to sell you about their qualifications rather than the recruiter or hiring manager trying to sell them.

Over the course of this recruiting ride there will be plenty of bumps along the way in the form of objections and concerns, but the purpose of the ride must be made clear: it's to review the candidate's background and present the job as a potential career move if it is. Frequently you'll come to a fork in the road or need to take a detour. If the job doesn't offer a good career move or the candidate isn't strong enough for the role or is too strong, you'll need to network with the person, asking for other potential passengers who might find the current drive more interesting. This is the referral and networking process covered in depth in the previous chapter.

The key to success in this entire process involves the recruiter, or the hiring manager in some cases, to "Control the Conversation" to ensure the candidate doesn't opt out before fully understanding the career merits of the opportunity, despite their initial hesitancy to do so. If the job doesn't represent a possible career, the person should decline moving forward, but far too often recruiters give up too soon before ever getting to that point.

Here's how this full disclosure Win-Win Hiring bus ride maps out the route you must take.

First, Put Only Semifinalists on the Bus

All of the sourcing tools and tactics covered earlier involve identifying semifinalists and convincing them to at least contact you to discuss the career potential of your open opportunity. It's important to go slow, but you'll need to persist to get at least 50–60% of the small, prequalified talent pool you identified to engage in at least a preliminary conversation. This requires that your messages emphasize the idea of having an exploratory conversation about a possible career move, rather than pushing the open job. The big theme here, and one worth repeating often, is simple: "Sell the ride, not the destination." Alternatively, "Sell the discussion, not the job." By removing the time pressure and going slow, you'll get more people open-minded enough to at least take the first short drive.

Only Ask "Yes" Questions and Don't Take "No" for an Answer

As shown in Figure 13.2, getting to a very weak "Maybe" is good enough for starting the bus ride. But even getting a maybe is often a challenge. One way to do this is to avoid any questions that can be answered with a "No." For example, asking, "How would you like to discuss an awesome cost manager job for a small manufacturing company?" won't interest anyone who doesn't want to be cost manager or work for a small company. However, asking the question this way will get more interest: "Would you be open to discussing a financial management spot if it represented a significant career move?" It's possible that working for a small company implementing a state-of-the-art cost system would put the person on a better career trajectory, but this will never be uncovered without a preliminary conversation.

You can also be vague about the title by asking the same question this way: "Would you be open to exploring a situation if it was clearly superior to what you're doing today?" This is the universal "Yes" question since 90% of all candidates will answer yes to it whether they're looking or not. In my mind this is the most important question a recruiter can ask to get a person to at least consider a very preliminary discussion.

From my experience, even people highly satisfied with their current jobs are often still willing to discuss opportunities simply as a means to network with and build a relationship with a top recruiter for future ones.

Once you get the person on the phone, it's important to still be vague about the job. A very short (one to two minutes) high-level

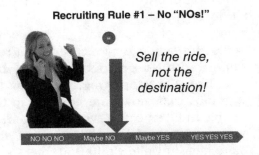

Recruiting Rule #1 – No "NOs!"

Sell the ride, not the destination!

NO NO NO   Maybe NO   Maybe YES   YES YES YES

Figure 13.2 The First Rule of Recruiting.

summary is all that's necessary. Or just say you're handling a number of related positions and you want to see if one of them makes good career sense for the person. This is the type of introductory statement that keeps the recruiter in the driver's seat. Too many recruiters start off describing the job, which is a sure way to stop the conversation if there's no instant interest. In this case you've not only lost a future prospect, but also a current networking opportunity. Just as important, you might be able to modify the role somewhat if the person is truly outstanding. For example, one executive search firm now using Performance-based Hiring just told me that on one project their international automotive client increased the job two management levels to hire someone they recommended because they persisted this way. While the candidate initially was not interested in the original role, the recruiter asked, "What if we could make the job bigger?" The answer was "Yes." That's why it's important to keep the conversation going regardless of the concerns or objections the person raises.

Overcome Preliminary Objections and Concerns

While most people will agree to a preliminary conversation, some will ask about the compensation before they're even willing to agree to any type of discussion. This is actually a good sign; it means they are at least somewhat interested in leaving their current job. However, under no conditions tell them what the compensation is. Instead, if they ask, say something like, "If the job doesn't represent a good career move, it doesn't matter what the compensation is. So let's first see if the job represents a career move and then we'll see if the compensation fits. Worst case, we can network for future opportunities if it doesn't."

There are a number of other common concerns candidates often raise when first contacted by a recruiter that recruiters must learn to handle in order to get prospects onto the bus. The most important of these, like "I'm happy where I am" and "I'm not in a position to change jobs right now," are covered in Chapter 14 on recruiting and closing, but it's best to avoid them entirely if you can by asking only yes questions initially, being vague about the title, or suggesting you're handling a few different roles.

How to Answer the "What's a Career Move?" Question

Since you've already expressed the idea that the decision to proceed is based on the potential of a better career opportunity, you'll need to describe what this is early in the conversation. Often candidates will ask about this, but if not, it's important to proactively explain it. The graph in Figure 13.3 will help clarify the factors involved in a career move.

I typically set the stage for a career discussion by first explaining the Win-Win Hiring concept and why it's important to measure hiring success over the course of the year and at the anniversary date, not just based on the size of the offer package. Then I say a good career move needs to provide a minimum 30% nonmonetary increase. I call this the "30% Solution." This 30% is a combination of a number of different factors, including more satisfying work, a job with more impact, one that offers more stretch and learning, and most important of all a chance to continue this growth over multiple years.

This is a good way to explain your company's hiring process, too, by saying that your company's interviewing approach is dual in nature. Part of this is to assess the person in comparison to the real performance objectives of the role and the other part is for the candidate to gather the necessary information in order to make a proper long-term decision if an offer is made. This approach

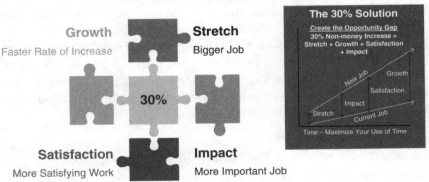

Figure 13.3 Factors in a Career Move.
© 2016. All Rights Reserved. The Adler Group, Inc.

changes the role of the recruiter to more of a career advisor than just someone trying to fill a job. This will be important as you move the candidate through the interviewing process. Overcoming concerns along the way will help minimize the chance the person will opt out before fully understanding the career merits of the role.

This career-oriented focus drives the point home that in order to achieve a positive Win-Win Hiring outcome the nonmonetary factors in the 30% Solution need to be fully understood. Once explained this way, most people agree these longer-term factors are at least as important, if not more so, than the compensation received on the start date. Yet for most candidates considering different opportunities, these nonmonetary factors are vague at best. Describing and closing this gap with specific details is the key to recruiting stronger talent, increasing assessment accuracy, and hiring people for the right reasons without the compensation package being a make-or-break factor. Repositioning the assessment process this way gives the recruiter a significant advantage when negotiating offers, especially when the person has other opportunities to consider or might get a counteroffer.

This dual assessment approach is embedded in all of the interviewing techniques described throughout this book, with the candidate learning the specific details of what comprises the 30% nonmonetary factors during the questioning process. This all comes together when recruiting the candidate and making an offer, but explaining it starts with the first phone call. In my mind recruiting is not something done at the end of the process; it needs to be embedded at the beginning of it. This prevents surprises when offers are made, reduces opt-outs before the candidate learns about the career merits of the opening, minimizes the need to pay compensation premiums, increases the acceptance rate, and, most important of all, ensures the candidate accepts your offer since the job represents the best career opportunity for the person in comparison to everything else being considered.

Review the Person's Profile Before Describing the Job

Once you've addressed the preliminary concerns and the person has agreed to engage in an exploratory discussion, don't launch into a sales pitch about your job opening. Instead say something like, "Great.

Let's first review your LinkedIn profile for a few minutes and if it seems like the potential for a career move exists, I'll describe the role in more detail. Then we can make a mutual decision if it makes sense to get more serious and determine next steps."

As you're reviewing the person's profile, look for areas where your opening might offer a 30% nonmonetary increase. Consider things like the scope and focus of the job, the size of the team and budget, the importance of the position and its impact, and the person's previous rate of growth in comparison to what you have to offer. Since you're comparing the person's background to the performance profile and the EVP, you'll have enough information to craft a statement about the career merits of your opportunity, if appropriate.

Build a 10-Minute Relationship by Controlling the Conversation

It's essential that you don't let prospects opt out before they have a full understanding of your opportunity. By controlling the conversation around the career opportunity and the 30% Solution, and by getting the candidate to describe his or her background first, the recruiter can then figure out if the job represents a career opportunity. It takes at least 10 minutes for both the recruiter and the prospect to share enough information for both to feel comfortable with each other about moving on to a more serious in-depth discussion, if warranted. The recruiter must not rush the process, nor let the candidate rush it, either. Then, even if the person isn't ideal or interested, you'll at least be able to network with the person.

You need to invest at least 10 minutes to build a worthwhile networking relationship. Don't short-circuit it. If you do, it could derail the entire process before it even begins.

Recognize that as the search process progresses, things often change. Sometimes the job gets bigger or the compensation budget is increased. By developing a professional relationship as described here, it's possible to reach out to the candidates again later to see if the changes made make the job more appealing. Just as important, you can proactively search on the person's connections using LinkedIn and ask if the people found are worth contacting for this or other opportunities. This would not be possible without developing the relationship first.

■ RECRUITING IS GETTING THE CANDIDATE TO SELL YOU, NOT YOU SELLING THE CANDIDATE

In Appendix 2 you'll find an Exploratory Phone Screen Talent Scorecard. Chapter 8 describes how to conduct this full phone screen interview. While you should review this approach ahead of time, I wouldn't suggest using the complete guide during the first call with a candidate. Regardless, portions of it are useful to get a sense of the person's general fit for the role and if the person has elements of the Achiever Pattern. Just as important when conducting this initial screen is to look for components of the 30% Solution to see if the candidate is likely to be interested in your open job.

Assuming the candidate is a good fit for the role, it's now appropriate to provide a high-level summary of the job, describing some of the big challenges and the importance of the role to some big company initiative or project. Then highlight areas in the 30% Solution that show why exploring the job in more depth might make sense. You might even want to highlight one area where the job offers the most career growth for the candidate as a means to get the person more invested in wanting to learn more. For example, I told a person who was a tax director at a big company that in the new job he'd be reporting directly to the CFO and setting up the tax strategy for the entire company. At the same time I expressed some concern that this might be too big a stretch. I then asked him to describe the biggest international tax strategy project he had ever worked on to see if his background was appropriate. He gave me a great example in an attempt to prove he was certainly capable of handling the larger role.

This is a good example of how to recruit top-tier talent. It isn't by overselling the role with a bunch of hyperbole and empty promises. It's by spending the time to understand what motivates a candidate to excel and then presenting your opportunity as a means to achieve this. It's important to note than when it comes to dealing with strong people, recruiting is not you selling the candidate; it's setting the stage to get the candidate to sell you.

The value of this approach cannot be overstated. It's important to recognize that unless they're desperate, people don't change jobs without seeking the advice of their friends, family, coworkers, other recruiters, and even their boss when they turn in their resignation letter. So if they can't convince themselves of the career merits of the job early on, they won't be able to convince anyone else either unless it's for a compensation increase. That's why you have to take money off the table as the criteria for moving forward in the process. When done correctly, when the candidate is asked, "What's the money?" when he or she tells their significant other or best friend that they're considering changing jobs, their answer will be, "It's not about the money; it's about the career opportunity."

How to Handle Compensation by Not Discussing It Too Soon

In Chapter 2 introducing the Performance-based Hiring business process, I made the contention that candidates should never be screened in or out based on their compensation requirements until they have understood the job. By delaying the discussion this way, compensation becomes a negotiating factor, not a filter for having the conversation. And if the job represents a true career move, compensation is of secondary importance when it comes to accepting or rejecting an offer. Just as important with the delay is that if the candidate is not perfect for the role for whatever reason, you might otherwise lose the chance to network with the person and get some strong referrals of people who are.

On the other hand, once both the recruiter and the candidate agree that it's worth getting more serious about the role, it is important to begin the compensation discussion. One way is to just ask. For example, on a recent executive-level marketing search I suggested to the candidate that since she was with a bigger company, her compensation expectations might exceed my client's budget. Then I asked her to provide a broad range of what she'd consider fair. I specifically said this was not a negotiation but just to see if arranging another call – in this case with the hiring manager – made sense. It turned out she was in the high end of the range. Based on this I suggested we move forward but, in the process, she would need to recognize that if an offer were to be made it would be for a very modest increase. More important, though, was for her to make her decision on the career opportunity and if a 30% nonmonetary increase could be achieved. I didn't press her for a decision, but the next day she agreed to proceed.

While this candidate didn't get an offer, she had thought it over and agreed it was worth moving forward due to the opportunity the role represented rather than the size of the compensation package.

In another case, for a senior executive role, the candidate's current package far exceeded the compensation budget. When I suggested we weren't even in the ballpark he pushed back and wanted to proceed saying the chance to become the CEO of a publicly traded company was far more important than the compensation. This person ultimately got the job, he did become the CEO, and his compensation two years later far exceeded what his current earnings were at his prior company. The point here is that if you talk about compensation too soon, you lose the chance to develop a relationship and fully understand the person's personal reasons for changing jobs. This will be important for current networking purposes as well as for future opportunities that might develop.

From a practical standpoint there's no need even to discuss compensation until both the recruiter and the candidate agree it makes sense to get serious. Some recruiters would argue they don't have time to do this with every candidate since they're pressed to fill roles quickly and efficiently. My counter to this is that if you've only sourced potential semifinalists to begin with, the recruiting role is fundamentally changed from a transactional process to one based on mutual discovery. By spending more time with fewer people, and as long as they're the right people, you'll be able to network with them to get strong referrals if they're a not a good fit for the current role. Just as important, you can reach out to them again if the job changes or as other more suitable jobs become available. This is how you build a deep network of superior talent that can be called upon when needed.

Gain Concessions to Negotiate the Offer as a Series of Steps

Once you've established mutual interest, have discussed compensation in comparison with a 30% nonmonetary increase, and have determined the candidate could be a potential semifinalist, the last negotiating step before letting the candidate off the Big Red Tour Bus involves getting concessions from the candidate as a prerequisite before moving forward in the process. This may include simply asking if the person is willing to consider the job from a longer-term career perspective for only a modest increase in compensation.

If so, say you'll try to arrange the next meeting. Don't push this idea too aggressively. Give the candidate time to ponder the trade-off and get back to you if they want to proceed. This was the situation with the marketing position described earlier. This way when you do make offers there will be few deal-breaking surprises. In another case I told a candidate for an HR director-level position that the benefit package wasn't as good as the one she had, so if she got an offer she shouldn't be surprised. She agreed with this condition to move forward in the process and wasn't fazed at all when the offer was made and accepted a few weeks later.

Changing jobs for someone who is fully employed and not actively looking, or has other opportunities to consider, is a big decision involving many variables and one that takes time to consider. By highlighting the need to achieve a Win-Win Hiring outcome, the importance of this type of decision is put in proper perspective. Doing so also sets the stage to ensure your candidates make the right decisions and get all of the information needed to make them properly.

In Chapter 14 on recruiting and closing, the importance of this initial setup will become more obvious. When you're actually negotiating the offer, you want the candidate to weigh the nonmonetary factors associated with a career move just as heavily as those contained in the offer package. This way even if your compensation isn't the best, you'll still be able to get your offer accepted if the career opportunity is superior to the other situations being considered. In most cases the candidate's competing opportunities will be vague on these nonmonetary factors, increasing the likelihood more of your offers will be accepted, and more important, they will be accepted for the right reasons.

■ SUMMARY

The Performance-based Hiring business process described in this book has been designed to hire top-tier candidates on fair and equitable terms. The measurement of success in this case is consistent and numerous Win-Win Hiring outcomes. As far as I'm concerned, a company's entire hiring process must be considered ineffective or at least suspect if this goal isn't regularly attained. Achieving it doesn't happen by churning through lots of people and hoping a few great people somehow fall through the cracks and wind up being great hires. Instead, it involves spending more time with a few prequalified prospects and convincing them of the career merits of what you're offering. Learning to drive the Big Red Tour Bus is a critical part of this entire process from first contact to the final close. This is the glue that holds the entire process together. And without this high-touch approach, including full engagement by the hiring manager, success as measured above is unlikely.

Chapter 14

Recruiting and Closing Top Performers

■ THE BASICS OF RECRUITING AND CLOSING

Once a person has been confirmed as a semifinalist by the hiring manager and both want to move forward in the process, it's important to start the closing process immediately. Begin with the end in mind (i.e., one of Stephen Covey's Seven Habits) by telling the candidate that in a few weeks there is a good chance the person will be getting an offer for this job. Then go on to say that a few days before this happens, you're going to present this scenario to the candidate:

Put the money aside for a moment; do you really want this job? If so, why? Because if you can't tell me in specific detail why this job represents a great career move and will likely result in a Win-Win Hiring outcome, I'm going to recommend that an offer shouldn't be extended.

Of course, then you have to remind the person that a career move requires a minimum 30% nonmonetary increase consisting of stretch, growth, impact, and satisfaction. This is the 30% Solution described in Chapter 13. The point of this question is to remind the candidate that one of their roles is to get this information during the interviewing process in order to make the right career decision. This way, if an offer is extended, the candidate will have all of the information needed to compare other opportunities being considered and make the best career decision possible. In fact, you should tell the candidate that just by asking the questions about these nonmonetary factors there's a higher probability an offer will be extended since it demonstrates that the person is very career focused.

But this is just a start to the closing process. As important, hiring managers need to agree with this approach, since they're the ones who provide the necessary job information for the candidate to make the proper decision. This agreement isn't hard to get, though, since it was fully explained when the performance profile was prepared and a Win-Win Hiring outcome was presented as the objective.

Recruiting Is Not Selling, It's Listening

Hiring a top person requires much more than conducting a professional interview and making an accurate assessment. In addition, getting a candidate to accept an offer requires exceptional recruiting and negotiating skills. If the person is top-notch and in high demand, he or she will likely receive a counteroffer or an offer from a competing organization. Too many hiring managers, and most recruiters, think recruiting is mostly selling and wooing by using hyperbole, extra compensation, and multiple levels of pressure to seal the deal.

This is exactly the wrong way to recruit a top person. It's more important to ensure the candidate clearly sees the job as the best career opportunity among competing alternatives. If the offer package is competitive, even if it's not the best compensation-wise, then closing the deal should be focused on having the candidate understand the short- and long-term value of each of these other opportunities. Much of this can be accomplished using the Performance-based Interviewing process described in this book. When candidates know they've been evaluated properly and in comparison to real job needs, they consider the subsequent advice provided by the recruiter and hiring manager as more meaningful.

Recruiting starts by conducting an in-depth professional interview. The inquisitive and job-focused nature of this interview sends an important message to the candidate that the company has high selection standards. On a more micro level, using the interview to seek out differences in what the candidate has accomplished in comparison to the performance profile is a powerful means to demonstrate the actual career opportunity you're offering. The sum of all of these differences is the 30% Solution or the "opportunity gap" the open role represents. These differences could include the size of the project or team, the importance of the work, the opportunity for accelerated growth, and what the candidate can learn, do, and become. Collectively, these gaps represent a significant career move for the candidate, and if big enough they can more than offset the need for a significant compensation increase. Positioning the job this way maybe shouldn't even be called recruiting. "Career-based consulting" might be more appropriate.

It's somewhat surprising that many hiring managers still think there's an endless supply of top talent who meet all of the criteria on the job description and are willing to accept ill-defined lateral moves. This is unlikely in most cases but truer when dealing with any strong person who has multiple opportunities to consider. It's also unwise when hiring anyone, even if they have few other options.

Hiring a person based on an economic need is unlikely to inspire the person to work at peak levels, especially once the economic need is met. In my opinion, it's better to offer a person an incentive to grow, a chance to maximize their abilities, and to become better at what they want to do. This way, the person views the new job as a worthwhile career move, not as just a means to a paycheck. With the 30% opportunity gap as an underpinning, negotiating the offer then involves getting the person to make a tradeoff between career growth and the compensation package. Providing someone with a chance to become better every year is a great way to increase job satisfaction, motivation, and on-the-job performance. The tradeoff for the candidate in this situation might be a little less on the compensation side. Making this case, though, is where good recruiting and negotiating skills are required.

While the Performance-based Hiring process is an easy-to-use and practical way to assess a candidate and set up the recruiting process, it offers the following less-obvious benefits:

➤ Focusing on the career opportunity minimizes early opt-outs, increasing the chance the best person is hired, not the most desperate. Just as important, not as many people need to be interviewed to make one great hiring decision.

➤ When candidates see the job as a stretch move, they have the information needed to convince their family members, friends, coworkers, and personal advisors as to why the position is the best long-term career move among other competing alternatives.

➤ Describing the dual decision-making process required to achieve a Win-Win Hiring outcome minimizes the chance of the candidate accepting a counteroffer or another offer where money could become the main factor in the candidate's decision.

➤ Investing more time interviewing fewer prequalified top-tier people improves assessment accuracy and increases the likelihood of raising the talent bar. Part of this involves converting strangers into acquaintances before they become employees.

Despite the obvious benefit, these outcomes are not possible without a performance profile to make the comparison and the Performance-based Interview to obtain the information. Given this, here's how to achieve these multi-level objectives.

Stay the Buyer from the Beginning of the Process to the Very End

If a candidate has an economic need for your job, it's pretty easy to stay the buyer. Needy candidates are always in sales mode, trying to convince you they're worthy. However, any high-demand candidate who has multiple suitors has a totally different perspective. Unfortunately, when interviewing someone in this situation who clearly is an outstanding performer, managers and recruiters quickly switch roles and go into sales mode, using hyperbole and exaggeration in an attempt to convince the hot prospect of the worthiness of their offer. Even if the person doesn't opt out under the company's apparent desperation, there ends up being a bidding war if you ultimately decide to make the person an offer. Worse, the person hasn't even been fully assessed since too much time has been spent selling rather than questioning and listening. Staying the buyer not only prevents the problem, but also increases interviewing accuracy while minimizing the need to pay compensation premiums.

Start by listening four times more than you talk. Asking tough, detailed questions about the person's accomplishments is the best way to do this. By prefacing the most significant accomplishment question with a description of what you need accomplished and why it's important to the company, the best and most worthy candidates will naturally get interested and try to convince you they're qualified. This is called the "pull-toward" interviewing technique. Don't accept superficial answers. Peel the onion and get facts and specific details about the accomplishments. Challenge the person. This part of the discussion is called the "push-away." When both techniques are used in tandem, top people will leave this type of interview knowing they've been assessed properly, and if the job appears to be a real career move, thinking about why they want it, not why they don't.

In order for a job to represent a career move it needs to offer both stretch and growth. Stretch represents the actual difference between the person's current position and the job you're offering. It covers the scope and scale of the job in terms of team size, overall responsibility, budget, what the person can learn, and the challenges involved and their impact and importance to the company. A more important job in a smaller company represents stretch from an impact standpoint. Growth is the future. It represents what the person can become if the job is handled successfully. This relates to taking on bigger assignments with more significance, promotional and unique learning opportunities, and getting exposed to more challenging situations and senior executives.

While hard to quantify, a job 15–20% bigger than the person now holds would represent an excellent career move, especially if there is another 5–10% annual growth on top of it. If the combination of stretch and growth is less than 10%, the job is more a lateral transfer. As part of demonstrating this type of opportunity, have the candidate meet other people who have been successful and have taken on bigger roles in the company. You need to prove the company's claims of growth opportunities; otherwise you're being deceptive. These situations quickly lead to disappointment, underperformance, and unnecessary turnover.

The Performance-based Interviewing process can be used to help both the interviewer and the candidate figure out the size of this opportunity gap by comparing the candidate's accomplishments to the performance objectives listed in the performance profile. The differences represent the opportunity gap. Then use the push and pull techniques as part of the follow-up questions to get the candidate to "own" the opportunity gap.

Make Passive Candidates Earn the Job to Increase Its Value

Good candidates will not be deterred or offended if the assessment is accurate. Instead, they'll try to convince or sell you as to why they're qualified. This is a good sign when it happens, especially if the person wasn't actively looking to begin with. Some candidates might be overly concerned by the size of the challenge. This is one way to have candidates self-select themselves out of the job.

Strong candidates will likely want to better understand the challenge involved and ask a series of appropriate follow-up questions. Expect this. Be concerned if the questions are not forthcoming or not relevant.

By challenging or subtly pushing the candidate, the person understands clearly why the job represents a possible growth opportunity. A bunch of small gaps can often represent a big career move. A slightly bigger team, more influence, bigger impact, and broader responsibility combined with a faster-growing company, is often all you need to convert what seems like a lateral transfer into a significant career opportunity. A Performance-based Interview achieves this far better than overt selling. If an offer is made, the candidate is then in a better position to favorably compare your opportunity among others from a long-term growth perspective, rather than strictly on the size of the short-term compensation increase.

Minimize the Negatives; Accentuate the Positives

While Year 1 and Beyond criteria represents the bulk of why top people select one offer over another, minimizing the candidate's current company frustrations is often another unstated factor involved in their decision. Leaving a bad boss, doing work that's stifling, sacrificing quality for expediency, or not being respected or heard are common reasons why fully employed people begin looking for new opportunities. Just as important is attempting to get a better work-life balance, if possible.

As you begin the phone screen, ask the person why he or she is looking for a new job, and what the person would need in a new job if they were to switch companies. Then ask them why this issue is personally important to them. Getting the answer to "Why is this important to you?" will get at some of the person's underlying frustrations. If you can minimize these problems, you'll increase your odds that you'll be able to hire the person on reasonable terms. Eliminating these current negatives needs to be considered as much a component of the 30% nonmonetary increase as any of the more positive factors.

■ DON'T MAKE AN OFFER UNTIL YOU'RE 100% SURE IT WILL BE ACCEPTED

For a top person, especially a passive candidate, taking a new job represents a critical personal decision, one that affects family, friends, and close associates. These decisions are not made quickly or lightly. Too often, companies hurry the process to fill an opening. This clash of needs often precludes either party from making the best decision. By moving as fast as possible, but not faster than the prospect is able to digest and consider everything, you can achieve an optimum balance.

But don't wait until you're finished interviewing to start the offer testing process. By then too many things are left uncovered and the unexpected "surprise" is likely to pop up at the worst possible time. With these unknowns hanging over the candidate's head, upon getting the offer the typical candidate response is, "I'll have to think about it." This noncommitment also gives the person the chance to shop the offer around and accept an offer from the company with the deepest pockets. This converts the negotiating process into a series of reactions and counterreactions. You won't have to endure this if you test every aspect of the offer before it's made, and then don't make the offer formal until the candidate is 100% committed to accepting it with little delay.

Testing and Negotiating the Offer by Getting Continuous Concessions

It's never too soon to start testing interest early. In fact right after the first phone screen with the hiring manager is a good place to begin. Here's how this is done. First, you need to stay the buyer throughout the process and create the career opportunity gap as described earlier. Second, lengthen your interviewing process to add an exploratory step with the hiring manager at the beginning and add one or two additional steps during the assessment process. A second round of interviews, including a panel interview and a problem-solving take-home question, should be part of this expanded assessment. Regardless of what you add, the key is to not allow the candidate to proceed to a subsequent step without getting some type of concession.

For example, if you're a recruiter, suggest early on that while the candidate is a bit light in comparison to the other candidates being considered, you'd like to present the candidate to the hiring manager as a high-potential person worthy of serious consideration. However, since the candidate's compensation is already at the high end of the range, going forward would mean any potential salary increase would need to be modest. Don't proceed unless the candidate agrees to this concession.

Position Your Job as a Career Move

In most cases when getting an offer, candidates have only a limited understanding of the real work itself, the environment in which this work takes place, and the potential career opportunity the job actually represents. In these cases the offer-negotiating process emphasizes the compensation package and everything a candidate receives on the start date (i.e., the job title, the location, the benefits package, and some perks). None of this will have any impact on the likelihood of a Win-Win Hiring outcome. Using a performance profile and a Performance-based Interviewing process changes everything by focusing on what a person will be doing and what he or she could become by doing it successfully over the course of the first year. To ensure that this longer-term point of view is fully appreciated and understood, it must be formalized, not just preached. That's the purpose of the career decision comparison table shown in Figure 14.1 and in Appendix 2. The purpose is to clearly demonstrate that the "Year One and Beyond" factors are more important than the Day One compensation package and the location.

The table offers a useful way for candidates to compare different job opportunities on three time-based dimensions: the start date offer package, the work the person will be doing in the first year and the underlying circumstances, and a realistic understanding of the potential that the job represents. You should give your candidates this table early in your hiring process to demonstrate the importance of each of the factors and what's needed to determine if a Win-Win Hiring outcome is likely.

This table came about in this formal way when one of my first candidates rejected a job offer from my client for another role for what seemed like very superficial reasons. In this case it was for a

A Win-Win Hiring Approach for Comparing Job Offers and Opportunities				
Decision Stage	Primary Criteria	New Opportunity	Current Position	Other Opportunities
Day One Criteria *The Offer Package*	Compensation			
	Location			
	Company Brand and Reputation			
	Job Title			
Year One Criteria *The Actual Work, Team, and Challenges*	KPOs and Work Mix			
	Chance to Make an Impact			
	Personal Interest in Work			
	Bigger Job or Lateral			
	Hiring Manager's Style			
	Quality of Team			
	Company Culture and Pace			
	Learning Opportunities			
	Work/Life Balance			
Beyond Year One *The Career Opportunity*	Long-term Growth Opportunity			
	Visibility and Mentors			
	Business Conditions			
	Leadership Team			
	Total Rewards			

Figure 14.1 Comparing Job Offers and Opportunities.
©2020 All Rights Reserved • performancebasedhiring.com
• info@performancebasedhiring.com

job with a better title, one that offered slightly more money and for a much shorter daily commute. I pressed the candidate, hoping I could save the deal. Everything turned around when he told me it was for a company in a slow-growth industry.

Given this critical piece of information, I told him he was making a long-term strategic career decision using short-term tactical information. This statement alone got his attention. I then pointed out the year one differences amounted to spending most of his time on maintenance-type activity and minor improvements versus implementing new automated assembly equipment and establishing a lean manufacturing process. I went on to say that making matters worse for him was that in a few years his career options would be limited since he was working on old technology. The next day he agreed to accept my client's offer and he thanked me nine months later after he received a big promotion.

I learned my lesson after this encounter: don't leave the critical career decision information gathering to chance. Instead of reacting to candidates who tell you they're not interested in your job for lack of knowledge or a series of short-term reasons, it's far better to proactively give them the information needed to make a correct long-term yes or no decision. While this won't eliminate all of their concerns, it will prevent the most important from becoming deal-breakers.

As described in the first paragraph in this chapter, the setup to this type of decision-making is made as soon as the prospect agrees to become a candidate for the role. The information needed to make an appropriate career decision approach is embedded in this table. That's why giving them the table up front sets the stage for everything that follows.

It turns out this information is useful for everyone (i.e., candidates and their advisors, recruiters, and hiring managers) to understand what's at stake for candidates when comparing opportunities and changing jobs. While all of the specific details shown in the table aren't necessary to make an accurate comparison, the segmented approach allows a candidate to compare different opportunities based on the offer package, the work itself, and the long-term career opportunity the job represents. The overall idea is that in the long run, career growth will have a far greater impact on compensation than getting a big initial bump just for changing jobs. Whether you're the recruiter or hiring manager, the information in the table is what you need to pull together and provide the candidate to demonstrate that your opening is in fact a career move, not a lateral transfer.

Avoid Job Hopping Syndrome

One aspect of the work history review covered in Chapter 9 on conducting the Performance-based Interview was to ask candidates why they changed jobs and if the purpose of the job change was realized. The point of this was to understand if their recent changes were mostly for short-term compensation reasons with little thought to the long-term career aspects of the job change. Frequently, good people do change jobs with the best intentions and things still don't work out as hoped. In some situations this can be used to your advantage if the person is on the fence about your open job.

What you'll discover is that most people believe they're changing jobs for career reasons, but in most cases this is not what actually occurs. The problem is that just about everyone overvalues what they'll be getting on the start date and accepts the vague promises about the future opportunity as quite realistic. Only the most diligent and truly career-minded candidates recognize that changing jobs is one of the most important life decisions they make. These are the people who make sure they fully understand what the work actually entails and have reasonable proof that if they're successful the future opportunities are promising.

It's important that your candidates hear this important message – even those who are not likely to get hired by your company. They'll thank you for it later on. But if an offer is possible, this long-term versus short-term message needs to be stressed, especially if the person's last one or two jobs didn't turn out as promised. I tell candidates in this situation that they can't afford another mistake and that more due diligence on their part is essential. The problem is that when this happens too often the person has wasted critical years standing in place without gaining much career progress. This is similar to the oft-repeated idea of getting the same one year of experience year after year.

Taking too many jobs for short-term reasons and ending in this type of endless rut is what I refer to as "Job Hopping Syndrome." I advise candidates in this situation that they must overemphasize the career opportunity at the expense of the compensation package in order to get their careers on a better trajectory.

This message is also something passive candidates need to hear if they've been coasting along for the past few years without much career progress to show for it. In some cases this is often all they need to understand to at least consider what you have to offer. When a candidate says to me, "I'm happy where I am," on the first call I typically respond with something equally meaningless like, "That's exactly why we should talk." This is a great conversation starter and one that can be used to get reluctant candidates to at least consider the idea that there is sometimes more risk in not changing jobs despite how happy they are.

■ TESTING OFFERS

Part of hiring the strongest talent is overcoming objections at every stage in the recruiting funnel. Many of these top-of-the-funnel concerns were covered in Chapter 13 on driving the Big Red Tour Bus. Others will come up once you've started interviewing candidates. It's important that all of these are fully addressed before an offer is extended. Otherwise, you'll lose too many good candidates for avoidable reasons. There is no issue when candidates opt out of consideration for a job with full knowledge it's not a worthy one, but too often candidates opt out for superficial reasons like, "I'm not looking for another job," or "I just took on another role." My counter to this is typically something like, "That's the best time to look – when you don't need to." That's why it's important to persist until the candidate has enough information to decide whether pursuing the opportunity is worthwhile.

While keeping strong candidates in the process is critical, just as important is that there should never be a surprise rejection when an offer is actually made. In fact, an offer should never be made until you're 100% sure it will be accepted. This minimizes the chance the person will shop your offer around or accept a counteroffer. Establishing the 30% nonmonetary career opportunity and formalizing it with the career decision matrix is part of achieving this goal. The other part involves testing every aspect of the offer before it's formalized in writing.

Assuming the person has indicated serious interest after the first round of in-depth interviews, testing could be a simple as, "When do you think you could start if we could put together an acceptable offer in a few weeks?" There are a number of other tests of interest described as follows that should also be asked, but this "start date" test question is a great way to find out how interested the candidate is in your job. If the person gives specific details about a start date, it's a sign the person is quite interested. If the person is vague or noncommittal, it's clear the person isn't yet all that serious about your job.

Use 1–10 Test of Interest to Uncover Concerns

Before you can overcome objections and test offers, you need to identify any unspoken concerns the candidate might have. A reluctance to move on to the next step in the interviewing process is an obvious clue that you have a problem. Unfortunately, by this time it might be too late to rectify it, but asking why is a good way to at least give it an attempt. A better way is to proactively find out any potential concerns before they become deal-breakers and use the next meeting to resolve them. The 1–10 test is a simple way to achieve this.

After the first meeting with someone whom the hiring manager considers a possible finalist, ask the person how your job ranks in comparison to other opportunities he or she is now considering on a 1–10 scale. Describe a 10 as a job the candidate clearly sees as superior to everything else being considered from a short- and long-term perspective. Describe an 8 or 9 as a job that is of serious interest and a 6 or 7 as a remote possibility. If you've done your sourcing and interviewing properly, the candidate will likely rank your opening somewhere in the 8 to 9 range. Then ask the person what he or she would need to know to make your opening one point better or the best among everything else being considered including a potential counteroffer.

With this 1–10 test you now know your chance of hiring the person and what you need to do to increase your odds. As long as the candidate is seriously interested, he or she will likely mention the need for more information about resources, more clarification about the role, the upside opportunity, the leadership team, the hiring manager's style, and the compensation and benefit package.

For example, one of my candidates for a senior engineering role wasn't sure the R&D budget would support the company's aggressive new product growth plans. Another person was concerned about the hiring manager's style since he was very low key. A third wanted to meet some other team members who had recently been promoted to see if this was a realistic option. In each of these cases we made sure the candidate got the information necessary to make a more accurate decision.

Regardless of the concern, using the 1–10 test of interest you also learn how active the person is from a job-hunting standpoint and what you need to do to fight off the competition and close the deal. Most often when your job is not number one on the list, it's likely the person is overvaluing the short-term convenience issues (e.g., commute, current frustrations, etc.) and the compensation package. This is when it's essential that you reframe your opportunity using the career decision table described earlier, prefaced by a statement like, "It's important not to make long-term strategic career decisions using short-term tactical information."

Closing, Testing, and Negotiating Offers

If a candidate says, "I have to think about it," after you've made an offer, assume you've made the offer too soon. While we want all candidates to seriously consider all aspects of an offer before it's extended, it's better to delay the actual offer until all of the facts are on the table. Just as important is to be the last company to make an offer to ensure yours isn't used as leverage to negotiate something better elsewhere. Assuming you've done everything right, an appropriate response from a candidate after an offer is extended should be something like, "Yes, this is just what we discussed, and I will accept it on these terms. Let me review the details just to make sure everything is covered and if so, I'll sign it in the morning."

Getting this type of low-key and affirmative response is unlikely unless you've tested every aspect of the offer ahead of time and gotten verbal agreement that the terms are acceptable. The following techniques can help you get there.

Closing Upon a Concern

Closing upon a concern is an important closing test you can use to assess the validity of any issue raised. For example, if the candidate is concerned that the resources available might be insufficient, say something like, "If we can address this to your satisfaction, would you be willing to become a finalist for this role?" If the candidate won't agree to this, you can assume the concern is a smokescreen for a bigger problem. Of course if the person agrees to this condition, you need to address the issue to his or her satisfaction, or the person will opt out.

For one mid-management spot I asked the candidate if he'd be open to accept the job based on the discussions he had at the time, including the compensation package. He said yes, but he was concerned the title wasn't big enough. I then asked him if he'd be willing to meet the hiring manger again for a lunch meeting if they could make the title more appropriate. He wouldn't commit to this next step. This was a clear indication something else was the problem, not the title. After pushing it a bit, it became clear he just wanted an offer to use for negotiating better terms on another job he was considering.

Sometimes minor concerns can become deal-breakers when they're not uncovered and addressed ahead of time. This is especially true if they become last minute surprises. This happens often when these issues relate to components of the benefits package. For example, when changing jobs people often have to give up a week or two of a three- to four-week earned vacation benefit for the standard two weeks. Anticipating problems like this and getting agreement ahead of time that the person will accept an offer if this extra vacation is provided is a good way to prevent the negative surprise during the closing process. These and related issues can be uncovered before an offer package is presented by asking, "Are there any other issues we need to consider before we go ahead with putting a formal offer package together?"

A few years ago this happened on a director of HR search we were conducting when the candidate said she couldn't even verbally accept an offer without reading all of the fine print in the offer package first. We then gave her the unsigned offer letter without any of the detailed compensation information to review. She was mostly concerned about the insurance plans and when her family would be fully covered. A few minor adjustments were made, and the candidate then said she was now ready to accept an offer based on all of the terms agreed upon.

Use a Secondary Close to Test Seriousness

You don't always need to ask if the person will accept your offer directly. A secondary close is a good indirect way to determine this. Saying something like, "If we can get the offer presented later in the week, when do you think you could start?" will accomplish the same thing. If the candidate can give you a reasonable start date and specific details about how they will turn in their resignation letter at their current job, you can feel comfortable the person is seriously interested in your job. Be very concerned after all of this time has been spent on multiple interviews and conversations if the response is vague or noncommittal. This is a clear sign the person has never seriously considered your opportunity.

If you've been through the job changing process more than a few times with different candidates, you know that those who are interested in your role start mentally going through the logistics and timing of what it would take to change jobs. This includes figuring out how they're going to finish up projects or if they'll get their promised bonus if they leave too soon. The simple "When can you start?" question reveals this inner thinking; or worse, the lack of it.

Use a Counterproposal to Get 100% Commitment

Here's the recruiting problem once you make an offer formal: candidates stop telling you what they're thinking about and whether they'll accept it or not. This is when the recruiting rule "Stay the buyer throughout the process!" becomes even more important to follow. By delaying the actual formal offer as long as possible, you'll still be able to know what the candidate is thinking regarding accepting your offer and give yourself another chance to address any potential issues.

Despite the fact that you've done everything as described in this chapter, it won't be enough. You'll still have many candidates call you a day or two before they're to receive your offer and complain for some reason that it's not fair. Normally this is about the compensation package they've already verbally agreed to accept, but it could be anything. Despite what it is, you have to deal with it professionally and assertively.

First, recognize that a concern raised at the last moment could turn into a positive if handled properly. A situation like this provides another opportunity to minimize the chance the person will get and accept a counteroffer or accept a competing offer from another company. It starts by understanding that a candidate's negative feeling about your job is comparable to buyer's remorse. This is the uncomfortable reaction buyers get after purchasing something thinking they either shouldn't have bought it in the first place, or they paid too much for it. When it comes to accepting a job offer it's better when buyer's remorse comes before the offer is made rather than afterwards. By then it's too late to do much about it.

It's common for a candidate to experience buyer's remorse when accepting any job that's filled with a lot of unknowns. It could be they're concerned they're not making the right decision, the job might not be the best, the hiring manager might not be as good a leader as hoped, or the company has a problem given something that just showed up in the news. Despite the cause, this uncomfortable feeling becomes even more pronounced when it's coupled with the emotional stress involved with resigning from a job. Under these circumstances candidates can often be seduced into accepting a counteroffer when it's combined with some compensation increase. While accepting a counteroffer may provide some immediate stress relief, it's often short-lived when the candidate realizes months later that little has changed. But for the outside company making the offer, this "I told you so" insight is too late to do much good. That's why having buyer's remorse occur before your official offer is made, and before the candidate resigns, gives you time to still do something about it.

When the candidate's concern is about the size of the compensation package, I just ask them if they're rejecting the offer or if they just don't think it's fair. If it's not an outright rejection, the situation can typically be resolved with a bit of negotiating. In this situation, start with a review of all of the preceding conversations and offer tests, especially the one about asking if the person really wants the job for something other than the money. Go through this test again and get the person's agreement that the job represents the best career opportunity among everything else the person is considering, including a possible counteroffer. Then ask if the financial terms could be improved somewhat, would the person accept the new offer.

But a yes is not enough in this case; an unconditional yes is required.

You need to tell the candidate that in order for you to attempt to get the offer increased, you must have the person's 100% commitment to accept it under the revised terms. Without this, no one will be willing to fight for an increase. Don't force the person to agree to this provision on the spot. It's an important decision and you want to give the person time to think it over. This could be a few hours or until the next morning. In most cases the person will agree to move forward based on this new condition. Push this a bit and make sure the candidate will formally agree to the "no counteroffer" discussion and will sign your offer letter right away if the compensation can be increased to the level desired.

A lot of recruiters push back on this negotiating idea, saying that once an offer is set in stone the compensation can't be changed. Others don't like it since they believe it's too aggressive. I push back to the first group by saying since the official offer hasn't been made, the compensation hasn't been solidified yet. To both groups I say that the test compensation should be a little bit lower than what you think is appropriate. This way you have some wiggle room if needed. More important, though, is to recognize that a great deal of time has been spent up to this point to ensure the right person has been found and offered a job that represents the best career possible given everything else being considered. An inability to close this offer at this late stage means every preceding effort has been wasted and the person is making a career mistake by accepting any other offer. If you're convinced a Win-Win Hiring outcome is likely, then you have to persevere to make sure your offer is accepted.

While this assertive closing approach won't be needed every time, it's important that all candidates recognize the primary reason for accepting any job offer is the career opportunity it represents. Sometimes extra energy is necessary to overcome a candidate's reluctance to proceed or to prevent them from taking what appears to be the safer decision based on some short-term or promised benefit. This is when recruiters and hiring managers need to exert some pressure to push the process across the finish line.

■ SUMMARY

Hiring the best people, especially passive candidates, requires much more than an accurate interview. It's also much more than reactively moving into a hyper-sales mode to convince a strong person of the merits of your job opening. Done properly, it's an end-to-end process starting with a clear understanding of real job needs and the use of an in-depth interview that's been integrated with a professional recruiting process that also maps to the decision-making process of top professionals.

By testing each aspect of the offer before making it formally, you're in a position to ensure the candidate has all of the information needed to fully evaluate your opportunity in comparison to everything else being considered. While you want candidates to think about your offer, you'll know exactly what the person is thinking if you don't rush to make it. Once you make a formal offer, candidates are less open. Just as important is being the last company to make a formal offer. This has obvious advantages, including increasing the likelihood your offer will be accepted by getting a commitment that it will be.

Chapter 15

Leveraging HR Technology to Implement Performance-based Hiring

In the introduction to this book the point was made that many hiring problems are strategic in origin, using a surplus of talent strategy to screen out unqualified candidates rather than spending more time on attracting stronger talent. By spending more time with fewer prequalified prospects, it's possible to improve quality of hire efficiently, quickly, and at less cost. This chapter demonstrates how to leverage existing HR technology using a Win-Win Hiring focus. The technologies mentioned in the following examples are worth considering as part of implementing Performance-based Hiring but are recommendations only, not specific endorsements.

■ USING THE TRICKLE-UP APPROACH TO VALIDATE THE IMPACT

Getting a company to overhaul its entire hiring process and implement Performance-based Hiring is a daunting task.

Don't even try. It won't work.

On the other hand, having one recruiter and one hiring manager complete just one search assignment using the techniques described in this book is the best way to get started. After two or three hiring assignments completed this way, you'll have a sense of what works best for you and what you need to do to gain acceptance across a broader group of hiring managers. Based on our experience in over one hundred implementations the biggest obstacle to get even one hiring manager to try it out the first time happens during the intake meeting. This is when you declare that a list of skills, experiences, and generic competencies is not a job description, it's a person description. Once you get the hiring manager to agree to prepare a performance profile, you're well on your way towards attracting stronger talent, increasing interviewing accuracy, and improving your ability to negotiate offers based more on the career opportunity the role represents, not the size of the compensation package.

Despite the commonsense logic of defining work as a series of performance objectives, there's a lot of historical inertia causing it to be an uphill battle. This story from a very experienced recruiter who went to our live training course in 2020 and who has crossed the chasm will help you understand the importance of persevering.

I have to admit that before this class I was skeptical about how this process could be so much better than what I was currently doing. It was difficult at first to retool my 20-some years of recruiting to think a different way. The performance profile I believe is the real heart of the process. It also requires a lot of work to get onboard mentally, and to be able to sell the hiring manager on why we were taking such a different approach to an intake session. Once we jump this hurdle, the real validation for the hiring manager is the comparison of the original posting and the results of the retooled job description. Gaining this new knowledge sets up the foundation for the posting. Taking key words important to the position, the and hiring manager targeted the types of applicants I would need to attract.

Where the real results began to become apparent, from the recruiting perspective, was the detail I gathered about what the real job is about, not the static HR template of essential duties. Tying together the key performance objectives of the position and chatting with the high-level referrals I received let me know I was on the right track.

I think of recruiters as generalists. We know lots about many different fields but getting to the heart of the role allows for a better fact-focused interview with candidates. We gain respect by actually understanding what they do and are able to build a conversation around what we need and what they desire in a long-term position. This is far more productive than speaking in bullet points.

Successfully implementing Performance-based Hiring and achieving consistent Win-Win Hiring outcomes requires the proper blending of high tech with high touch. Following are some examples of how this has been and can be achieved.

■ USE SEEKOUT TO BUILD A TALENT PIPELINE OF OUTSTANDING DIVERSE TALENT

Throughout this book I've contended that a prerequisite to achieving consistent Win-Win Hiring outcomes was the need to fill the talent pipeline with only semifinalists. Here's a quick summary of how this is done:

1. Define first year job success as one or two major performance objectives and four or five key subtasks.

2. Develop an employee value proposition – the EVP – that captures the ideal candidate's intrinsic motivators.

3. Identify 20–30 likely prospects who have been recognized for doing outstanding work in the required field AND who would also see the role as a likely good career move.

4. Do whatever's necessary via a series of compelling, customized, and career-focused messages to engage with at least half of these people.

5. Persistence is critical when first engaging with these people. It's important not to take "No" for an answer until it's clear the role doesn't represent a good career move. If the role is not a worthy move, get a few referrals of outstanding prospects by searching on their LinkedIn connections.

6. Move the process forward by getting the candidate and the hiring manager to agree to an exploratory phone call to determine if there's serious interest on both sides.

7. Rethink all of the above if after two or three exploratory calls with different prospects either the candidate or the hiring manager doesn't want to proceed. This is a strong indicator of a problem with how the role was defined or with the sourcing, assessment, or recruiting process. Don't continue to send out more candidates in this situation; instead, fix the problem.

It turns out SeekOut[1] does much of the heavy lifting involved in making this happen. That's why it's an extraordinary high-tech tool for managing a high-touch process. For one thing, it offers multiple ways to find just about any resume and job profile for every possible job imaginable. In combination with their AI and diversity filters and the "clever" Boolean and achiever terms described in

[1]https://seekout.com.

the sourcing chapter, it's relatively simple to build a target pool of 20–30 likely prospects within a few hours. Their CRM campaign automates the outreach, so within a day or two recruiters should be on the phone with potential candidates. By leveraging SeekOut this way, you'll be setting up exploratory calls for the hiring manager within one week after opening the search project.

For example, this past year one of SeekOut's clients – a high-tech data analytics company with a commitment to building a diverse workforce – wanted to hire an outstanding woman for a senior tech leadership role. Within a week of using SeekOut's diversity search capability, hundreds of previously hidden candidates were identified for this role. A few weeks later a highly qualified female senior engineer leader was hired.

In another situation, for a case study project for one of our LA-based clients, we used SeekOut to find a few high-potential mid-level software developers. In this case we combined a number of achiever terms like intern, award, honor, mentor, and teach to find some people who only had a few years of experience but who were already doing more senior-level work. This is a great way to spot some very strong candidates who would also likely see the role as great career move.

■ HIRETUAL.COM OFFERS A UNIQUE AI APPROACH FOR SOURCING THE HARD TO FIND

Hiretual's enterprise software, in my opinion, is an essential tool every recruiter who handles critical technical and management searches must have. Hiretual is a robust AI-powered sourcing platform that rapidly expands talent pools beyond LinkedIn to include other open web platforms your candidates network on and is easily linked to most applicant tracking systems (ATS) for internal sourcing and candidate rediscovery. Even better, it can be turbocharged when the clever Boolean and high-touch recruiting techniques described in Chapter 12 are incorporated.

For example, we recently helped a UK-based company find a director of data analytics. To begin the process we used Hiretual's built-in filters in combination with our Achiever terms (i.e., honor OR award OR prize OR patent OR speaker OR whitepaper) and were presented with a dozen interesting candidates. We selected three who looked very strong for Hiretual to "clone" using their AI search tool and found three others, giving us a total of six likely semifinalists to begin our outreach program. Since we had previously integrated our email with Hiretual and uploaded a batch of templates, we were able to reach out to the candidates a few hours after preparing the performance profile. Since Hiretual gives instant access to the social media sites the prospects are on, we were able to connect with two who were on LinkedIn and one on Facebook. We also sent text messages to five of the six prospects since their cell phone numbers were also listed.

Of course, we still need to talk to these prospects and determine if the role represents a worthy career move, and if not, get a referrals. But using Hiretual gives us a great head start.

■ EIGHTFOLD TAKES A COMPREHENSIVE AI-APPROACH FOR MATCHING PEOPLE WITH OPPORTUNITIES BASED ON POTENTIAL

While defining work as a series of performance objectives is essential for all important staff and management positions, this is not often possible when hiring, promoting, or redeploying talent at scale. In this case, Eightfold[2] offers a unique solution to identify best-fit candidates who possess the required skills, can quickly learn the missing skills, and have the potential for successfully handling the job. Their AI-powered Talent Intelligence Platform has learned from over a billion profiles, over a million skills, and over a million titles, allowing Eightfold's algorithms to identify personalized career paths for every individual.

For example, one situation the company shared with me was hiring military veterans who did not initially appear to be the best fit for corporate sales roles since they lacked the traditional sales experience. However, it turned out that a better predictor of sales success was using Eightfold to consider candidates who have highly developed adjacent skills like leadership, task management, and the ability to learn. Using this approach, it was possible not only to widen the talent tool but also better predict on-the-job success.

Presenting a complete and diverse pool of talent to interview that includes employees, contractors, and external candidates

[2]https://eightfold.ai.

allows hiring managers to make better hiring decisions. More important, these candidates are highly likely to accept these offers, since the jobs will be better matched to their actual capabilities and potential to succeed. All of these conditions are essential in order to achieve positive Win-Win Hiring outcomes. What's most exciting is that Eightfold's AI-powered Talent Intelligence Platform allows companies to accomplish this at scale for all types of roles.

■ PHENOM CONVERTS WORKFORCE PLANNING INTO A STRATEGY ASSET

Many recruiters complain they don't have enough time to do anything but post a job since hiring managers are always in a hurry to get their jobs filled once the requisition has been formally approved. This seems a bit reactive since in most cases these jobs were approved on a preliminary basis as part of the company's annual budgeting process. This is the value of workforce planning.[3] Knowing months ahead of time based on sales forecasts and financial projections allows you to start building deep talent pools long before these people are going to be hired. With just a rough estimate of the types of jobs that need to be filled by location, it's possible to conduct the supply versus demand analysis described in Chapter 12 on sourcing to determine the best means to identify the people needed to fill these roles. It's important to note that for any high-demand positions you'll need to start months earlier to be able to hire these people within 30 days after the job requisition has been formally approved.

In many ways this workforce planning process is equivalent to just-in-time inventory management. The idea behind this is to have the right amount of material needed to meet production forecasts exactly when it's needed but never later. When it comes to hiring, this is accomplished using a good workforce plan, building a deep network of strong talent and referrals, and nurturing it with a robust CRM system built into your ATS. With this in place it's possible to start presenting potential semifinalist to the hiring manager for preliminary review within a few days of getting the requisition formally approved.

[3]"Practicing Workforce Planning." Society of Human Resource Managers, SHRM, www.shrm.org/resourcesandtools/tools-and-samples/toolkits/pages/practicingworkforceplanning.aspx.

Phenom[4] seems to do a great job of managing the workforce planning process, building the appropriate talent pools, and managing the nurturing process. Phenom is a technology that sits on top of the ATS providing companies a better means to manage their hiring needs, including forecasting and real time analytics. Especially important are their tools for managing the entire recruiting funnel, including source of candidate and conversion rates at each step.

Another important Phenom feature is their chatbot. Utilizing a sophisticated and programmable decision-tree using AI that incorporates self-learning and manual feedback loops, candidates can find open jobs that best meet their career needs rather than searching an endless list of irrelevant jobs. This alone reduces the number of unqualified people applying to jobs. The design is equivalent to a hub-and-spoke job board, allowing companies to push candidates to a group of related jobs, while the backend system finds the most appropriate roles for candidates.

■ AI FOR SCREENING HAS A POWERFUL TOOL WITH PYMETRICS.AI

While this book is largely written for improving hiring results when the demand for talent is far greater than the supply, many of the principles can be applied to high-volume needs. The most important is to write job postings that are compelling and customized by role in some story-like fashion. Just as important, these postings must be easy to find. With this list of people who have applied, it's still imperative that the list be prioritized in some way that brings the most suitable candidates to the top of list. Many new technologies make this claim, but it seems like pymetrics.ai[5] has done a remarkable job on a number of fronts.

By conducting a detailed job analysis and evaluating top performers doing the same job, it's possible to discover the common attributes, largely soft skills, that drive their success. Using this information it's then possible to screen candidates on the same factors to predict their subsequent performance. One example pymetrics shared with me was using their approach for a major U.S.-based debt collection agency to identify candidates for their account representative role. The role is stressful, resulting in very high

---

[4]https://www.phenom.com.
[5]https://www.pymetrics.ai.

rates of turnover. By benchmarking 144 of the company's strongest employees for performance and cultural fit, pymetrics developed a screening tool for job candidates. The results were quite impressive. After six months on the job, candidates who ranked "highly recommended" by pymetrics had a median collection rate that was 53% higher than those ranked "recommended." For candidates who were hired despite a pymetrics "not recommended" score, the differences were even more dramatic, with significantly lower collection metrics, and they tended to stay in the role for less than half the time of the "highly recommended" group.

■ CREATING AN INTERNAL MOBILITY PLATFORM USING SMARTRECRUITERS

SmartRecruiters[6] is a user-friendly and enterprise-capable ATS helping companies manage their entire front-end hiring process, including improving post-hire success. One example with one of their clients – one of the largest employers in the financial services sector – clearly demonstrates this full-cycle capability. The company partnered with SmartRecruiters to address what they saw as two critical retention challenges. The first was reducing their high attrition rate for lower-level positions, including call center staff and retail bankers. The second challenge was improving the overall job engagement, satisfaction, and retention rate for highly skilled technical staff and experienced managers. Given the company's brand and market leadership, these more senior people were consistently targeted by both competitors and external recruiters alike.

While the problems were complex, SmartRecruiters created a robust internal job site that solved both problems simultaneously. Now, as new jobs are opened, the system automatically searches for current company employees who would be likely strong candidates who are then proactively contacted to determine their interest. It's important to note that before implementing this program the company got the full support of their managers in order to ensure companywide adoption.

Obviously, there is a lot of behind-the-scenes technology involved in developing this matching process, but by proactively reaching out to current employees the company has taken internal mobility to a true Win-Win Hiring level. The results are impressive:

[6]https://www.smartrecruiters.com.

within 90 days the company doubled their internal moves, cut turn-over rates in half for high volume hires, increased employee referrals by about 30%, and significantly increased new employee job satisfaction during the first year. This is a great example of using advanced HR technology at scale to address critical hiring challenges from a very personal and high-touch perspective.

■ USING GREENHOUSE TO MAXIMIZE QUALITY OF HIRE

Pollen – a U.K.-based company – is a firm adherent of the Performance-based Hiring process and is now implementing it using their Greenhouse[7] applicant tracking system to effectively manage it at every step. While other ATSs have similar capabilities, we've had more success with Greenhouse due to its flexibility in scheduling interviews and managing interview guides and talent scorecards. For Pollen we've built a series of performance profile templates by function that can be modified based on the complexity of the role. The company is using the talent scorecard to predict Quality of Hire during the assessment, comparing who should be hired based on these rankings and then reevaluating candidates using the same scorecard every 90 days to compare predicted to actual performance. This is possible since the pre-hire assessment is based on actual job needs. The variances highlight the areas that need to be improved either in how the job was initially defined or the specific factors where the assessment was flat wrong. In most cases these relate to intrinsic motivation to do the actual job in the actual environment and whether the new employee and hiring manager's working styles mesh.

We are now working with Greenhouse to develop better approaches to predict quality of hire more accurately and track it more efficiently post-hire. The idea is to embed feedback process control at every stage in the pre-hire funnel to ensure the candidates being considered are likely semifinalists, and if hired, will raise the talent bar.

[7]https://www.greenhouse.io.

■ CONDUCT A REFERENCE CHECK BEFORE MAKING AN OFFER USING CHECKSTER

While I'm not sure this is always true for everyone else, I've never had a problem getting the names of former hiring managers who would fully endorse a candidate and provide an honest reference. In fact, during the first in-depth interview I ask candidates if they have a few hiring managers they could use as references who would also validate the information they're providing regarding their accomplishments. When they balk at this, I get concerned that everything they're saying might be suspect.

A thorough reference check should include conversations with hiring managers, peers, and subordinates. The following list highlights a few of the steps involved. You'll see a somewhat cynical or forensic theme in this approach. Part of this is the need to confirm the candidate's actual accomplishments and how the fit factors will impact the person's performance if hired.

Step 1: Understand the relationship between the candidate and the person giving the reference, the length of time the two worked together, some of the projects they collaborated on, and the role each person played.

Step 2: Validate the accomplishments the person described during the interview with a focus on the pace, the team involved, and the person's role on these teams. Find out how the person's strengths impacted their work with the teams and if the person was recognized in some formal way for this, like being assigned to handle some difficult problems or influencing others.

Step 3: Ask if the reference would recommend the person to be rehired and under what circumstances. Flip this around and find out under what conditions would they not recommend the person to be rehired. This process will reveal strengths and weakness and many of the fit factors.

Step 4: With subordinates, ask if they would want to work with the person again and why. Ask under what circumstances they would not want to work with the person again.

Step 5: Ask the reference how they would rank the person on a
1–10 scale, with 10 being outstanding. If the person says a 9
or 10, ask for examples of where this type of ranking was justified. The detail provided will validate the quality of the
person giving the reference. Most people will rank the person a 7 or an 8. In these cases, ask what the person would
need to do or improve in order to be ranked one point
higher. This will also reveal some weaknesses.

Although this isn't the complete reference checking process, it
will provide a great deal of insight into the strengths and weaknesses of the candidate and how the fit factors impacted these.

While reference checking tends to be a very personal process,
Checkster[8] automates this process by having candidates submit a
list of people they've worked with in the past who are willing to rank
the person on a series of attributes that best predict fit and performance. The anonymized collective results are then used to help
companies make more informed hiring decisions. This is powerful
information that can increase the likelihood of a positive Win-Win
Hiring outcome especially if the information is used to development
customized onboarding and development programs for the new hire.

■ USE ONBOARDING TO START DELIVERING ON THE PROMISE

One way to increase the likelihood of a Win-Win Hiring outcome
is to review, clarify, and prioritize the performance objectives in
the performance profile within a few days after the person starts
on the job. During the interviewing process these performance
objectives should have been discussed in enough detail for the
candidate to fully understand real job needs and justify accepting
the offer based on the career opportunity the position represents.
There should be no surprises during the onboarding review as a
result. During the review session the hiring manager should explain
how he or she will support the new hire to address any training
requirements involved or fill in the development gaps while the
new hire comes up to speed.

The new hire's performance should be tracked and discussed
regularly and formally for the first few months. Extra diligence and

support during this period are especially important if the person is struggling at all. On a quarterly basis the new hire should be reevaluated on all of the factors on the combined Quality of Hire Talent Scorecard used before the person was made an offer. Any major differences should be highlighted. On one level these will help identify areas where your interviewing process can be improved. On a personal level, the variances might help you spot development areas to help the new hire improve his or her performance if needed. Most often these variances relate to lack of clarity around the job when the person was initially hired, or the job requirements were changed post-hire. The other variances relate to the fit factors, including (but certainly not limited to) how well the new hire's and the hiring manager's styles mesh. The importance of getting the "managerial fit" factor right was covered in depth in Chapter 10 on making the assessment.

Clarifying expectations during the onboarding period is the first step in delivering on the Win-Win Hiring promise. Without this focus built into the process from the beginning, it's hard to achieve it reactively after the person is hired. If it's been short-circuited at all, it's important that the hiring manager and the candidate review the key performance objectives in detail while negotiating the offer. This is often the tipping point for a candidate who's on the fence about accepting an offer, especially when the role presents the best opportunity among other jobs being considered. Just as important, the hiring manager might decide to modify the job a bit, up or down, to make the fit even better.

■ FEEDBACK PROCESS CONTROL WITH OUTMATCH.COM

Achieving a Win-Win Hiring outcome requires ongoing insight into the hiring manager's satisfaction with the new hire and the new employee's satisfaction with the job. Outmatch.com[9] provides a good approach for tracking this using the Net Promoter Score[10] approach. By asking employees a series of questions about their overall satisfaction with the job on a regular basis post-hire, companies are able to pinpoint areas where some type of intervention might be necessary. As important is to get hiring managers to assess

[9]https://outmatch.com.
[10]https://www.netpromotersystem.com/about/measuring-your-net-promoter-score/.

their new hires the same way, asking about their performance and if they would rehire the person and why or why not.

While this feedback is essential for improving the employee's ongoing performance, it's also invaluable for improving the overall effectiveness of the company's entire interview and selection process. By identifying the factors that were improperly evaluated during the assessment, it's possible to modify the job analysis and interview guides to prevent future hiring problems. This can only be effective, though, when post-hire performance is tightly integrated with the ongoing pre-hire process. Otherwise any changes made are too late to have much impact or even to know if they're effective.

One example Outmatch uses to describe the value of its ability to improve job satisfaction and quality of hire relates to an ongoing project with a large U.S. retail organization with over 28,000 employees. Prior to having this feedback loop in place, newly hired associates just left the organization. With it, though, they're now able to intervene quickly to minimize involuntary turnover. As a result of this, turnover was reduced significantly in the first year. More important is that by knowing the causes of potential employee dissatisfaction the company modified their selection process to minimize the most common of these post-hire problems. This is how a reliable feedback loop like this can become a great way to improve the selection process and achieve more Win-Win Hiring outcomes.

■ CREATE A WIN-WIN HIRING CULTURE

While some remarkable tools and technologies are now available to find outstanding diverse talent, they will be ineffective if the recruiter who first connects with these candidates doesn't know the job and can't position it as a career move. From what I've seen, effectively balancing this intersection of high tech and high touch is the tipping point for raising the talent bar and building a diverse workforce. It turns out creating a Win-Win Hiring culture starts one job at a time during the intake meeting by asking the hiring manager this question: "What does the person need to do to be considered highly successful in this role on their first-year anniversary date?" That's all you need to do to get started, but sometimes it's the biggest first step you need to take.

Chapter

16

Use Performance-based Hiring to Create a Win-Win Hiring Culture

In the past 25 years since the first edition of Hire with Your Head was written, many changes have been made in the hiring process and billions of dollars have been invested in making them. However, other than reducing time-to-fill, the needle hasn't moved much when it comes to improving Quality of Hire, decreasing first year turnover, increasing job satisfaction, or lowering cost per hire. In fact, one could argue that emphasizing time-to-fill exacerbated these problems by rewarding short-term thinking and superficial decision-making when just the opposite was needed. By spending more time with fewer people, as long as they're the right people, all of these problems can be minimized or avoided altogether. Describing how this can be done was and is the purpose of this book.

I've called the process for accomplishing this Performance-based Hiring, but what it's called matters less than what it does: achieves consistent Win-Win Hiring outcomes for all levels of jobs in all types of companies. The paradigm-shifting idea of not declaring hiring success until the first-year anniversary date rather than the start date is the game-changer behind this. With this long-term hiring objective in mind, designing a hiring process to achieve it requires a reevaluation of every step involved in order to determine whether it enables or prevents a positive outcome.

Practically speaking, companies typically have three big hiring needs. One is to fill rank-and-file jobs with good people quickly at a reasonable cost with the fewest mistakes possible. Another is filling important staff and mid-management positions with strong and diverse talent who have significant upside potential. The other is filling critical technical and senior-level roles with absolutely the best people possible. Performance-based Hiring was designed primarily to meet the second of these two critical hiring requirements, but many of the ideas presented can help improve all high-volume needs, including entry-level and university hiring requirements. One big problem that should be avoided at all costs is using a high-volume high-tech process to fill important positions where those hired will directly impact a company's performance.

Regardless of the position, delivering on the Win-Win Hiring promise should not be compromised.

■ DELIVER ON THE WIN-WIN HIRING PROMISE

Doing the wrong things more efficiently never seemed like a good idea to me. That's why I contend that nothing much has changed since I had the image in Figure 16.1 drawn in 1998 that was first mentioned in the introduction to this book. The fundamental reason for this lack is using a process designed for high-volume hiring and trying to force-fit it to a process that requires more customization and more high touch.

By redesigning the hiring process to focus as much on first-year performance and job satisfaction as well as filling these roles with the strongest talent available, it is possible to deliver on the Win-Win Hiring promise and create a company culture that sustains it. That's why, despite the earlier misgivings, I believe we're now at a tipping point where significant change is achievable in terms of improving Quality of Hire, raising the talent bar, increasing job

Figure 16.1   Hiring circa 1998.

satisfaction and on-the-job performance, and in the process dramatically reducing turnover.

The Performance-based Future of Hiring

I asked the illustrator who drew the hiring bucket of inefficiency in 1998 if he could create a new vision for hiring based on this Win-Win Hiring objective. He came up with the graphic in Figure 16.2. As you can see, getting to this destination requires a different road, a different map, and a different vehicle guided with some type of GPS course-correcting device. This book covered all of the details. Here are some of the big directional themes.

Create a Win-Win Hiring Culture

Hiring needs to be considered a long-term investment, not a short-term expense.

Figure 16.2   Win-Win Hiring circa 2021 and Beyond.

Hiring for the start date is a transactional process driven by productivity and cost metrics. The cost for this type of hiring process is budgeted in the company's annual operating plan. What's interesting is that this budget ignores the hidden cost of bad hiring decisions. A good estimate of this is the percent of new hires who underperform or leave in the first year times the total increase in annual payroll for these people. For example, the annual fully burdened payroll expense for 100 new professional staff hires is about $15 million. This is a waste of $3 million if 20% of these people either leave the first year or fall short of expectations.

What's surprising is that most companies ignore this unbudgeted loss, focusing instead on the cost of hiring these people, not if these people are being hired properly. By thinking of hiring as a long-term investment in people and justifying it on a ROI basis, these mistakes can be cut dramatically. This is a huge and recurring annual unbudgeted expense. Much of it can be eliminated by getting each hiring manager to recognize that great hiring is not only equivalent to every other important performance objective he or she has but is a prerequisite for achieving them.

Although unconventional, you might want to start the creation of Win-Win Hiring culture by giving every one of your new hires a guarantee that they will be fully satisfied with the job on their first-year anniversary date. But to get this guarantee the person has to agree to describe in detail why the job being offered is the best career move among competing opportunities before being made an offer. Go further with this idea by making your hiring managers responsible for getting the candidate the information needed to make the comparison with full transparency. Then make the hiring manager and new hire both responsible for doing what they said they'd do once the person is on board.

As wild as this guarantee idea sounds, surprisingly, this happens all of the time when a person who has worked with the hiring manager before is hired for a new role. While this guarantee might not be stated, it's certainly implied. There is no reason this same information-sharing process used to get a hiring manager and new hire who know each to take shared responsibility for making the one-year guarantee can't be applied when they don't know each other. Performance-based Hiring is that process. And using it for every job and at every step in the process pre- and post-hire will be the basis for creating a self-sustaining Win-Win Hiring culture.

■ BUILDING A WIN-WIN HIRING CULTURE STARTS WITH THE RIGHT TALENT STRATEGY

Simply put, you can't use a hiring process built under the assumption that there's a surplus of talent strategy when the assumption is flat wrong. I've been around longer than 95% of the people reading this book, and ever since I entered the workforce in the late '60s, there has always been a scarcity of outstanding and diverse people who can raise the talent bar. In these situations you can't hope someone applies. Instead you have to proactively identify and attract these people to consider your openings using some type of high-touch nurturing process. Despite this commonsense idea, for most positions companies continue to use processes designed to weed out the weak, assuming that by casting a bigger net and expanding the talent pool a few good people will be caught. This will never happen when boring job postings represent your company's idea of a great and compelling career move.

Many HR and talent leaders take exception to this "attract in" idea using legal compliance, privacy, cost, effort, insufficient resources, or lack of executive sponsorship as the reason why little progress has been made. On the other hand, billions have been spent on new applicant tracking systems, interview training, competency models, and AI-infused HR tech with scant evidence to justify the enormous investment. Yet when one looks at the advances made in global manufacturing, distribution, and logistics; and enterprise-wide software development; HR processes, systems, and procedures seem archaic and disjointed in comparison.

Building an outstanding and diverse workforce starts with the right talent strategy, not with making excuses about why it can't be done. In this case, it's attracting the best, not weeding out the weak. That's what the Performance-based Hiring process described in this book has been designed to accomplish.

Hiring as an Integrated System, Not a Sequence of Separate Steps

While duct tape has thousands of uses, integrating a bunch of interdependent processes is not one of them even if you call it an API. While an API does link data interactions between different applications, it doesn't mean the individual applications were designed to collect the proper information to be transferred. For example, if the best candidates don't apply to a job posting it doesn't really matter if those who do apply are rank-ordered properly even if the most sophisticated AI has done the ranking. Just as bad is asking an outstanding person a bunch of behavioral questions when the interviewer can't tell the person anything relevant about the job. Without the job analysis it's not even possible to make an accurate assessment about the candidate's ability and motivation to do the actual work despite having the proper skill set, all of the right competencies, and a perfect personality style just as described in the job description.

Yet these types of situations happen frequently whenever individual steps in a business process are optimized rather than optimizing the entire business process. Successfully managing this type of system-level balancing act is not unusual. In fact, it's an everyday activity for all other business functions. For example, consider the challenges faced by product managers who are constantly making tradeoffs when developing the product specifications given shifting customer needs, tight budgets, changing business conditions, new technologies, and moving delivery schedules. Imagine what would happen to the product cost and its success if the design team insisted on including some feature the customer didn't want or the operations group couldn't build. Systemic problems like these are caused by suboptimization, and when it comes to hiring processes the damage it causes are costly and most often unrepairable. If your hiring managers need to see too many average people to make one decent hire, you're experiencing some of the damage. But it's far worse after the person is hired or the best one wasn't even seen.

These and similar problems can be minimized by applying system-level design thinking to the entire hiring process. When making the decision to add some step in the process or to balance the competing needs of different users, it's important to focus on the primary customer as the ultimate decider. In most cases this will be an outstanding person, whether active or passive, who will ask lots of questions about the job, who is not in a hurry to change jobs, and who will either get a counteroffer or a better one compensation-wise elsewhere. All of this detailed analysis is required in order to build a hiring process designed to achieve consistent Win-Win Hiring outcomes and raise the talent bar. Performance-based Hiring has been designed to accomplish this objective.

Benchmarking Best Practices

It's important to note that all of the techniques comprising the Performance-based Hiring process described in this book are regularly used to find, interview, and hire someone who is known to the hiring manager or when promoting someone internally. In these cases the person's subsequent performance is highly predictable and the likelihood of achieving a positive Win-Win Hiring outcome is expected. Not achieving it is the big surprise. Similar results are possible by applying these same basic principles for external hires with a few benchmarking adjustments based on how the best candidates find new jobs and how the best hiring managers hire them.

Hiring managers who consistently hire the strongest talent tend to clarify job expectations up front; they conduct multiple interviews before making someone an offer; they dig deep into the person's past performance; and they tend to coach and mentor the people they hire after they're hired. As important, they'll connect with prospects before they become serious candidates as part of the recruiting process.

For the best prospects − those who would qualify as semifinalists − the list of shared and common characteristics is a bit longer and more complex. For one thing, many have no need to change jobs. Convincing them to do so requires extra effort on the part of both the hiring manager and the recruiter. Here are some of the other factors that need to be considered when working with candidates who haven't directly applied:

➤ They're more discriminating and ask lots of questions about the job, the resources available to do the job, the company culture, why the position is open, and everything related to the compensation and benefits package.

➤ They're generally not in a hurry to change jobs, they often get counteroffers or competitive offers, and since they're human, they can still be seduced by the size of the start date package.

➤ They will take the advice of a good recruiter who knows the job and who can present the role as a worthy career move. They also get instantly turned off by a recruiter who oversells the job, is hustling for the quick close, or one who can't describe the role in other than vague terms.

➤ They want to work for managers who can help with their career development. In fact, this relationship is often the tipping point in why one offer is accepted over another. Hiring managers who want to hire these types of outstanding people need to make a time investment with them, especially with those who are on the fence about moving forward.

In order to hire any of these people, it's important to meet their needs by emulating the traits of the best managers who do whatever is required to hire these people. Just as important is the recruiter who needs to orchestrate the entire process overcoming concerns and challenges every step of the way. As a practical matter, all of these techniques have been captured in the Performance-based Hiring process described in this book, including how to negotiate and close offers based on the career opportunity it represents.

■ MEASURE AND MANAGE QUALITY OF HIRE

Past performance doing comparable work is a good proxy for measuring and predicting Quality of Hire. The actual measurement is made in a formal debriefing session where the interviewers share their evidence for each of the factors on the Quality of Hire Talent Scorecard. This turns out to be quite accurate as long as each interviewer understands his or her role and is using the Performance-based

Interview to assess the candidate's ability, fit, and motivation based on the performance-based job descriptions. This same scorecard can then be used to measure Quality of Hire based on the person's actual performance once on the job.

Comparing the differences in pre- and post-hire scores provides the feedback needed to improve the assessment process based on the factors on the scorecard that were the least accurate. From what we've seen, most of these post-hire differences are due to lack of clarity around real job needs and not enough effort assessing the fit factors, especially the working relationship between the hiring manager and the new hire.

Practically speaking, if you can't measure a performance objective, it's pretty hard to figure out how well you're doing or if you're getting better or worse. Quality of Hire is one of those more elusive metrics that people find difficult to get their arms around. Part of the difficulty is that there are so many variables involved in making the assessment, including if the strongest candidates are willing to accept your offers. Most of the factors involved in predicting quality of hire and their interrelationships are captured in the Hiring Formula for Success. While using this as the basis for measuring quality of hire might not be perfect, perfection is not what matters. What matters is that you approximate Quality of Hire at every step in the process to make sure your hiring process is producing enough high-quality candidates and where it might be falling short.

For example, start measuring it at the top of the funnel to ensure the quality of the people being targeted make them likely semifinalists. In this case it means the person is performance qualified, possesses the Achiever Pattern, and would see the job as a likely career move. If the hiring manager won't agree to at least talk to the best of these people, it doesn't really matter how you measure Quality of Hire; you'll be spending too much time chasing the wrong candidates.

After the hiring manager talks to these people, you'll have another data point to determine the effectiveness of the process. If both the hiring manager and top person agree to move forward in the process, the likelihood of hiring a top performer is quite high. It's an indication there's a problem if either one is reluctant to proceed, especially if it happens frequently. The cause of the problem then needs to be identified and fixed before presenting additional candidates. This is how a metric – like Quality of Hire or a proxy for it – can be used as a trigger in a process control feedback loop to keep the overall process on track before too much time is wasted seeing candidates who will never get hired.

■ USE HIGH TOUCH TO CREATE AN OUTSTANDING CANDIDATE EXPERIENCE

By spending more time with fewer but stronger people, it's possible to achieve consistent Win-Win Hiring outcomes often more quickly, typically at lower cost, and always with fewer mistakes in comparison to existing high-tech solutions.

In the past year I've spoken with a few dozen talent leaders in just about every industry imaginable, from electronics and software to energy, financial services, and food service. All of them described their increased investment in a variety of new sourcing and recruiting software and tools but were disappointed in their company's overall lack of effectiveness in hiring more diverse talent, measuring and improving Quality of Hire, hiring more passive candidates, and getting their hiring managers more engaged in the hiring process.

I suggested the problem was too much emphasis on technology and not enough on high-touch recruiting like talking to people on the phone. A better balance of this type of high touch with high tech might be the solution.

One of my favorite of Stephen Covey's seven habits is: Put First Things First.[1] The idea behind this is to prioritize work by order of its importance and urgency with the less important, administrative, and day-to-day activities put at the bottom of the list. When it comes to recruiting and hiring, the highest value activities are recruiting top-tier prospects, collaborating with hiring managers, understanding real job needs, networking, and getting referrals. Yet in our analysis we find that not enough time is spent on these critical high-touch tasks, with most recruiters handling too many requisitions, chasing down hiring managers for feedback, sending emails

---

[1]Covey, Stephen R. The 7 Habits of Highly Effective People. Franklin Covey, 1998.

to candidates hoping they'll respond, or sending more emails to more candidates if the earlier emails aren't productive.

It's possible to end this reactive tail-chasing process by spending more time with only prequalified prospects. This is what putting first things first means and how it's possible to provide a remarkably positive candidate experience for everyone involved. In most cases, candidates who apply to jobs get little in the way of personal feedback as to where they stand in the process. This is true even for candidates who have been interviewed. Part of this is lack of meaningful feedback from the hiring manager to provide to the candidate. Regardless of the cause, it lessens the chance good people will stay interested in the role if they believe they've been demeaned in any way. The need to provide every candidate a positive experience with a company cannot be understated, but it's almost impossible to provide this at scale using technology to replace the human touch. However, an exceptional and personalized candidate experience is possible when only 15–20 people are being considered for any role. In these situations, a blend of high tech and high touch can provide every prospect and candidate the appropriate mix of feedback and hand-holding they need.

Finding a job, going through the interviewing process, and accepting an offer, if one is extended, is a very personal process for the candidate. In the high-tech world of filling jobs at scale, this personal side of recruiting is often just an afterthought. In a surplus of talent situation, where the supply of qualified people is greater than the demand, this problem is manageable. Ensuring a reasonably positive candidate experience will typically suffice. However, in a talent scarcity world where the demand for talent outstrips the supply, ignoring the high-touch requirement is downright foolhardy. This is where great recruiter skills are not only essential but represent the difference-maker in seeing and hiring the best people available, not just the best people who apply.

■ TAKE THE RISK AND BIAS OUT OF THE "YES" DECISION

The risk of being wrong drives safe and conversative hiring decisions. This is a recipe for replicating a workforce, not for improving it. Bias makes this risk even greater.

When it comes to hiring, there's less risk in saying no than yes. That's why most hiring managers need to see too many candidates to make one hire. In the process they hire the safest and often least diverse candidates who check most of the boxes on the job description, not the candidates with the most potential or ability.

Removing the risk in the hiring decision starts by recognizing that it's hard to be objective, especially when you're meeting someone for the first time. On the other hand, there is much less risk when you know someone personally and make judgments about them based on their work quality, their team skills, and their reliability, work ethic, and consistency. This same insight can be achieved when it comes to hiring strangers by sharing evidence around these same performance factors allowing everyone to be more objective and confident about their decisions. While this is easy to conceptualize and intuitively accept, it does require some aggressive intervention when making the decision of whom to hire or reject. It's best if this intervention takes place long before the in-depth interview. This starts with defining performance as the criteria for success and conducting exploratory phone screens with candidates before they're considered true semifinalists. The use of more panel interviews in combination with formal debriefing sessions sharing evidence will also help. But this might still not be enough to take the bias and risk out of the hiring decision.

You can assume an assessment is incorrect whenever you hear an interviewer making judgments about a candidate either negative or positive that emphasize feelings, subjective criteria, shallow thinking, or superficial evidence. For example, statements that include phrases like *not sure, bad feeling, just wouldn't fit, great first impression, too soft, smart as a tack, real go-getter, too light, overqualified*, or anything related, require you to push back. Providing detailed evidence of a candidate's major accomplishment related to a real job need is the best way to counter these emotion-packed assessments.

By making the process of making the yes decision safer by making it more objective, less biased, and evidence-based, the whole team can feel more comfortable making the no hire decision, too. While this will begin to sound repetitious, it's important to reenforce the idea that by comparing a candidate's past performance doing comparable work in similar circumstances, the risk of making a hiring mistake is greatly reduced. In these cases, the bigger risk is being too safe and not hiring the best person.

■ HIRING STRONG PEOPLE IS THE FIRST STEP IN MANAGING A GREAT TEAM

Performance-based Hiring is a process not only for finding and hiring outstanding people but also how to best manage and develop these people once they're on the job. This is why achieving more Win-Win Hiring outcomes is the expectation, not the hope. This tight integration has been achieved by embedding many best management practices directly into the hiring process. The most important of these are clarifying expectations up front, assigning people important work they find self-motivating, and giving them the direction and support they need to be successful. These are the Q1–Q4 factors in Gallup's Q12 list of criteria that separate the world's greatest managers from those who aren't.[2] Google's Project Oxygen[3] echoed the same theme based on thousands of surveys of what it takes to be a great manager at Google.

Without this understanding of what drives individual performance, it's easy for employees to waste time, flounder on less important work, get frustrated, demotivate themselves and others, and become disengaged and dissatisfied. This is a recipe for underperformance and unnecessary turnover. This situation is far worse for new hires, especially if the work assigned does not meet their initial expectations or understanding of what they thought the role entailed.

Hiring the best talent is not just about better interviewing skills, although this is a part of it. It's also not about better sourcing, networking, and recruitment advertising, although these are all critical parts. It's also not just about better recruiting and negotiating skills, although they're both critical since you can't afford to lose good people for the wrong reasons. Hiring the best talent is about having the right talent acquisition strategy, a fully integrated hiring process based on how top people get jobs, and a fully committed management team that believes hiring great people is how you build great companies.

That's what is meant when people say hiring top people is the most important thing every manager needs to do.

This is how you deliver on the Win-Win Hiring promise.

---

[2]Harter, J., 2016. *First, Break All the Rules.* New York: Gallup Press.
[3]"Project Oxygen," re:Work, Google. https://rework.withgoogle.com/subjects/managers/.

Appendix 1

Performance-based Hiring and Legal Compliance

David J. Goldstein[1]

Businesses hire people because there is a job to be done. The goal is to find the right people, bring them on board, and get them to work. When the wrong person is hired, the work doesn't get done. Worse yet, the productivity of others may be disrupted. And in the worst case a bad hire can lead to litigation. Employment-related litigation is extremely costly and legal fees represent just the tip of the iceberg. Litigation distracts managers, impacts employee morale, and often breeds additional litigation.

[1]David J. Goldstein, a shareholder in Littler Mendelson's Minneapolis office, has over 35 years of experience working with in-house counsel, business leadership, and HR professionals to proactively identify and implement creative solutions for complying with legal and regulatory requirements, avoiding liability, and resolving internal and external disputes. An experienced trial lawyer, David's clients include healthcare providers, construction companies, financial institutions, colleges and universities, and professional sports teams. David devotes a significant portion of his practice to assisting employers with the implementation and maintenance of effective affirmative action programs and representing contractors before the OFCCP. David has a JD from Harvard Law School and a BA from Haverford College. While in law school he also taught freshman economics at Harvard College. Additional information on David is available at http://www.linkedin.com/in/davidjgoldstein and http://www.littler.com/people/david-j-goldstein.

For these and other reasons, successful companies need to adopt an effective approach to recruiting and hiring. Performance-based Hiring provides such an approach.

By creating compelling job descriptions that are focused on key performance objectives, by using advanced marketing and networking concepts to find top people, by adopting evidence-based interviewing techniques, and by integrating recruiting into the interviewing process, companies can attract better candidates and make better hiring decisions.

Nevertheless, because the Performance-based Hiring system does differ from traditional recruiting and hiring processes, questions arise as to whether employers can adopt Performance-based Hiring and still comply with the complex array of statutes, regulations, and common law principals that regulate the workplace. The answer is yes.

In particular:

➤ A properly prepared performance profile can identify and document the essential functions of a job better than traditional position descriptions, facilitating the reasonable accommodation of disabilities and making it easier to comply with the Americans with Disabilities Act and similar laws.

➤ Even employers that maintain more traditional job descriptions may still use performance profiles or summaries of performance profiles to advertise job openings. Employers are not legally required to post their internal job descriptions when advertising an open position. Nor is there any legal obligation to (or advantage in) posting boring ads.

➤ Under some circumstances, federal government contractors will want to include in their job postings objective, noncomparative qualifications for the position to be filled. Using SMARTe, employers can create performance-based job descriptions that include such objective, noncomparative elements. Requiring applicants to have previously accomplished specific tasks represents a selection criterion that is no less objective than requiring years of experience in some general area.

➤ Focusing on "Year 1 and Beyond" criteria may open the door to more minority, military, and disabled candidates who

have a less "traditional" mix of experiences, thereby supporting affirmative action or diversity efforts.

➤ The law permits employers to define who will be an "applicant" by limiting consideration to individuals who fulfill
certain procedural requirements such as fully completing
an application form. Requiring interested individuals to
complete a short write-up of some accomplishment related
to the job to be filled (the "two-step") can serve as such a
requirement. Individuals who do not submit the required
write-up need not be considered as applicants for record-
keeping purposes. Of course, while individuals can be
rejected based on the quality of their submission, those
individuals who do submit the write-up will need to be
counted as applicants.

➤ Conducting Performance-based Interviews ensures that
the interviews will be structured and properly focused and
minimizes the risk of an interviewer inquiring into pro-
tected characteristics. Moreover, since the Performance-
based Interviews are conducted pursuant to a common
methodology, one is assured that the candidates are being
fairly compared.

➤ Performance-based Interviewing promotes fair consideration of the different skills and experiences that each candidate has to offer – which is essential to promoting diversity.

➤ One obstacle to diversity in hiring is the greater effort
required for an interviewer to connect with a person who is
different. Hire with Your Head offers techniques for controlling
this type of bias. Waiting 30 minutes and using the Plus or
Minus Reversal Technique will reduce the impact of such
biases and promote greater diversity in hiring.

➤ Although employers are generally required to maintain
records of the actual applicant pools considered for each
hire, a single posting may still be used to cover multiple
openings by narrowing the pool through the two-step process
and maintaining appropriate applicant tracking systems.

➤ Performance-based Hiring is a business process for hiring
top talent. While the process will be useful for filling many

different types of jobs, there may be some jobs (for example, lower-level, lower-skilled, high-turnover positions) for which it doesn't make sense to use Performance-based Hiring. That is not a problem. Employers need to be consistent in their hiring processes for similar positions but remain free to adopt different processes for different positions.

Appendix 2: Forms

A complete full-size set of these forms is available for the purchaser of this book at hirewithyourhead.com and hiring.tips/HWYH4_forms. After completing the form and agreeing to the usage terms you'll need to use this password to open the documents: HWYH4

Exploratory Phone Screen Talent Scorecard

The Performance-based Phone Screen

Quality of Hire Talent Scorecard

The Performance-based Interview

The Ideal Candidate Persona

Exploratory Phone Screen Talent Scorecard

Based on Lou Adler's *Hire With Your Head* & *The Essential Guide for Hiring & Getting Hired*
Use this recommendation form after completing the "Exploratory Phone Screen" course on *The Hiring Machine* learning platform. It will save time, raise quality of hire and minimize hiring mistakes due to first impression bias.

Performance-based Hiring

Candidate: _____ Position: _____ Interviewer: _____ Date: _____

Factor	Not Recommended for this Position	Need More Info to Advise Yes or No	Recommended for Further Assessment	Rank
Work History Review				
General Fit for Open Role	Little or no match on title, company, scope and scale.	Reasonable fit but it's not clear all of the core factors are fully covered.	Strong fit on all core factors. Brings other strengths with good track record.	
Team Skills and Impact	Team makeup not comparable. Little growth shown on size and/or role.	Team makeup is comparable but inconsistent growth. Not sure of role and impact.	Growing role and impact with cross-functional teams.	
Achiever Pattern and Growth Trend	Trend of growth inconsistent. No recognition for exceptional work.	Some recognition and growth but pattern is not consistent.	Positive trend with evidence of achievement and recognition for exceptional work.	
Factor	Not Recommended for this Position	Need More Info to Advise Yes or No	Recommended for Further Assessment	Rank
Most Significant Accomplishment (MSA) Questions				
Comparability of Accomplishments	Accomplishment is a clear mismatch on many factors.	Accomplishment is reasonably similar, but questions remain as to actual role.	Accomplishment is a strong match and person had positive role in project success.	
Organizational and "Soft Skills"	Unorganized. Reactive. Misses most deadlines. Makes excuses.	Planning and project management efforts seem a bit reactive and less organized.	Strong planning and organizing skills. Logical and proactive. Meets goals.	
Problem-solving and Thinking Skills	Biggest problems and challenges faced are not comparable.	Has faced similar problems and challenges but it's not clear if successfully handled.	Has successfully handled problems and challenges at least consistent with needs.	
Factor	Not Recommended for this Position	Need More Info to Advise Yes or No	Recommended for Further Assessment	Rank
Fit Factors and Recruiting Issues				
Culture and Environmental Fit	Mismatch on pace, resources, intensity, sophistication and decision-making.	Reasonable match on most issues driving culture but not sure it's a good fit.	The person has successfully worked in similar situations at similar pace and intensity.	
Job Interest, Compensation and Recruiting Issues	Not a fit for the job on too many issues. Job is not a career move.	Reasonable candidate, but many issues to overcome to recruit and hire the person.	Strong candidate and worth pursuing. Job represents a good career move.	
Recommendations and Next Steps				

Summarize why the person is worth seriously considering and the issues that need to be addressed in subsequent interviews. If rejecting the person, describe why.

Describe the recruiting issues that need to be considered including compensation, how active/passive the person is and if the person is considering other opportunities.

Exploratory Phone Screen Talent Scorecard

The Performance-based Phone Screen

November 2020

Performance-based Hiring

Note: This is a semi-scripted interview to determine if a candidate should be invited onsite. It's okay to stop the interview after the Work History Review if there is not a fit. If there is a reasonable fit, ask about the person's major accomplishments. This is enough info to determine is the person should be invited onsite. Recruiting is embedded into this process as a means to represent the opening as a true career move.

Step 1	Welcome and Review Job/Motivation	More Information
Opening question to determine job-hunting status and motivation for looking	Provide a 1-2 minute overview of the job, then ask: *Can you provide a quick overview of how your background relates?* *What's your current job-hunting status? How long have you been looking?* *What factors are you looking for in a new job?* (pause) *Why is having (factor1) and (factor2) important to you?*	For the initial phone screen find out how long the person has been looking and how actively. Asking the "Why?" follow-up question allows you to understand the person's reasons for looking and what the person would require in a new position.

Step 2	Bring Impact of First Impressions to Conscious Level	Information & Hot Tips
Action: Be aware of your biases	Write down your immediate emotional reaction to the candidate. Measure this again at the end of the interview when you're less affected by it. Determine if the person's true phone personality and communication style would help or hinder on-the-job performance.	o Collect evidence to decide yes/no o Ask same questions to all candidates o Ask about details, examples, facts o Assume competent at beginning

Step 3	Review Work History and Achiever Pattern	Fact-finding & Hot Tips
Use this to develop structure behind experience and accomplishments Look for "Achiever Pattern"	*Please tell me about your most recent job. What was your position, the company, your duties, the teams you've been on and the big projects handled?* (Do this for the past few jobs.) Spend 10-15 minutes on this. For each position obtain: title, promotions, basic duties, 360° team chart, impact made, challenges faced, any recognition received. Ask why the person changed jobs, looking for a career growth decision pattern. If the person is an achiever, but growth has stalled, or the current job is not highly satisfying, your job might be a good move.	Look for basic fit and Achiever Pattern. **Achiever Pattern:** o Faster growth, more promotions o Special awards, bonuses, raises o Assigned to bigger projects o Hired or pushed by mentor **Look for career opportunity gaps** o Differences in scope and span o More important projects o Broader influence and exposure o Faster growth

Step 4	Most Significant Accomplishment Question (MSA)	Fact-finding & Hot Tips
Ask this question to determine if person meets the criteria for inviting onsite or for continuing the conversation.	Ask about the person's biggest career accomplishment and the one most related to the open role if the candidate seems to be a strong possibility. *Can you please tell me about your most significant career accomplishment or consider a project or event you're quite proud of.* *One major project we're now working on is* (describe). *Please tell me about something comparable you've worked on.* Spend 10-12 minutes to fully understand the accomplishment. If the person possesses the Achiever Pattern and the accomplishment is reasonable, the person should be seriously considered.	o Overview of job, company o Person's role and how assigned o Team, role and if changed over time o Snapshot of beginning and end o Environment – pace, resources o When? How long? Results? o Walk through plan and results o Describe tech skills and how applied o Obtain 2-3 examples of initiative o What did you change/improve? o Describe biggest problem solved o Walk through biggest decision made o Describe likes, dislikes o Where did you exceed expectations? o What recognition did you receive?

Step 5	Determine Interest and Recruit	Fact-finding & Hot Tips
Question & Discussion Create Job Stretch	*While we've seen a few other very strong candidates, I'm also impressed with some of the work you've done. Based on what you know now is this something you'd like to consider more seriously?* **For potential semi-finalists** Describe why the position could be a career move and worth a more in-depth interview. Focus on job stretch, more important and more satisfying work, and faster growth rate.	o State sincere interest o Make candidate earn job o Listen 4x more than talk; don't sell o Describe concerns to create gap o Mention other strong contenders o What other jobs are you considering? o Link job to big company projects o Ask about interests and concerns

The Performance-based Phone Screen

Quality of Hire Talent Scorecard

Based on Lou Adler's *Hire With Your Head* and *The Essential Guide for Hiring & Getting Hired* and the training programs on WinWinHiring.com. It's important for the hiring team to complete this form together by sharing their evidence after conducting a Performance-based Interview. (Revised Oct 2020)

Performance-based Hiring

Candidate: _____ Position: _____ Interviewer: _____ Date: _____

Factor	Level 1 Minimal	Level 2 Adequate	Level 3 Strong	Level 4 Great	Rank
BASIC COMPETENCIES					
Primary Skills	Bare minimum.	Has the basics but needs training.	Covers all direct job needs well.	Extremely strong in all job needs.	Broad. Brings far more to the table.	
Experience	Minimum threshold.	Meets most, but not all needs.	Meets all experience needs.	Broader and related experience.	Excellent background for role.	
Achiever Pattern & Growth Trend	No evidence the person is in the top 50%. Spotty trend.	Some, but not sure if person is in top 50%. Flatter trend.	Evidence clearly indicates person is in top third. Upward growth trend.	Evidence clearly indicates person is in top 10-15%. Steep upward path.	Evidence clearly indicates person is in top 5%. Handles big stretch roles.	
ESSENTIAL CORE COMPETENCES (In Comparison to the KPOs/OKRs for the Role)					
Talent & Overall Technical Ability	Nothing remarkable. Needs too much extra training and support.	Can do the work, but needs added training, support or coaching.	Technically tops. An asset. Can learn quickly. Covers all job needs.	Top-notch. Trains others. Constantly improving. Brings more to the table.	Brilliant. Sets standards. Leader in field. Sought out. Recognized.	
Management & Organizational Ability	Seems reactive. Misses most deadlines or projects aren't comparable.	Projects are comparable but seems more reactive than forward-looking.	Has planned, organized and executed comparable projects.	Excellent. Plans, anticipates, communicates, and succeeds.	Outstanding organizational results with comparable projects and teams.	
Team Skills (EQ) & Development, Leadership	Hasn't worked on comparable teams or little team growth.	Has worked on comparable teams and has some team growth.	Good fit on comparable teams. Has developed strong comparable teams.	Clear positive team track. Coaches others. Recognized for strong team skills.	Impressive x-func team growth. Asked to lead. Persuades, motivates, coaches.	
Thinking & Job-related Problem-solving	Didn't understand any key issues or develop any solutions.	Understood most job related issues, developed okay solutions.	Clearly understood all key issues and developed strong solutions.	Understood all key & less obvious issues. Reaches out for best solutions.	Provides deeper level of insight. Offers multiple unique solutions.	
SITUATIONAL FIT FACTORS – WEIGHT THESE FACTORS HIGHER					
Job Fit with Recent Comparable Results	Accomplishments are not directly comparable or not recent.	Some comparable accomplishments, but inconsistent or not recent.	Major and subtask accomplishments are recent, strong and comparable.	Achieved outstanding results under similar conditions.	Full job match with exceptional results – scope, pace, team, resources.	
Managerial Fit	Mismatch between candidate's & manager's style.	Limited, but has worked with similar managers.	Successfully worked with similar managers.	Person easily adapts to a variety of manager styles.	Super fit. Coaches upwards. Both are flexible.	
Culture & Environment	Complete mismatch on culture & environment.	Reasonable match on culture and environment.	Close match on culture and environment.	Excellent match and has made similar transfers.	Thrives in this type of environment, culture.	
Motivation[2]	Little evidence of motivation to do this type of work.	Will do the core work but needs extra pushing.	Self-motivated to do work with normal supervision.	Takes initiative to learn and do more, faster and better.	Totally committed to get it done. Constantly gets better.	

OVERALL FIT BASED ON SHARED EVIDENCE and RECRUITABILITY

(Provide evidence below used to rank each factor using the _Performance-based Interview_. Have everyone explain their evidence to determine total score. As part of the assessment determine if the person is likely to accept and offer based on the career merits rather than the size of the compensation package.)

The Adler Group, Inc. • Irvine, CA • www.winwinhiring.com • info@performancebasedhiring.com
©2020. All Rights Reserved. The Adler Group, Inc.

The Performance-based Interview

November 2020

Performance-based Hiring

Note: Before interviewing anyone it's important to define 3-4 key performance objectives for the job and 1-2 problems or challenges the person hired will be asked to handle. Some of the questions below relate to these to these job-related factors.

Step 1	Welcome and Review Job/Motivation	Information & Hot Tips
Opening question to determine general fit and motivation for looking.	*Let me give you a short overview of this job.* (provide one-minute summary). *Given this, can you give me a quick overview of how your background relates to this job?*	Ask for clarifying details to understand how the candidate's background, trend and current role fits with the current job requirements.
	What are you looking for now in a new job? (pause) *Why is having ___ and ___ important to you now? What's your current job hunting status? How long have you been looking?* For subsequent interviewers: *Based on your other discussions please give me a quick overview of your thoughts about the job, and what you've discussed with others so far.*	Asking the "Why?" follow-up question gets at the true source of motivation. Determine if person wants any job, or if person is looking for a career move. Mention that the purpose of this interview will be to determine if a win-win hiring outcome is possible.

Step 2	Measure Impact of First Impression	Information & Hot Tips
Action: be aware of your biases	Write down your immediate emotional reaction to the candidate – relaxed, uptight, or neutral. Write down the cause. At the end of the interview you'll measure your first impression of the candidate again, when you're less affected by it.	o Wait 30-minutes o Do opposite of normal reaction o Like: prove incompetency, be tough o Dislike: prove competency, be easy o Ask same questions to all o Be cynical, get proof, examples, facts

Step 3	Review Work History and Background	Fact-finding & Hot Tips
Use this to develop structure behind experience and accomplishments Look for "Achiever Pattern"	*Please tell me about your most recent job. What was your position, the company, your duties, and any recognition you received?* (Do this for the past few jobs.) Spend 20-25 minutes on this as part of a one-hour interview. For each position obtain: title, promotions, basic duties, 360° team chart, impact made, challenges faced, any recognition received. Go back 5-10 years looking for upward trend of growth. Ask why the person changed jobs and if the job achieved the reason for changing. Avoid *Job Hopping Syndrome*. If the person is an Achiever (top 25% in peer group), but growth has stalled, or the current job is not highly satisfying, your job might be a good move.	Look for an Achiever Pattern: major accomplishments in each job, upward progression, significant recognition. **For each job obtain:** o Overview, title, type of work o Draw org chart & how team was built o Dates, why left, explain gaps o Highlights, big projects, major focus o Recognition, raises, promotion **Look for stretch gaps such as:** o Project size and span of control o Influence and exposure o Impact and growth

Step 4	Assess a Few Major Accomplishments	Fact-finding & Hot Tips
Question for a few projects to determine impact and trend line	*Can you please tell me about your most significant accomplishment at (company)? Or, consider a project or event that you're quite proud of or where you excelled* *One major project we're now working on is (describe). Please tell me about something comparable you've led.* Spend 12-15 minutes (each) on 2-3 different major accomplishments in order to develop a trend line of accomplishments over time. Note the type of work where the person excelled and/or was highly motivated. Other interviewers can use this modified form of the same question but focusing on different attributes, like project management skills or technical skills. *I'd like to focus on (attribute). Can you tell me about a major accomplishment that best demonstrates this?*	o Overview of job, company o Team and org structure o Environment – pace, resources o When? How long? Results? o What results were expected? o How did you plan project? o Obtain 2-3 examples of initiative o What did you change/improve? o Big challenges or conflict faced o What did you learn about self? o How did you grow as a result? o What would you do differently? o What (technical) skills needed? o How were these enhanced? o What (technical) skills learned? o Describe likes, dislikes o Where did you exceed expectations? o How did you improve yourself? o What would you do differently? o What recognition did you receive?

The Performance-based Interview (1/2)

The Performance-based Interview
November 2020

Performance-based Hiring

Step 4a	Assess Major Team Accomplishments	Fact-finding & Hot Tips
Question for few teams & observe impact and trend line	*Can you please tell me about a major team accomplishment? Consider one where you led the team, and one where you were a key member of the team.* Spend 10-12 minutes on each team accomplishment. Observe trend line and changes in scope of team. Make note of the types of people on the team, variety of functions worked with, and how influential the person was in changing the direction of the team.	o Draw an org chart w/title o What was your role, why you? o What were biggest team problems? o How did you influence results? o 3 examples of initiative helping others o Examples of being influenced o How could you have been better? o Describe biggest conflict & resolution o Examples coaching others o Examples of being coached o Did you receive any team recognition?

Step 5	Discuss Major Job-related Problems	Fact-finding & Hot Tips
Repeat question 1-2 times using real problems Anchor with real project	*One major problem we're now facing is _____. How would you go about addressing this? What would you need to know and how would you plan it out?* *What have you done that's most similar?* (This is an anchor to ensure that the candidate doesn't just talk a good game. This might have been covered above.)	o What would you need to know? o What would you do first, why? o Who else would you involve? o How would you prepare? o How would you prioritize tasks, why? o How would you find critical issues? o What resources needed o How long would it take, why? o What would you do if…? o How would you make this trade-off? o How would you make business case?

Step 6	Let the Candidate Ask Questions	Fact-finding & Hot Tips
Tell candidates they can ask questions at the end	*Based on what we've discussed so far, do you have any questions?* It's important to delay candidate questions until the end. Meaningful questions at the end of the interview are insightful, since they demonstrate that the candidate has processed all she/he has heard so far.	o Evaluate if the questions were meaningful, appropriate, and relevant o Determine if the candidate is focusing on the long-term career opportunity or just short-term issues

Step 7	Recruit Using the Win-Win Hiring Opportunity	Fact-finding & Hot Tips
Question & Discussion Create Job Stretch	*While I've seen a few other very strong candidates, I'm also impressed with some of the work you've done. Is this role of interest? Why? Why not?* Only the hiring manager and/or recruiter need to spend too much time on this. Others can ask "What are your thoughts about the job?" For candidates who are possible finalists explain how the 30% solution might represent a good career move. *A win-win hiring outcome requires a job to offer a combination of stretch, growth and impact. Let's work on getting you more info around these factors.* Describe next steps and the person's availability given other roles he/she is considering.	o State sincere interest o Make candidate earn job o Listen 4x more than talk; don't sell o Describe concerns to create gap o Mention other strong contenders o What other jobs are you considering? o How interested on 1-10 scale, why? o What's needed to know to get to 8-9? o Link job to big company projects o What do you like/dislike? o How does job meet your needs? o Compensation needs, availability o When can you come back, next steps

Step 8	Measure First Impression Again	Information & Hot Tips
Compare candidate's true personality to 1st impression at opening of interview	Measure first impression again at the end of the interview. Determine how the candidate's first impression will impact on-the-job performance. Consider the actual impact on you, the actual impact on others (customers, peers, superiors, staff). As part of this compare the candidate's first impression when measured at the end of the interview to your initial reaction to the person. Keep track of this difference for every interview. The pattern will reveal your own personal biases.	o Did first impression change? o Become more/less nervous? o Open up more, talk more? o Did you observe true personality in accomplishments? o Did this change your decision? o Is true personality consistent with job needs?

The Performance-based Interview (2/2)

The Ideal Candidate Persona

Performance-based Hiring

Step-by-Step Guide	Comments	Notes
The Basics, Job Branding, the Employee Value Proposition (EVP) and Messaging		
Identify the core components of the 30% Solution	The 30% non-monetary increase (i.e., stretch, growth, impact and satisfaction) needs to be the foundation for the career and one the prospects need to understand in the first email and conversation.	
Candidate's intrinsic motivator	Determine what motivates a person to excel at this type of work. Once this is understood, messaging can be created to leverage this idea. Consider Internal vs. External and Team vs. Individual motivators.	
Determine the Employee Value Proposition (EVP)	Why would a top person want this job if he/she is not looking and if the person has other offers that are paying more? Then prove it with specifics and examples. What would the logical next step be?	
Create a customized "Job Brand"	Tie the job to a bigger mission. This could be an important project or company strategy or value. This needs to be customized by job, not generic boilerplate. Job branding is the idea of capturing the intrinsic motivator and linking this to a bigger purpose. Job branding is more important than employer branding for attracting passive candidates.	
Survey people currently in the role	Ask people in this role what they find most satisfying about the job. Use this to prepare the EVP and related messages.	
Tag line	Add a short clever tag line to the job title for emails and job postings. For example, "Prepare whitepapers in any color you want."	
Prepare email to drive person to the job post and your LinkedIn profile	Sell the discussion, not the job! Mention multiple positions. Take off the time pressure. Mention the hiring manager viewed the person's profile and was impressed.	
Sourcing – Defining, Understanding and Finding the Ideal Candidate		
Understand the typical progression of someone in this role who is a top performer	Understand where the person went to school or areas of specialized training received. What types of jobs would the person have held previous to your current opening? You'll use this to search for the candidate.	
Find out ideal candidate's job hunting status. What is the candidate looking for in a new job?	Use Career Zone Analysis to find out the job hunting status of your ideal candidate. The four types are Passive, Explorer, Tiptoer, and Active. On the Maslow scale does the person want a career move or a lateral transfer?	
Types of jobs previously held	Consider comparable positions in other industries or vendors and consultants servicing the industry.	
Direct and functional competitors	Consider industries or companies where the person would obtain similar experience.	
Comparative titles	Consider all types of titles including those that are more generic.	
"Cherry Pick" the ideal candidate as part of a "High Touch, Small Batch" sourcing approach. These all must be potential semi-finalists.	Determine the demographics of a person who would quickly see your opening as a possible career move. For example, this could be a senior manager at a big company who would see being a director at a small company as a good career move if it had more impact.	

The Ideal Candidate Persona (1/2)

The Ideal Candidate Persona

Performance-based Hiring

Step-by-Step Guide	Comments	Notes
Direct Sourcing – Searching Directly for the Ideal Candidate		
Define typical places the ideal candidate would use to find another job including job boards, associations and networking groups	Reverse engineer some ideal candidates' profiles to find groups (consider online and LinkedIn) or create one that you develop. Figure out where these people "meet up" and then join the group.	
Achiever and recognition terms that indicate the person is a top 25% person	An achiever term indicates the person is in the top of their peer group and indicates remarkable progress. As you search for candidates review their awards and honors for other achiever terms. Then search on these terms.	
Professional societies and specialty groups the person would join.	Include honor societies, professional groups and LinkedIn groups. If possible, join them or start one. Use the important terms in your Boolean search.	
2-3 most critical skills	Highlight the essential few. Consider all-inclusive "master" terms.	
Demographic or diversity terms	Consider groups, pronouns, programs, organizations, colleges.	
PRP: Proactive Networking – Who Knows the Ideal Candidate?		
Ask, "Who would know this person?" Build a 360° network of the ideal candidate's likely co-workers to get referrals.	Describe the types of people the person would work and interface with. You'll be able to connect with these "nodes" and search on their 1st degree connections for referrals. Consider vendors, consultants and customers.	
Implement a Proactive Employee Referral program (PERP) at your company	Connect with people in your company who are likely to know or who are connected to your "ideal" candidate. Then search on their connections using clever Boolean and ask if the person is strong. Have your co-worker reach out to the person.	

The Ideal Candidate Persona (2/2)

Index

08 ◄ INDEX